New Directions in East Asian History

This series addresses the ways in which history influences the political, economic and social development of East Asia, a region which now plays a pivotal role in our world's multipolar international system. The series provides new perspectives on East Asia's distinctive economic and political situation through the lens of 20th century history, with a particular focus on Pre-War and Cold War periods. It argues the need to re-examine the history of East Asia and provide new historical approaches to a vibrant and constantly changing region.

Highlighting that history is at the root of many modern day conflicts in Asia, this series provides a global forum for rigorous academic research and timely debate by scholars worldwide, and showcases significant new research on East Asian history and politics in the contemporary era.

The series will appeal to specialists in the history and politics of Asia; international history; scholars of modern and contemporary Japan, Chinese and Korea as well as international relations.

More information about this series at
http://www.palgrave.com/gp/series/15870

Aleksandra Babovic

The Tokyo Trial, Justice, and the Postwar International Order

palgrave
macmillan

Aleksandra Babovic
Osaka University
Osaka, Japan

ISSN 2522-0195 ISSN 2522-0209 (electronic)
New Directions in East Asian History
ISBN 978-981-13-3476-4 ISBN 978-981-13-3477-1 (eBook)
https://doi.org/10.1007/978-981-13-3477-1

Library of Congress Control Number: 2018965192

This Palgrave Macmillan imprint is published by the registered company Springer Nature Singapore Pte Ltd.
The registered company address is: 152 Beach Road, #21-01/04 Gateway East, Singapore 189721, Singapore

Contents

PART I

CHAPTER 1

The Tokyo Tribunal, Justice, and International Order

The Tokyo Tribunal, also less often referred to as the International Military Tribunal for the Far East (IMTFE), tells the story of how 28 Japanese civilian and military leaders conspired to wage an aggressive war against the Allied powers in the period from 1928 to 1945. There is much more to it than the Japanese leaders' punishment through judicial mechanism. The Tokyo Tribunal bears potential to illuminate on the important concepts of international criminal justice and international order, which could give a whole new perspective on this, at various levels, important judicial mechanism.

Together with its European counterpart, or the International Military Tribunal (IMT) at Nuremberg, it represents the first institutional manifestation of the idea that war can amount to not only an illegal act triggering international state responsibility, but also a criminal act allowing for individual criminal responsibility of high state and military representatives. The premise that the war crimes tribunals can constitute an integral cooperative component of the post-World War II international order establishing process and, furthermore, deter future aggression had been tested by the two tribunals. The results were, to say the least, mixed as this book intends to demonstrate.

At the heart of the IMTFE is the crime of aggression, contrary to modern international criminal tribunals whose material jurisdiction exclusively focuses on war crimes, crimes against humanity, and what has been often labeled as the ultimate crime in international law, genocide. Transitional

A. Babovic, *The Tokyo Trial, Justice, and the Postwar International Order*, New Directions in East Asian History,
https://doi.org/10.1007/978-981-13-3477-1_1

justice constitutes a panoply of mechanisms for dealing with international crimes, international criminal tribunals being only one of them. It is important to mention hybrid courts and truth commissions as other available processes for dealing with the responsibility for crimes committed in post-conflict societies. International criminal justice is not a permanent mechanism; international criminal law has been applied only sporadically in the postwar period by the International Criminal Tribunal for ex-Yugoslavia (ICTY) and the International Criminal Tribunal for Rwanda (ICTR), which are its two most notorious examples.

In 2002, with the entry into force of the Rome Statute establishing the International Criminal Court (ICC), international criminal justice was given a more permanent character. However, the ICC does not have universal reach as many states regularly involved in warfare around the world are not its members (the US, China, Russia, Israel). While the ICC is highly consensual in character, the above-mentioned ad hoc international criminal tribunals (ICTs) were imposed on states by UNSC (UN Security Council) resolutions. Also, the Court's activities are subjected to the UNSC that can intervene to postpone or stop the investigation or trial, for six months renewable, if it deems that a specific trial is obstructing the peace process. Contrary to the above-mentioned ad hoc mechanisms, the ICC has material jurisdiction over the crime of aggression since 2017; however, as the crime remains poorly defined and member states can prevent their statesmen or military from facing charges by using the available "opt out"[1] clause, it remains largely unused. This strongly shows that what Chief Prosecutor Joseph Keenan at the IMTFE called "the supreme international crime,"[2] referring to the crime against peace or the crime of aggression, has remained dormant and highly controversial to the present day.

The Tokyo Tribunal, which is the exclusive focus of this book, was officially established on May 3, 1946. Symbolically, the rooms of the Imperial War Ministry that were not so long ago the place where Japanese leaders made war plans were remodeled to host the historic Tribunal to prosecute 28 Japanese military and civilian leaders for waging aggressive war in the Asia-Pacific region. Two perspectives emerge. The first one is the perspective of the victor and, at the same time, victim nations which did not observe these selected Japanese politicians and military as statesmen, but as criminals who ought to be severely punished. Above all, they were targeted for planning, waging, and instigating aggressive war and war crimes inflicted upon prisoners of war and civilians throughout the Japanese Empire. The second one is the perspective of defendants, mostly prominent figures in Imperial Japan, who felt that they did their best to discharge official duties and to faithfully serve Japan's national interest. In their eyes, they failed to win the war for which they were being prosecuted. To them, the issues lay in their miscalculated political and strategic decisions, but not guilt related to the violation of morals, ethics, and international rules that they did not know about.

The Tokyo Tribunal is a part of the Allied powers' occupation policy. The early occupation plan was articulated around disarmament, demilitarization, and democratization which would allow Japan to reintegrate a newly created postwar international order, open and multilateral in nature.[3] Its jurisdiction was imposed upon defeated Japan that signed the Instrument of Surrender on September 2, 1945, by which it accepted the unconditional surrender and military occupation which was to be led by the Supreme Commander Douglas MacArthur, on behalf of the 11 Allied powers (the US, Britain, Australia, Soviet Union, the Netherlands, New Zealand, Canada, France, China, Philippines, and India). These nations were all represented at the Tribunal both within its prosecution section and panel of judges. A legal basis for the war crimes program in Japan is contained in the Potsdam Declaration of July 26, 1945, which read that stern justice should be meted out to all war criminals. At that time, the Allies' war crimes trials were already under way in Germany which put the pressure for a similar program to be implemented in Japan. It was expected that trials in Japan would start as soon as the roadmap had been paved by the German experience. The IMTFE Charter was unilaterally proclaimed by the Supreme Commander on January 19, 1946. Legal precedents such as that the aggressive war was an international crime triggering individual criminal responsibility of heads of states and their military had already been agreed upon in fastidious rounds of negotiations between the four allies in London in July 1945.

These were groundbreaking changes for international law and exercise of traditional statecraft which considered war to be a political act of state, not a criminal one. Present-day mechanisms of international criminal justice have become mainly preoccupied with the application of humanitarian regimes that regulate state and non-state actors' behavior in times of both war and peace. These judicial mechanisms particularly excelled at further development and refinement of crimes against humanity, war crimes, and genocide, thus addressing mass atrocity. Post-Cold War era's predominant legal, political, and societal discourse displays unquestionable support for respect and, when political willingness is present, the application of human rights and humanitarian regimes. Although World War II had the character of total war in which the brutalization of entire societies and cruelty of its participants gained momentum, the Allies were using these as a moral pretext to address what was considered at that time a greater issue—the individual responsibility for starting the aggressive war in both Japan and Germany. The deficit of international humanitarian norms was not at stake. The laws of war had existed but were ignored and downplayed as inept to respond to the complexity and scale of events which aimed at the utter destruction of the enemy.

Invariably, in the words of Brian Orend, every war is a "nasty business which, ultimately, calls forth more vice than virtue,"[4] and this applies to the case in point—the Pacific War. Despite the normative distinction between aggressive and defensive wars, ethically, such differentiations do not stand—if the ultimate test of morality is killing, then every war is immoral.[5] At the outset, it is necessary to clarify that this book does not question the veracity of Japanese atrocities nor exculpate or justify the behavior of wartime leaders in Imperial Japan. Rather, by adopting a posture of "moral minimalism," it remains focused on understanding the *mentalité*, political decisions, and international dynamics of the postwar period in which the prosecution of crimes of aggressive war or crimes against peace took place.

Contrary to the trial records of the International Military Tribunal at Nuremberg that were almost immediately published by its Secretariat in separate volumes from 1947 to 1949, the IMTFE records were lying in obscurity until the 1980s. In addition to this, academic debate was clearly distinguished between legal scholars and historians. Since 2008, the effort to reconcile the gap between the two disciplines and their respective methods and objectives has been reflected by publications where legal scholars and historians worked together[6] on treating important aspects of the Tribunal as it is, after all, both a historic and a legal event.

The classic works about the Tokyo Tribunal aim to assess the quality of justice at Tokyo and lie between the extreme views that qualify its justice as "victors' justice" or "justice of civilization." The volume *Victors' Justice* by Richard Minear published in 1971 offers a fierce critique of the Tribunal's legal postulates that were straightforwardly violated by American engagement in the Vietnam War. Minear rejects the legality of norms and procedural rules that were created ex post facto by the victorious Allies in order to get rid of Axis leaders and assign the ultimate responsibility for the Pacific War to the Japanese top brass. The selection of the members of the Tribunal was not merit based, but rather politically motivated to create a group of individuals who would be willing to carry out the postwar goals set by their respective governments and the Supreme Commander Douglas MacArthur—thus being prejudicial to the impartiality of justice and due process of law. He strongly argued that victors' justice was blind to similar atrocities committed and brutality used by the Allied powers to achieve victory. The rationale behind the Tribunal required 17 years of Japanese history to be rewritten in order to fit the dominant narrative of Japan's conspiracy to wage aggressive war, which resulted in history being profoundly flawed and simplified. In the author's words, the historical complexities leading towards the Pacific War could not have been grasped by the legalistic framework.

On the opposite spectrum of Minear's reasoning stands the work of Japanese historian Kentarō Awaya, whose book *Tōkyō saiban e no michi* criticizes the Allied powers for their half-hearted effort in prosecuting Japanese war crimes as well as the Allies' crimes against the Japanese such as atomic bombing and firebombing which fell into oblivion. As he contends, the probative evidence for these crimes—bacteriological tests and vivisections, sex slavery, opium and drug war—was available throughout the Trial while the former Japanese colonies were omitted from the bench. From the 1980s, with declassification of archives in the US, Japan, New Zealand, and Australia, a new potential was born for the research field to thrive and produce an expanded, yet more balanced narrative about the Tokyo Tribunal. Departing from the extreme views, a series of books by Japanese historian Yoshinobu Higurashi, based on archival materials from the Allied powers' countries and Japan, offer a new perspective on the Trial as a place of diplomacy, an institutional framework where the postwar international order was negotiated and created to reflect a new balance of power. This approach allowed for a broader perspective, both thematically and temporally, while his analysis transcends the strictly legal framework and embraces a broader perspective of the Tribunal. As part of the same effort the work of Yuma Totani, a Japanese historian based in the US, stands out as an invaluable contribution for the extensive new evidence that it brought to light which had a transformative effect upon the conventional knowledge regarding specific themes of the Trial such as the disharmonies of the work of the prosecutorial unit, non-evidence-based criteria for the selection of the defendants, the existence of abundant evidence about Japanese atrocities in its former Empire at the time of the Trial, and the legal incompetence of the members of the Court.

As the archives in the former Japanese colonies and certain Allied powers' countries were made available only from the 1990s, it is logical that the researchers' focus was exclusively placed upon the Tokyo Tribunal. As a consequence, other important trials of lower-rank Japanese military officials, for violations of laws surrounding armed conflicts or *jus in bello*, performed in national courts of the Allied powers for crimes committed against their prisoners of war (POWs) and populace in the former colonies, were rather marginalized. The proliferation of publications on these trials that extend beyond the 1950s offers a better understanding of the former Japanese Empire and acknowledges the existence of a more inclusive and contrasted view of the Allied powers' war criminal justice effort that does not only revolve around the Tokyo Tribunal. The latter enjoyed the position of a war criminal trial star not only in that it took place in Tokyo, but in that it was widely publicized as the most important trial as it was prosecuting the main architects of the Pacific War effort. However, that is only one piece to the war effort puzzle as other parts of society, beyond lower-rank soldiers, such as the business sector and different organizations and associations without which the war would not have been possible, were left outside of the picture. The 2017 multi-authored volume *Japanese War Criminals: The Politics of Justice After the Second World War* offers findings on Japanese Class BC war criminals who were tried throughout the former colonies of the Japanese Empire, tracing their fate from their prosecution to their release. Class BC trials are the theme that this book explores only obliquely, but recognizes them as crucial for understanding the wider Allied powers' war crime program in postwar Asia targeting Japan.

In 2018, *Transcultural Justice at the Tokyo Tribunal: The Allied Struggle for Justice, 1946–48* edited by Kerstin Von Lingen opens the Tribunal's "institutional black box" by offering experiences and interactions of its legal personnel. Its actor-based approach gives another layer of meaning to the dominant state-based approach literature by giving it a more democratic, inclusive, and multicultural view. This level of analysis portrays the Tribunal as an international, multicultural exchange and experience rather than subscribes to the narrative of American hegemonic influence. The Allied powers' legal representatives proved to be much more significant to the way work, dynamics, and outcomes of the Trial unfolded.[7]

In the immediate postwar period, political and intellectual milieu in Japan as well as its public opinion predominantly held onto *Tōkyo saiban shikan* or "the Tokyo Tribunal view of history," which nurtured a "masochistic" view when it comes to war responsibility. The 2008 *War Crimes Tribunals and Transitional Justice: The Tokyo Trial and the Nuremberg Legacy* by Madoka Futamura discusses the limits of the Tokyo Trial reflected in its inability to foster a broader sense of war responsibility in Japan, thus making it rather an obstacle for the Japanese people to come to terms with their past.[8] Futamura asserts that popular response towards the trial ranges from "passive acceptance to apathy," while criticism of the Trial and its denial are equated, which leaves little room for a meaningful discussion.[9] The manifestation of this kind of criticism gathered momentum from the 1970s and was primarily shaped by the dissenting opinion of Indian Justice Radhabinod Pal whose arguments were singled out and made to fit revisionist historical narratives. His dissenting opinion discusses the war of aggression as ex post facto *law* and stresses the defective procedure and partiality of justice at Tokyo, thus implying that all defendants should have been acquitted. Pal's dissent has further been arbitrarily distorted to serve the nationalistic discourse in Japan, which has been on the rise since the 1990s. As the Trial's criticism and atrocities denial equate, the nationalistic view justifies Japan's Great Asia War and refutes the legal validity of and subsequent verdict given by the Tokyo Tribunal.

This book builds upon the existing body of research and gives its contribution by shedding new light on the Tokyo Tribunal in several aspects. First, it observes the Tribunal as a politico-legal event, thus addressing its nature by discussing the postulates on which international criminal justice rests as a precursor for proper understanding of the Tribunal. The concept of international criminal justice has been often evaluated in strict terms, against justice administrated in domestic courts or, ideally, as an entity free from interference of politics. However, international criminal justice not only touches at the core of the once sacred domain of state sovereignty, that is, to punish its citizens, but it cannot be born without the political support of its sponsor states. They use their political values and strategic goals (geopolitical, security, or material) to formulate broader policies that are supposed to be channeled through the creation of international tribunals, their mandates, and rules, thus pointing out the idea that justice is not an end in itself.[10] Whether states will prosecute atrocities committed by parties involved in war is not a result of consistent practice, but rather careful calculations of self and collective interest which introduces the idea of international law being the "architecture of political compromise."[11]

American political philosopher Judith Shklar in her discussions on legalism introduces the general idea that "law is politics [...] but not every policy is legalistic."[12] Legalism as ideology[13] argues for a strict dichotomy between law and non-law. It observes law as a space where citizens are free of arbitrary acts of government, thus providing for stability and certainty within the social order. Legalism, in her view, ought to be liberated from this ideological divide and understood as "the policy of justice," a "form of political action," thus never isolated from the essential components of politics—power, prudence, and expediency.[14] However, faced with public outrage at the Axis atrocities, the grand scale of human, economic, and military devastation caused by World War II, the victorious Allies felt compelled to create an ex post facto law that would allow for criminal punishment of leaders they considered responsible before the law. They believed that this way they would avoid the judgement of the past and provide for a brighter future by outlawing war as an instrument of national policy for aggressive purposes. In these exceptional circumstances, the call to act came from the suitable opportunity and intention to avoid what is in Kantian words called "blood guilt" or *blutschuld*, which is implied complicity from ignoring crimes.[15] In addition, this highly moralistic narrative would be incomplete without taking into consideration the broader political objectives, the strategic and pragmatic ones. Shklar's ideological discussion of the relation between law and politics served as a departure point for scholars who researched on international criminal law or the Tokyo Tribunal more specifically.

The concept of legalism in endeavors of criminal justice was further refined by Johnathan Bass who described it as "liberal states' belief in the rule of law" and moral urge that perpetrators of atrocities ought to be punished. This view of legalism does not recognize the lack of consistency in application, and even misuse, of legalism by the same liberal states due to geopolitical and practical concerns related to their national interest and security. To remedy the latter purely liberal view of legalism, Peter Maguire offers a more appealing explanation of the policies underpinning international criminal tribunals that he denominates *strategic legalism*—that is, "the use of law and legal arguments to further larger policy objectives, irrespective of facts or moral considerations."[16] Another part of his argument, of importance to the subject matter and scope of this book, is that in the post-trial phase, when the war criminal issue started hurting US foreign policy goals, the US resorted to extrajudicial means to secretly reduce the defendants' sentences which would ultimately lead to their release.[17] In the same vein, Zachary Kaufman observes international criminal justice as an exercise of *prudentialism*.[18] He explains that international criminal tribunals are the product of "case-specific balancing of relevant politics, pragmatics, and normative beliefs."[19] Kaufman's argument appears to be more refined than that of strategic legalism, and the term *prudentialism*, defined in a multitude of ways, has been understood as choice of action that best serves one's interests without moral considerations, or, it could be added, at least not as its main motive. These two approaches are relevant to the effect that they add a realist component, that is, power and national interest, thus contrasting the liberal notion of legalism which entails consistency and commitment to the rules of law and advancement of morality. However, in case of strategic legalism and prudentialism normative beliefs are unstable and unpredictable when applied to the realm of international relations. However, the term prudentialism involves prudence or cautiousness in decision-making which, according to this book, did not reflect the Allied powers' choices at all times. For reasons pertaining to semantics, the term *strategic legalism*, borrowed from Maguire, will be used as it allows for a better understanding of the coherence and utility of legalistic policies used by the Allied powers in relation to their larger diplomatic and political goals for postwar Japan. This book, however, considers that moral component is more often than not present to support these legalistic policies.

Second, the analytical grid takes into consideration the factor of time when looking at different stages of international military tribunals. Political goals, values, and intentions professed in the moment of their establishment, investigative phase, and later, trial phase, adjudication, and, finally, execution of sentences phase which entails releases and pardons before the serving of the full sentence do not coincide. These "behind the curtain" realpolitik considerations to which tribunals are submitted, in a more or less subtle way,[20] are not visible on the institutional record of the tribunals which makes "the true story of these institutions rather incomplete."[21] Due to this "compartmentalization"[22] of the trials it is difficult to assess "the nature, intent, and impact of the political decisions which created, administered, and ended these trials"[23] under a single label of victors' justice or justice of civilization. In the case of the Tokyo Tribunal, its establishment period reflected the power dynamics, principles, and goals of the immediate postwar international order which in turn dramatically transformed throughout the Trial as the regional dynamics of the Cold War took precedence over lofty goals proclaimed in 1945. Events ought to be analyzed within the context peculiar to them—circumstances, timing, and mentality—which act as transformative forces guiding actors' intentions and decisions at a given moment. The context has a significant role in making sense of concepts, institutions, actors, decision-making processes at a given time. Thus, this book aims to emphasize the evolving circumstances that were reflected in the very unfolding of two distinct phases of the international justice in Tokyo. The book makes sense of justice rendered by the Tokyo Tribunal by prioritizing the establishment of the Tribunal and the execution of sentences stages. The two distinct moments are the most revealing of the Allied powers' evolving intentions, dilemmas, and strategies—the immediate postwar context when the urge to establish the Tribunal was at its highest and the post-institutional phase where the Cold War context challenged the dynamics of justice. These shifts were mirrored upon and changed the dynamics and quality of what can be called the end product—that is, the criminal justice at IMTFE. This approach adds a new layer of meaning to the extant political, legal, and historical narratives surrounding the Tribunal presented by its main stakeholders—the Allied powers, postwar Japan, and victims—each using different phases of the Tribunal at their convenience in gauging the war criminal trials program in Japan.

Third, the story behind the Tokyo Tribunal does not end with the delivery of the majority judgement. Certainly, it implied the institutional closure of the Tribunal's activity, but what came after—the execution of imposed sentences—is often a disregarded piece of the puzzle. The "execution of sentences" phase also involves parole, clemency, or pardon before the complete execution of the sentence by the prisoner. In the practice of modern international criminal tribunals, it has become a rule rather than an exception that convicted war criminals are released by default after having served two-thirds of their sentence.[24] In the case of the Tokyo Tribunal, it was not the composite part of the war crimes program; although its Charter did grant the Supreme Commander Douglas MacArthur with "the power to approve, reduce or otherwise alter any sentence" imposed by the Tribunal, the formal system of clemency and parole was not formally established until 1950. The rationale behind the clemency and parole system was meant to be a corrective to initial injustices in sentencing, but more importantly to adapt to the increased strategic value of Japan that transitioned from being a foe to becoming a friend. This post-institutional dimension of the Tribunal has been rather neglected and left out in assessing the overall quality of the Allied powers' justice. Usually, the extant research, with few exceptions, mostly takes as its analytical grid the trial process and adjudication when assessing the Tribunal. Yet, the inclusion of the post-institutional phase of the IMTFE bears potential to shed a new light onto the nature and meaning of justice administered at Tokyo that has a property of being evolving, in motion rather than static in character. Yoshinobu's book *Tōkyō saiban* is chronological in its approach and the author does include a section on the release of Class A war criminals. However, Class A war criminals' release is not observed as part of the overall justice process of the IMTFE as it does not belong to its two-and-a-half-year-long institutional lifespan.

The central research questions that this work aims to address are: What was the purpose of using the international criminal justice in postwar Japan? Beyond retribution, what other goals were targeted by the Tokyo Tribunal, and how did these influence the nature of justice designed for this specific context? In what way did the post-institutional phase of the Tribunal, involving the parole and release process of the convicted war criminals, transform the nature and meaning of the war crimes program in Japan?

The present research will argue that the IMTFE, observed as a part of occupation, was established to fulfill the main Allied powers' postwar policies at the international and regional level. Beyond retribution, the Tokyo Tribunal served as a strategic legalism tool to complement newly created international rules on the use of force. These rules would constitute the basis for the post-World War II international order, primarily prescriptive in nature and meant to preserve peace. The creation of both a legal and a historical narrative on Japan's aggressive war constitutes its second largest goal. On a more local level, the Tokyo Tribunal served as a medium for the reeducation of local leaders. Japan's ascendance to the role of Western ally and its strategic value did not result in the prompt release of Class A war criminals; quite the contrary, it reached a deadlock in which legalism no longer played a strategic role. This issue exposed inconsistencies in US expectations regarding Japan's rearmament and started to inhibit progress on important security agenda in US-Japan diplomatic relations. The dynamics of US-Japan negotiations regarding Class A war criminals, as it will be shown, placed in the hands of the Japanese government a powerful tool to instigate its own minimalistic visions of security vis-à-vis the US. Consequentially, the IMTFE and Class A war criminals which once represented the symbol of Japanese defeat started to become an indirect asset for Japan in its aspirations to achieve postwar reintegration on its own terms. Hence, the justice meted out at IMTFE did not exclusively benefit the Allied powers, but had some utility for the defeated party in war. The book reveals that justice, in the Cold War context, lost its strategic character and started working against the Allies, but predominantly US larger diplomatic goals.

The argumentation is based on findings from the archival documents predominantly from the US National Archives related to the work of US government agencies which had to strike a delicate balance between war criminal policies and other strategic goals. International conferences in the interwar and war period set in motion the establishment of the Tribunal, whereas the Far Eastern Commission plays an important role in amending the occupation policies and enhancing the international experience at the Tribunal. The International Prosecution Section plays instrumental role in elaborating the historical narrative of Japan's aggressive war and refining the newly created law. The documents and minutes of the Clemency and Parole Board, which was the main body in charge of the release of Japanese war criminals, was the place where the strong legal mentality in the post-war period was reflected. The minutes and reports of the Allied representatives' meetings in Washington reveal the Allies' deliberations behind the decision-making process in relation to the release of Class A war criminals. Findings in relation to the Japanese side of the story draw predominantly from authoritative secondary sources on the topic and in minor part from the archival documents of the Ministry of Foreign Affairs and Ministry of Justice which, each in their own right, played an instrumental role in the process of releasing war criminals.

Before proceeding to the organizational aspects of the book, it is important to clarify a few points. The term justice is used to designate international criminal justice which consists in international criminal law application by the Tribunal from its establishment to the release of the convicted war criminals. Although Class A war criminals or major war criminals were convicted by the IMTFE, after the occupation, the campaign for the release of BC war criminals somewhat merged with the efforts for the release of Class A war criminals. In many instances, the war criminals question or issue encompassed both classes, but in the later stages of the decision-making process, their differences would reappear as Class A war criminals involved deliberations of all of the Allied powers which signed the Peace Treaty with Japan. In this sense, their paths occasionally converge and diverge. The present work uses diplomatic history so as to place the Tokyo Tribunal within the broader framework of US-Japan diplomatic relations which dramatically evolved over the period covered by the analysis. The occasional insights into the lower-level-placed actors aim to offer a better understanding of how policy choices adopted at the top level, mainly preoccupied by politics, principles, emotions, and exigency,[25] had to compromise with facts, law, and objectivity[26] once they reached the execution stage within the IMTFE. Also, the trajectory of the IMTFE from a high political level, passing through mid- to lower-level agencies (Ambassadorial, Clemency Parole Board), with its eventual resurgence at the top diplomatic level in 1955, is reflected in the narrative and political relevance of persons involved. The events are analyzed to reflect the dominant political ideas of the time in which they took place, whereas connections made with present-date similar events are made with the intent of showing the evolution of the principle or consequences of past choices that had been made. In order to respect the nature of the phenomenon studied which also pertains to the legal domain, minor parts of the present work address and discuss technical legal points and principles. This duality surrounding the Tokyo Tribunal is reflected in the agency of the second generation of *lawyers-statesmen* personified by Henry Stimson, Robert H. Jackson, John Foster Dulles, who were concerned with legal justifications, using moral or legal grounds, and lower-level *jurist-politicians*, who were part of the IMTFE representing justices and lawyers with a great sense of pragmatism, ready to bend their legal ideologies and convictions in order to implement policies they were assigned.

The book is organized in two parts. Part I articulates the argument that the Tokyo Tribunal was used as a vehicle to promote goals that were both international and regional in nature—to establish a law-based international order, to produce a self-serving historical narrative, and to fulfill three-pronged occupation policies in Japan. The chapters also aim to reflect the nature of the international criminal justice that is always strategic, selective, and partial. Chapter 1 introduces the Tokyo Trial and places it within larger strategic, legal, and history-related goals of the postwar international order. It further delves into the literature review on this subject, the book's central research questions, findings, and its contribution to the field. Chapter 2 shows the direct nexus between the 1919 Versailles Conference and interwar institutional and legal instruments to limit war which ultimately failed. It also looks at IMT Nuremberg as a starting point in criminalization of the aggressive war, a goal that the IMTFE would entertain in its own way. Chapter 3 illuminates on the inter-Allied powers' rivalry when it comes to the establishment phase of the Tribunal which initially weighed in favor of the US leadership role. It argues that the role of the Commonwealth nations would prove crucial for addressing the political imperative of expediting trials until the public interest was still high. Their power and influence would be most visible within the Tribunal, more precisely its International Prosecution Section, and not the little effective institutional mechanisms surrounding the IMTFE such as the Far Eastern Commission (FEC). Chapter 4 shows how the judicial narrative is used to manipulate the historical narrative regarding the nature and unfolding of the Fifteen Years War. The main argument is that the hegemonic nature of the historical narrative lies in its exclusive focus on the aggressive war charge which disregards interests of other nations in the Asia-Pacific, thus reflecting the still prevalent colonial and racial mentalities. The lack of political linearity of decision-making centers in Japan, along with the lack of direct evidence, as well as unified theaters of battle, furthermore, shows that the prosecution had to rely on suspicious legal concepts in international law to give coherence to the case. Chapter 5 reveals the motives behind the piecemeal inclusion of the mass atrocity committed against the population in the former Japanese colonies from the indictment, despite the fact that the evidence was available during the Trial, and the role the prosecution assigned to it. The chapter also analyzes instances of Allied atrocity against Japan in light of the newly established law. The chapter shows in what way the deliberate silence on these crimes impacts the historical record and how it complicates Japan's understanding of its own guilt. Chapter 6, the last chapter in Part I, turns its attention towards the arbitrary process of selection of the Japanese defendants and the poor standard of evidence used to make the case against them. The chapter illuminates on the reasons for absence of Emperor Shōwa from the dock given that he represented the only clear constant source of power and authority in Japan during the war. Part II of the book turns to the post-institutional phase of the Tribunal and the phase of the execution of sentences that happened in the changed geopolitical setting of the Cold War. The chapters articulate the argument that the strategic nature of justice, presented in Part I, had been lost and started to work against the larger interests of the US while it benefited, to some extent, the Japanese government. Chapter 7 observes the majority judgement and its dissenting and separate opinions as instances that offer legal and historical narratives to be instrumentalized by each stakeholder in the process. The chapter looks at how the already shifting policies towards Japan in the early Cold War context failed to be reflected when the window of opportunity opened for the review of harsh sentences imposed on the Tokyo Tribunal's defendants, Class A war criminals. As the chapter demonstrates, this sentence review episode provoked controversy between the Allies regarding the international character of the Tribunal. Chapter 8 treats the San Francisco Peace Treaty and its nature and provisions addressing the fate of war criminals and reflects contradictory postwar policies towards Japan. The concept of clemency and parole and their meaning for the war crimes program in Japan are explained. The institutional disputes within middle to lower levels of power in the US, in the context of its close relations with Japan, regarding the future course of the war criminal policies, shed light on the deep discrepancies existing between legal and political solutions. Chapter 9 treats Prime Minister Yoshida's position towards the war criminals as well as institutional cleavages when it comes to the release of war criminals in Japan. It goes on to show the persistent confusion between Class A and Class BC war criminals which complicates and converges their campaign for release. The chapter shows that Japanese public opinion played a crucial role in pushing the government into action, although the most important developments occurred starting with the Hatoyama Cabinet. In addition, the chapter analyzes the inter-Allied differences when it comes to the release of Class A war criminals, as well as the important role played by Communist China and the Soviets in impacting the process. Chapter 10 points to the persistent rigidity of the US policy towards the release of Japanese war criminals and the reasons for it, which stands in contrast with softening of the until then conservative policies of other Allied powers. The Hatoyama and Kishi Cabinets, which had a personal interest in the release of Class A war criminals, skillfully accelerated the release process. The chapter illuminates on the transformative role Class A release and rehabilitation had upon the sense of war responsibility in Japan. Chapter 11, the concluding chapter, discusses the limitations and few successes of the Tokyo Tribunal when it comes to the legal, strategic, and political goals it intends to fulfill. More generally, the chapter puts into perspective the expectations states can place into these war criminal tribunals as judicial instruments of peace when used in post-conflict societies. The chapter concludes that international criminal tribunals remain mostly beneficial to the hegemons and states they tend to patronize and, to a lesser degree, to states whose leaders they put on trial.

Notes

1. The Rome Statute of the International Criminal Court, Article 15*bis*.
2. Nuremberg Judgement, October 1, 1946, 25.
3. Akira Iriye, *Japan and the Wider World: From Mid-Nineteenth Century to the Present,* New York: Longman, 1997, 100.
4. Brian Orend, *The Morality of War,* Peterborough: Broadview Press, 2006, 247.

5. Larry May, *Aggression and Crimes Against Peace* (Cambridge: Cambridge University Press, 2009), 339.
6. Neil Boister and Robert Cryer, *The Tokyo International Military Tribunal: A Reappraisal*, Oxford: Oxford University Press, 2008; Kirsten Sellars, *Crime Against Peace and International Law*, Cambridge: Cambridge University Press, 2013; Kirsten Von Lingen, *Transcultural Justice at the Tokyo Tribunal: The Allied Struggle for Justice*, Leiden: Brill, 2018; Sandra Wilson, Krebb, Trefault, and Dean Aszkielowicz, *Japanese War Criminals: The Politics of Justice After the Second World War* (New York: Columbia University Press, 2017).
7. Kirsten Von Lingen, *Transcultural Justice at the Tokyo Tribunal: The Allied Struggle for Justice*, Leiden: Brill, 2018.
8. Madoka Futamura, *War Crimes Tribunal and Transitional Justice: The Tokyo Trial and the Nuremberg Legacy*, London: Routledge, 2008, 109–133.
9. Ibid., 72–74; 109.
10. Jackson N. Maogoto, *War Crimes and Realpolitik: International Justice from World War I to the 21st Century*, (London: Rienner Publishers, 2004), 10.
11. Jackson N. Maogoto, *War Crimes and Realpolitik: International Justice from World War I to the 21st Century*, 10.
12. Judith N. Shklar, *Legalism: Law, Morals and Political Trials*, Cambridge: Harvard University Press, 1986, 144.
13. Legalism as ideology is referred to in the sense that it defends the law from the world of politics, without its proponents acknowledging that in claiming so they are also positioning themselves among political values. See more in Shklar, *Legalism: Law, Morals and Political Trials*, 8.
14. Shklar, *Legalism: Law, Morals and Political Trials*, 126, 143.
15. Jonathan N. Choi, "Early Release in International Criminal Law," *The Yale Law Journal* 123 (2014): 1812.
16. Peter Maguire, *Law and War: An American Story*, New York: Columbia University Press, 2001, 9.
17. Ibid.
18. Zachary D. Kaufman, *United States Law and Policy on Transitional Justice: Principles, Politics and Pragmatics*, New York: Oxford University Press, 2017, 58–60.
19. Zachary D. Kaufman, *United States Law and Policy on Transitional Justice: Principles, Politics and Pragmatics*, 58–60.
20. M. Cherif Bassiouni, "From Versailles to Rwanda in Seventy-Five Years: The Need to Establish a Permanent International Criminal Court", *Harvard Human Rights Law Review* 10 (1997): 12.
21. Ibid., 12.
22. Ibid., 12.
23. Ibid., 12.

24. Jonathan N. Choi, "Early Release in International Criminal Law," 1791.
25. James Burnham Sedgwick, "The Trial Within: Negotiating Justice at the International Military Tribunal for the Far East, 1946–1948," (Phd Thesis, The University of British Columbia, 2012), 24–25.
26. Ibid.," 24–25.

CHAPTER 2

In the Shadow of the Paris Peace Conference: Behind the Scene of the International Military Tribunal for the Far East

International Law Awakens as an Instrument of Foreign Policy

The Paris Peace Conference along with institutional and legal developments that animated political and intellectual debates in the interwar period is instructive for understanding the purpose and goals related to the International Military Tribunal at Tokyo. In that sense, the establishment of the post-World War I international order, League of Nations, and related legal instruments in the interwar period had relevance extending well into the making of international order in 1945.

The end of the nineteenth and the beginning of the twentieth century featured the emergence of international law as an independent discipline which gave way to its growing professionalization.[1] International lawyers at the newly formed international law institute in Belgium saw the value of the discipline in it giving impetus or "new force" to "diplomacy and individual science" which they considered to be its essential components. In France, editors of *Revue générale de droit international public*, founded in 1894, and to this day one of the most prestigious journals of international law, felt committed to the development of the "science of international law" that was finding its place among other disciplines it overlapped with—philosophy, history, and politics. International law was conceived as a discipline that was suitable to serve as an extended hand of national politics and diplomacy. The newly granted power of international law as an

A. Babovic, *The Tokyo Trial, Justice, and the Postwar International Order*, New Directions in East Asian History,
https://doi.org/10.1007/978-981-13-3477-1_2

instrument for serving strictly national interests was particularly appealing in the US and Japan, both rising powers on the international scene. The US embarked upon expansion and creation of its informal empire, while Japan was eager to catch up with the West and become the first Asian power, an equal sovereign among countries that considered themselves to occupy the top of the "standard of civilization ladder," a legal concept that was advanced by international law to justify the right of European nations to colonize non-Europeans. National international law institutes and journals, created by nationalist legal elites who were supported by their respective governments, became an institutional driver for "nationalization of the study of international law."[2]

In 1897, the Japanese Society of International Law was formed and already in 1902 it started publishing *Kokusaihō Gaikō Zasshi* or *Journal of International Law and Diplomacy*. It is worth noting that in 1866, Shu Nishi and Tsu Shindō, whom the Bakufu sent abroad to study international law at the University of Leiden, brought to Japan the leading-edge knowledge on the Western law and disseminated the legal thought of Hugo Grotius who extensively wrote on rules of war and peace. Later in 1945, some of the Grotius natural law reasoning that war can be waged not only for the purpose of self-defense but also punishment of crimes and that those waging unjust wars cannot benefit from the same rights as those who do will be heavily deployed in interpreting the laws on the use of force at Tokyo. Nishi became the Japanese government advisor on European affairs in addition to his scholarly and teaching work at Kaiseijo.[3] The concept of modern international law was one example of the Western ideas and knowledge which were imported to Japan and proved to be the key to modernization process of the Japanese state and its ascension to the rank of a legitimate power on par with its European counterparts. In connection to this, Japan sought to be able to rectify unequal treaties, which presented it with burdensome demands, that it had been forced to conclude with the Western powers since 1858.[4] The most important diplomatic goals for Japan in the late nineteenth century would be its ascension to the status of power which would give Japan an opportunity to not only renegotiate the above-mentioned treaties in relation to the Western powers but also gain legal sovereign rights pertaining to "civilized nations" and thus legitimacy for its territorial expansion in Asia.

In the US, international law had a pivotal role in the backing of its expansionist foreign policy in the overseas territories, starting with the annexation of Hawaii and the Philippines following the Spanish-American

War of 1898. The period from the 1890s to the 1920s is considered to be a "progressivist era"[5] during which international lawyers in official capacities of secretaries of states, ambassadors, diplomats, professors shaped US foreign policy. The founders of the American Society of International Law (ASIL) represented a new generation of "legalistic moralistic"[6] international lawyers, among whom some became influential statesman, who created a whole set of "legal subterfuges" to justify what had started as an era of American interventionism. ASIL served as a platform for developing an American view of international law that was based in positive law and was meant to support US realpolitik. This early American community of international lawyers understood that international law needed some kind of power basis to be applied. This Hobbesian view of the function international law was to fulfill was highly sophisticated, pragmatic, and sensitive to the imperatives of fulfilling the national interest, thus mostly free from critique and divergent from Grotius natural law which was infused with morals and idealism. In essence, the American view of international law in this period was realist in nature.[7] American international lawyers were part of the elite that shared a strong sense of public service and believed that the US was a country of laws and that law was the best suited to support this transitional period in the US foreign policy—from tradition of isolationism to the path of imperialism.[8]

Limiting Peace Through Cooperation

The League of Nations was a clear departure from the above-mentioned American prewar realist tradition of international law, backed up by Wilsonian idealist and moralist vision of the international order which was to be kept by through international cooperation and threat of collective coercive action.[9] The war to end all wars did not live up to its expectations; however it did set into motion important changes to the international order and shifts in power dynamics, mainly in the European theater but also in the Asia-Pacific region. These profound changes set the international dialogue among the Great Powers regarding the premises upon which the new order should be based.[10] The 1919 Paris Peace Conference represented an important venue for victorious nations (America, Britain, France, Italy, and Japan) to divide war gains, to organize a new international order that would preserve the status quo, and to punish the defeated. The peace settlement involved, to a certain degree, a reluctant introduction of international law as its preserving agent. The consequences of the important decisions and choices made in 1919 would have immediate impact upon the developments of the interwar period, and, most importantly, percolate all the way into the post-World War II peace settlement. The war marked the end of the Ottoman Empire, "the sick man of Europe," and the Austro-Hungarian Empire giving birth to new independent nations, which started positioning themselves around the victorious European powers, their new patronizing states. Although the main theater of the Great War was Europe-centered, it had important repercussions for East Asia, a bastion of European imperialism, and Japan which had already started emerging as a regional power in the 1890s–1920s.

Following its victories in the first Sino-Japanese and Russo-Japanese wars in 1895 and 1905, respectively, Japan gained not only important spheres of influence in Manchuria and Korea but rose as an important force that "asserted greater political, economic, and cultural influence within Asia."[11] In the eyes of the US and certain European states, Japan, "a great and ambitious nation,"[12] posed a threat and was seen a potential challenger to the Western-led regional order that had been built on the ashes of the Chinese regional domination.[13] The Great War propelled Japan into a position of economic and military power among White nations at Versailles which it proudly assumed as the only Asian power to participate in the formation of new international order.[14] In the aftermath of the Great War, Japanese foreign policy, under Foreign Minister Yasuya Uchida, stayed faithful to the Meiji era imperatives of Japan, cooperating within the multilateral framework with the Western powers, the principle of non-intervention in China, and the protection of Japanese interests in Manchuria.[15] Nevertheless, it is important to mention that Japanese foreign policy had derailed from these principles and its traditional course on two occasions, under Foreign Minister Kato Takaaki and Prime Minister Masatake Terauchi, as they used military force to elicit territorial concessions. In particular, Takaaki's Twenty-One Demands presented to China in January 1915, by which Japan tried to gain similar rights to those that European powers already had, threatened to violate China's territorial and administrative integrity, while Terauchi's Siberian intervention in August 1918, in contravention to the agreed rules, was interpreted by the US as Japan's effort to secure exclusive control of northern Manchuria and Siberia. These represented the first examples of Japan's ambitions for exclusive control over these territories.[16]

At the Paris Peace Conference, the Japanese delegation became aware of its limited chances for territorial and economic expansion in the region due to the European powers' spheres of influence. They came to the negotiating table with an initially uncompromising demand on one point—the recognition of Japanese special rights in Shandong province. As the demand for the annexation was met with disapproval from other powers and US President Woodrow Wilson who wanted to break away from the old diplomacy that involved unequal treatment of third countries and secret alliances, the Japanese delegation changed its strategy by reframing its cause in a way to appeal to Wilson's idealism. In the end, Wilson accepted the Japanese demand for governing ex-German possessions, contrary to the proposed joint governance with other powers, with promise to give extensive rights and better treatment to the Chinese which was to be subsequently negotiated. In addition, the Japanese blamed the Western powers for the current situation in China by which they scored extra points that would make President Wilson succumb to their proposal.[17] Despite his plea against colonialism and the opposition of all members of his delegation, he saw value in what he thought would reshape the existent great power structure in East Asia, ensure the successful conclusion of the Peace Treaty, and secure the League of Nations project.[18] The dire consequences of this concession that others qualified as a "terrible mistake"[19] would be visible only later in the interwar period.[20] More importantly, this shift resulted in Japan drifting apart from its old and traditional ally, Britain, and gravitating towards more cooperation with the US that was championing the new principles. America was the only nation that did not possess an explicit sphere of influence in the region—it did not offer open support for the great powers system in the region—yet it benefited from rights and privileges as a favored nation.[21]

What presented itself as an opportunity for the US-Japan rapprochement was their shared interest in penetrating the order dominated by European powers.[22] While at the end of the nineteenth century the US was slowly joining the Big Powers, in 1919 the rise of the US to preeminence was evident against the European continent that suffered unparalleled human, material, and military losses.[23] Organizing new order under Wilson devalued the role of international lawyers, and it rather put into service historians, geographers, ethnographers, and economists. In the words of Stephen Wertheim, had it been any other president, the solution would be axed on "legalist-sanctionist world order" rather than one based on loose international organization that caters to the popular will and is devoid of power of physical sanction.[24]

In essence, the new peace settlement was supposed to keep "Germans down, the Americans in, and Russians out."[25] Germany, stripped of its colonies and burdened with heavy reparations, was subjected to a punitive peace that bred the revisionism in the interwar period and led to renewed hostilities. The destruction of the defeated enemy proved to be a detrimental choice for the international order and would constitute one of the most valuable lessons learned for the Allied powers in the aftermath of World War II. In 1919, the question of whether and in what way Germans and their allies ought to be punished for starting the Great War was entrusted to the Commission on the Responsibilities of the Authors of the War and on Enforcement of Penalties within the scope of the preliminary Peace Conference. The Entente powers were clearly divided: Great Britain and France supported the criminal prosecution of German Emperor Wilhelm II, while the US, cool-headed and sheltered from the miseries of direct war experience, refuted his prosecution as it considered statesmen business should be out of reach of judicial authorities for an offense that was clearly of a moral but not a legal character. When it came to the idea of international criminal punishment, President Wilson was more consumed with the League of Nations project than organizing trials, which he considered to be equivalent to a pure act of revenge.

The Report issued by the Commission was important in two aspects: it attributed the responsibility for waging war to Germany and rendered the immunity of heads of states obsolete for violations against laws and customs of war and humanity.[26] In 1919, Wilhelm II was not recommended for prosecution as the Report observed lack of legal basis and considered the matter suitable for study by statesmen and historians.[27] Articles 227, 228, and 229 of the Paris Peace Treaty vaguely stated his criminal responsibility for "a supreme offense against international morality and sanctity of treaties."[28] This provision did not contain any concrete definition of rule being violated or offense and was thus deprived of all substance. His apprehension for the trial was ordered, but it never took place due to his refuge to Holland. Lord Chamberlain questioned the efficiency of potential trials given the time length needed to convene the tribunal, investigate the crimes, and prosecute numerous German war criminals. After the passions of war subsided, he thought, the Allied war criminal program would face reduced interest in justice being served and lose support of public opinion.[29] This kind of dilemmas, as later chapter will show, was present in the hour of deliberations surrounding the utility and timeliness of the Tokyo Tribunal.

Particularly interesting for this book about the Tokyo Tribunal are reservations lodged by the American and Japanese delegations at the Paris

Peace Conference regarding the criminal prosecution of heads of states for violations of laws of war and humanity.[30] The US legal stance evidenced the moment of absence of jus gentium Americana that had developed in the whereabouts of the twentieth century and that was shortly abandoned during President Wilson's administration. Jus gentium Americana is here understood as the dual use of international law to protect and project US national interests in both restraining and enabling ways. More precisely, law is seen as an agent of restraint from action and enabler for legitimate action. In *Legalist Empire*, Benjamin Coates argues that this behavior is not "hypocritical" but a "particular" way of applying law. Yet, it could be further elaborated that this particularity consists in the view of international law as an instrument of power and, when suitable, force. The legality of state's actions ought not to be a matter of believing but the application of existent norms or their bona fide interpretation. In that sense, subjective element of belief is oftentimes connected to legitimacy of actions that are sought to be justified or validated in the absence of rules or their violation. The American view of international law is deeply infused with realism, thus inseparable from its national interest and power, and in that sense, it is hegemonic. Ironically, the American reservations exposed the novelty of the idea of an international tribunal and appropriateness of the national commission[31] to prosecute the offenders of laws of war and humanity to punish those who committed criminal acts. This led to the point of negative criminal responsibility which implied that that person of authority who failed to prevent or repress the violations of others—he should have had knowledge of or ability to prevent—is a liability criterion which would be hard to prove.[32] The Americans also advanced the lack of the legal precedent and state practice against the prosecution for initiating war which would lead to ex post facto or retroactive law, while the violation of immunity of heads of states, who can only be liable before their national courts, but not before a foreign jurisdiction, would be detrimental to state sovereignty.[33]

The Japanese stance towards what could have been called beginnings of international criminal law back in 1919 was in concert with American delegation. This was not surprising. Japan sat at the table with the Big Powers and as an expansionist power itself did not want to see its heads of states indicted for any war-related offenses in the future. The Japanese delegation shrewdly formulated its reservations around the issue of "victors' justice." They opposed the negative criminality and criminal liability of senior leaders that was problematic for their institution of the Emperor and even asked for the elimination of word "heads of the state" from the report. Japan's official position marked continuity as similar arguments were advanced against the legality of the Tokyo Tribunal by the Japanese defense team in 1946.

The League of Nations was another peace project to be achieved through rational debate and cooperation between its member states. The 1921 Covenant of the League of Nations was meant to preserve world peace from unilateral status quo usurpations by bringing a collective response against such state in any form deemed suitable, including force. Its Article 10 was the nucleus of collective security idea. The Covenant was prescriptive when it came to means of pressure to be employed against the aggressor state or state threatening to use force—economic, financial, and military[34]—while it remained indicative when it came to arbitration and adjudication in relation to questions of international law and treaties which were considered another important source of conflict between nations. Legalists wanted a compulsory judicial mechanism for state disputes outside of diplomatic core that will be able to enforce laws, albeit only upon states outside of the Western hemisphere.[35] For them, the League was an immense disappointment as it placed the matters in the hands of men, not laws.[36] As a result of the deep divisions within the Senate regarding the Covenant, the vote against its ratification put an end to the Wilsonian League. The League was simply devoid of any concrete and effective measures to prevent or deter war in the tumultuous interwar context of revisionism and expansionism.

In the 1920s the international legal momentum to prevent war and closely define aggression under the banner of *jus contra bellum* developed in response to the Covenant's lack of robustness. The above-noted collective security and sanctions were connected to the disarmament process as contained in Article 8 of the Covenant. The League's Treaty of Mutual Assistance of the Temporary Mixed Commission of 1923 held that war of aggression was an international crime that ought to be stopped by providing mutual assistance to attacked state due to the reduction of armaments. Yet, the challenge of clearly defining the act of aggression was not met which made the provisions on aggression being an international crime futile and the incentives for disarmament conditions slim. Another aggravating factor was that Britain, overwhelmed by the burden of postwar recovery, and in absence of the US that left the League, had less incentive in providing protection to other states which ended up in it leaving the treaty. This sent a strong signal to other states that mutual assistance would not serve as means to stop aggressive war.[37] The Geneva Protocol of 1924 or the Protocol for the Peaceful Settlement of International Disputes shifted the focus towards aggressive war prevention through compulsory judicial and arbitrational methods.[38] An aggressor could be automatically identified by its failure to accept judicial or arbitrary settlement by the Court after the violation of the provisions of both Covenant and Protocol. Once again, Britain withdrew from the document it supported to come to life as it threatened its right to resort to war without being stigmatized as an aggressor and it did not want the Protocol to be applicable to conflicts of little interest to it. These instruments sought to make aggressive war illegal and criminal, yet without defining it, and by creating conditions conducive to peace and security—disarmament, mutual assistance, and compulsory adjudication before the International Court of Justice prior to resorting to war. In essence, states could still have resort to collective coercive measures against state identified as an aggressor which did not change the already existent state of affairs when it came to resort to war. All these treaties were part of the effort to delegitimize war but were not widely supported and did not gain enough traction to become international law.[39]

The 1928 Kellogg-Briand Pact or the General Treaty for the Renunciation of War as an Instrument of National Policy that is discussed in the following section distinguished itself in that it aimed to condemn the unilateral use of war by states while it allowed for war in a form of a collective action against state identified as an aggressor.[40] Wars in self-defense were not prohibited, but they were mentioned in the notes attached to the Pact. This was a dangerous space to navigate as states preserved their discretion in deciding the threshold past which the actions committed by another state were requiring a military response. The Pact did expect contracting states to seek peaceful means in solving their international disputes, but did not prohibit the use of force should these prove ineffective. Also, civil wars and internal strife were not covered by it while non-signatories were out of the scope of the Pact which implied that wars with them were permitted. The high contracting states only condemned the resort to war as an instrument of national policy but did not renounce it. As a result, the Pact that gained wide support from state did not make war illegal in general, only war used as instruments for furthering national interest or unilateral wars. Once state resorted to war, other states were given free hand in waging war against it. The Pact did not refer to key legal terms used by the above-mentioned treaties such as "aggression," "international crime," "sanctions," and "adjudication" which gained it wide acceptance and ratification among the Big Powers, especially the US. The general language of the Pact and absence of clearly prescribed procedures to prevent war mounted up the already existent feelings of insecurity that reigned in both European and Asian theaters.

The subsequent invasions in the 1930s were the first signs of failure of postwar peace settlement and other instruments to prevent war which was reflected by 1931 Japanese invasion of Manchuria on the occasion of which Secretary of State Henry L. Stimson, in reference to the Pact, denounced Japan "as lawbreaker"[41] and advocated the "non-recognition" of the situation created in contravention to the Nine-Power Treaty and the Kellogg-Briand Pact.[42] In protest to the conclusions of Lytton report, issued by the commission approved by the League's Council to investigate Japanese intervention in Manchuria, which proposed a solution detrimental to what Japan considered its vital interests—that is, demilitarization of the region and placing its autonomous government under Chinese sovereignty[43]—Japan left the League in 1933.

According to Hersch Lauterpacht, the prominent British international lawyer and afterward judge at the International Court of Justice (ICJ), although the Pact did not have any "teeth," its importance lied in diffusing the idea that war, which was previously used as an instrument to alter the status quo and international law, became illegal with the exception of wars fought in self-defense or as a collective sanction against the aggressor.[44] The instances of military expansion in the 1930s—Japan invaded Manchuria in 1931, Italy invaded Ethiopia in 1936, and Germany invaded Poland in 1939—leading up to the outbreak of World War II would indeed evidence that legal innovation was in the realm of the ideas that were still not ripe to gain the support and observance from nation states which once again chose to settle their differences by military force.

Securing Peace by Law: The Return of 1919 International Order

The ideas and dilemmas released by the Great War regained their value as World War Two was nearing its end in favor of the Allied powers, and the need to lay the grounds of a new peace settlement appeared on the horizon. The kernel of the Allies' argument, stemming from 1919 international order failures, was that both Germany and Japan should be integrated within the new international order. They ought not be pastoralized but occupied following their unconditional surrender which would allow the Allies to demilitarize, democratize, and reeducate their elites.

Regarding the punishment, Winston Churchill, who was a strong advocate of legalistic solutions for the main villains of the Great War in 1915, disillusioned with the power of law to settle political and historical issues, preferred summary executions of few of the Axis leaders who bore the most responsibility for the war.[45] During the war, President Franklin D. Roosevelt had already made oblique warnings about the punishment of the Axis "guilty barbaric leaders," in his speech at the Casablanca Conference in February 1943, and more directly so, he referred to the efforts of the Allied powers to put an end and punish the Japanese aggressive war at the Cairo Conference in November 1943. The reasons behind these low-key statements regarding the punishment of the Axis leaders were the absence of concrete policies for war crimes program and the fear of retaliation against the prisoners of war who were captured by the Axis.[46] In planning the course of action for the final days of war at Quebec in fall 1944, Churchill and Roosevelt consulted on the question of prosecuting the major war criminals. The British plan, drafted by Chancellor Lord Simon, played a decisive role in swaying President Roosevelt towards a political solution as memorandum concluded that "it could not rest with judges, however eminent or learned, to decide finally a matter like this, which is of the widest and most vital public policy."[47] The summary executions were tempting as the leaders were aware of the fastidious process that the investigation, apprehension, and trial would entail. Ironically, in October 1944, Joseph Stalin, delighted at the opportunity to reap the benefits of the Soviet entry in the war against Japan, opposed summary executions and suggested that the world would be more impressed if the Axis leaders would be sentenced to life imprisonment following a legal procedure.[48] The Soviet version of legalism was unequivocally based on political criteria which established guilt of the defendants who were simply executed or imprisoned without any procedural rights.[49]

The end of 1944 marked a fierce battle within the US government between the Secretary of Treasury Henry Morgenthau Jr.—whose Jewish roots heavily weighted in his proposal for pastoralization of Germany—and Secretary of War Henry L. Stimson, a seasoned lawyer and "defender of laws and constitution,"[50] who argued for legal methods in the shape of the war crimes program. Although Morgenthau had the president's ear at the time of the Quebec conference, the leaking of passages from the vengeful report he authored to the press sealed its destiny as it was met with public indignation. In January 1945, President Roosevelt had a change of heart regarding the war crimes trials and decided to offer his support to Stimson as he acknowledged its added value laid in generating "historical record"[51] of the atrocities. The War Department, with Stimson at the helm, John McCloy, and Judge Advocate General Myron Cramer, who later joined the IMTFE as the US Justice, started making sketches of what would later become the war crimes trials program for both Germany and Japan. The awareness that the tribunals would be criticized and rejected as institutions of the purest form of political vengeance was palpable among its architects, and their anxieties were well founded. This created the imperative to ascertain the legal character of the program by adding tokens of legality—the guarantee of minimal procedural rights for the defendants—and in doing so to take care to spare the process of legal technicalities, often found in domestic criminal system. Another element to factor in was time which was reflected in requirement of promptness put before members of the tribunal in order to avoid "making martyrs of the individuals punished."[52] Despite this awareness, the IMTFE will be greatly impeded by protracted process that not only prejudiced the defendants for its rules of evidence that impeded defense[53] but also succeeded in making victims out of criminals for its lengthy procedure and harsh sentencing. The image of the convicted criminals as victims would become even more palpable during the post-trial stage of the execution of sentences where the legal minutiae surrounding clemency and parole process attracted public anger and burdened US-Japan postwar relations.

The United Nations Charter, the final product of the postwar settlement adopted on June 26, 1945, in its Article 2 paragraph 4 reads that states *shall* refrain from "threat or use of force against sovereignty, political independence, and territorial integrity of any state." Shall expresses the imperative for states not to use force in their international relations, but it does not prohibit war. Its Article 51 recognizes "the inherent right of sovereign states for individual or collective self-defense" in case of an armed attack against the member state. Law of the UN Charter restrains state behavior when it comes to the use of force but at the same time opens a loophole and space for enabling it through its general language. This "juridification"[54] of war in the sense that the law intervened to regulate the use of force came as a fruition of pre-World War II ideas of placing "crude political power" within the framework of "law and morality."[55] The intent was to preserve the postwar status quo by outlawing its violation to the dissatisfaction of many "have-not states."[56] It can be argued that international law is inclined to favor status quo powers over revisionist powers when it comes to rules that restrain the use of force. Juridification of war was complemented by its criminalization, strictly limited to wars of aggression—although these were not defined—which was a product of an uneasy compromise between four powers at the London Conference on August 26, 1945,[57] which was also occasion on which the Charter of International Military Tribunal (hereafter IMT) at Nuremberg saw the light of day.[58] Although the IMT and IMTFE were institutionally distinct entities created for two profoundly diverse war theaters, their raison d'être converged in their mission to validate the newly created norms by legally establishing the Axis leaders' criminal responsibility for aggressive wars. War criminal programs in Germany and Japan unfolded to reflect specificities in relation to wars they engaged in, but this shared political and legal goal of pursuing validity of the Allied powers' legal innovation would permeate into the late 1950s until the last prisoners were released on clemency and parole. The IMT Charter, created on a contractual basis between the Big Four at London—the US delegation was instructed to be uncompromising on definition of crimes and procedure[59]—served as a template to the US when it crafted the IMTFE Charter. Therefore, it is important to have a glimpse into the process of its creation that divulged the US legal position which was heavily rectified from the one opposing any criminal trials for the heads of state by international tribunals it had advanced back in 1919. At the London Conference, the Soviet and French delegations, which at first disagreed on placing the charge of aggressive war at the heart of the Tribunal's jurisdiction, finished by consenting to it under the promise that it would only be applicable to instances of the Axis aggression.[60]

Robert H. Jackson, American Justice at the Supreme Court and Chief Prosecutor at IMT, was another key and influential figure who propelled the development of the US legal position which recognized the criminality of aggressive war based on the previously discussed 1928 Kellogg-Briand Pact. Given that the Pact fell within the realm of state responsibility for aggressive war, legal categories pertaining to criminal law had to be fabricated in order to give life and meaning to the incrimination of aggressive war—a priori interpreted as illegal. The principle of individual criminal responsibility for aggressive war that disregarded immunity of heads of states—of pragmatic value when it came to continuity of state functions—came as a legal filler along with individual criminal responsibility of military personnel which previously used to avoid guilt for crimes committed by invoking the defense of superior orders. In his report to President Truman, who succeeded late President Roosevelt on April 12, 1945, Jackson stressed that the change in circumstances ushered in a new era in the growth and use of international law which, in Wilsonian spirit, ought to be "a real expression of our moral judgment."[61] Law was meant to be used as an expression of politics and its construed fluidity allowed it to keep up with ever-changing circumstances and respond to demands for expediency. The American legal stance was qualified as "relatively simple and non-technical"[62] and immune to "sterile legalisms."[63] Jackson's work was profoundly infused by the writings and advice from Sir Hersch Lauterpacht, who was at that time British professor of international law at the University of Cambridge. Jackson was also personally convinced that war of aggression constituted a punishable crime under international law.

The decision to pursue war criminal trials based on these newly announced principles were, in the eyes of Stimson, a victory for American legalism and his personal triumph over policy of isolationism that had gained a foothold in the US during the interwar period. The charge of aggression, which was severely disputed by European powers, was also a necessary package thought of as justification for the actions of the Roosevelt administration in relation to the US controversial position of neutrality[64] under which the US could engage in war with the Allies by providing them with economic and military assistance which all fell short of force. The US abandonment of neutrality although it did not directly suffer from German atrocities[65] and lend-lease that were badly needed by European states economically, militarily, and socially destroyed by war were valid reasons for which they decided to accept the US legal innovation. More importantly, they were aware that this would help the US administration address the potential domestic issue resulting from the fear of "perpetuating American internationalism" and the reversion to interwar isolationism.[66] That guaranteed US economic and military assistance without engaging in actual war as a belligerent.[67] Contrary to wars fought prior to the Treaty of Versailles, which punished a nation for losing the war, the German Empire and subsequently Germany and Japan would be punished for having started one.

Notes

1. Ignacio de la Rasilla, "A Very Short History of International Law Journals, 1869–2018," *European Journal of International Law* 29:1, 2018, 143.
2. Ibid., 142.
3. Oona Hathaway and Scott J. Shapiro, *The Internationalist: How a Radical Plan to Outlaw War Remade the World*, New York: Simon&Shuster, 2017, 57–58.
4. Ibid., 142. See Yasuaki Onuma, "Japanese International Law in the Prewar Period: Perspectives on Teaching and Research of International Law in the Prewar Japan," *Japanese Annual of International Law* 29 (1986).

5. Ignacio de la Rasilla, "A Very Short History of International Law Journals, 1869–2018,"143.
6. Francis A. Boyle, *Foundations of World Order: The Legalist Approach to International Relations, 1898–1922* (Durham: Duke University Press, 1999) Cited in Ignacio de la Rasilla, "A Very Short History of International Law Journals, 1869–2018,"146.
7. Boyle, Foundations of World Order: The Legalist Approach to International Relations, 1898–1922, 136.
8. Ibid., 17.
9. Benjamin A. Coates, *Legalist Empire: International Law and American Foreign Relations in the Early Twentieth Century* (Oxford: Oxford University Press, 2016), 152.
10. Tosh Minohara, Tze-ki Hon, and Evan Dawley, eds., *The Decade of Great War: Japan and the Wider World in the 1910s* (Leiden: Brill Academic Pub, 2014), ix.
11. Ibid., 3.
12. Ibid., 63.
13. Ibid.
14. Ibid., ix.
15. Ibid., 65.
16. Tosh Minohara, ed., *The History of US-Japan Relations: From Perry to the Present* (Singapore: Palgrave Macmillan, 2017), 54–57.
17. Ibid., 84–85.
18. Ibid.
19. Ibid., 87.
20. Ibid., 88.
21. Ibid., 79.
22. Ibid.
23. Coates, *Legalist Empire*, 152.
24. Stephen Wertheim, "The League That Wasn't: American Designs for a Legalist-Sanctionist League of Nations and the Intellectual Origins of International Organization, 1914-1920," Diplomatic History, Vol 35. No 5 (November 2011), 797–836.
25. Kirsten Sellars, *Crimes Against Peace and International Law* (Cambridge: Cambridge University Press, 2015), 3.
26. *Violation of the Laws and Customs of War. Reports of Majority and Dissenting Reports of American and Japanese Members of the Commission of Responsibilities. Conference of Paris 1919.* (Oxford: Clarendon Press), 1919.
27. Ibid.
28. Cherif M. Bassiouni, "From Versailles to Rwanda in Seventy-Five Years: The Need to Establish a Permanent International Criminal Court," *Harvard Human Rights Law Review* 10 (1997): 19.

29. Ibid.; Jonathan G. Bass, *Stay the Hand of Vengeance: The Politics of War Crimes Tribunal* (Princeton: Princeton University Press, 2000), 105.
30. *Violations of the Laws and Customs of War: Report of Majority and Dissenting Reports of American and Japanese Members of the Commission of Responsibilities*, Conference of Paris, (Oxford: Clarendon Press, 1919).
31. Ibid.,
32. Ibid., 72.
33. Ibid., 75–76.
34. Julius Stone, *Aggression and World Order: A Critique of United Nations Theories of Aggression* (Berkeley: University of California Press, 1958), 39–40.
35. Coates, *Legalist Empire: International Law and American Foreign Relations in the Early Twentieth Century*, 165.
36. Ibid., 166.
37. Sellars, *'Crimes against Peace' and International Law*, 19.
38. Ibid.
39. Ibid., 23.
40. Ibid., 25.
41. Ibid., 33.
42. Tosh Minohara, ed., *The History of US-Japan Relations: From Perry to Present* (Singapore: Palgrave Macmillan, 2017), 87
43. Ibid., 59.
44. Sellars, *'Crimes against Peace' and International Law*, 43.
45. Jonathan Garry Bass, *Stay the Hand of Vengeance*, 2.
46. Aleksandra Babovic, "Justice on Trial: The Establishment of International Military Tribunal for the Far East (1945–1946," (master's thesis, Kobe University, 2015), 20.
47. Memorandum by the British Lord Chancellor Simon, London, September 4, 1944. FRUS, 1944. *Conference at Quebec*, Washington: Government Printing Office, 1972, 92.
48. Prime Minister Churchill to President Roosevelt, Telegram, London, October 22, 1944. FRUS 1945. *Conferences at Malta and Yalta*, Washington: Government Printing Office, 1955, 400.
49. Higurashi Yoshinobu, *Tōkyō saiban no kokusai kankei: kokusai seiji ni okeru kenryōku to kihan*, Tokyo: Bokutakusha, 2002, 79.
50. Henry L. Stimson and McGeorge Bundy, *On Active Service in Peace and War*, New York: Harper and Brothers, 1948, xxii.
51. Ibid., 585–586.
52. Bass, *Stay the Hand of Vengeance*, 157.
53. Richard H. Minear, Victors' Justice: The Tokyo War Crimes Trial, Princeton: Princeton University Press, 1971, 122–123.
54. Term used to designate the use of law to regulate war.
55. Ibid.

56. Frederick S. Dunn, *Peace Making and the Settlement with Japan* (Westport: Greenwood Press, 1963), 9–11.
57. For more details on the negotiations leading to the IMT Charter, see Sellars, *'Crimes Against Peace' and International Law*, 84–112; London Conference, Report of Robert H. Jackson, *United States representative, to the international conference on military trials* (Washington: Department of State, 1949).
58. Ibid., 5.
59. The Assistant Secretary (McCloy) to the Secretary of State, Memorandum of Conference of the Secretary of State, July 26, 1945, FRUS, *The Conference in Berlin (The Potsdam Conference)*, Washington: Government Printing Office, 1960, 423.
60. Yuma Totani, *The Tokyo War Crimes Trial: The Pursuit of Justice in the Wake of World War II* (Cambridge: Harvard University, 2008), 21.
61. Justice Jackson's Report to President on Atrocities and War Crimes, June 7, 1945. http://avalon.law.yale.edu/imt/imt_jack01.asp (accessed on March 13, 2016).
62. Ibid.
63. Ibid.
64. Sellars, *'Crimes Against Peace' and International Law* (Cambridge: Cambridge University Press, 2013), 88–89.
65. Ibid., 44. Jackson defended the interpretation of "qualified neutrality" in the light of the Kellogg-Briand Treaty—aggressive wars made the traditional postulates of neutrality doctrine, that is, unquestionable absolute neutrality of states in any instance of war, inadmissible as the signatory states had the duty to militarily attack the aggressor.
66. Ibid.
67. Ibid.

CHAPTER 3

The IMTFE as a Venue for Legislating Process

The legal basis for the establishment of the Tokyo Tribunal was contained in Article 10 of the Potsdam Declaration of July 26, 1945, which specified that the punishment for crimes committed during the war would be individual rather than collective in nature. The Allied powers "[did] not intend that the Japanese [should] be enslaved as a race or destroyed as nation, but stern justice shall be meted out to all war criminals, including those who have visited cruelties upon [their] prisoners." The imperative of individual punishment stems from the bitter experience of the punitive Versailles Treaty that weakened Germany militarily and economically—the nation was punished as a whole—which led to revisionist aspirations in the interwar period.

Prior to these international deliberations, the United Nations War Crimes Commission (UNWCC), based in London, gave some hints on the general atmosphere among the Allies regarding the future tribunal. Its Special Far East and Pacific Committee broached the idea of a Central War Crimes agency to be placed in Tokyo to do the preparative work and assist the international tribunal.[1] Their draft recommendation envisaged the international tribunal to repose on Allied cooperation, without any reference to the US special interest for the Pearl Harbor Attack case. The American representative on the Commission, Colonel Hodgson, transmitted this draft to the Department of State (DoS) for a reference, but speculating that its certain provision might displease the dominant view that, although international, the US should take the main lead.[2]

A. Babovic, *The Tokyo Trial, Justice, and the Postwar International Order*, New Directions in East Asian History,
https://doi.org/10.1007/978-981-13-3477-1_3

The text of the Declaration did not include any reference to or hints regarding the future of the institution of the Emperor whose preservation was a matter of highest importance and frustration to the Japanese. This silence was reflective of important transitions in the power dynamics of personnel of the State Department which was reflected in changing views on what occupation policies would be adequate for postwar Japan. The death of President Roosevelt in April 1945 and the appointment of Henry S. Truman caused the above-mentioned transitions. The dominant influence of Japan hands personified by George Blakeslee, Hugh Borton, Joseph Ballantine, Eugene Dooman, and Joseph Grew, acting secretary of state, who were proponents of moderate policies was weakening in favor of harsher policies pushed for by new Secretary of State James F. Byrnes, new Acting Secretary of State Dean G. Acheson, and Assistant Secretary of War John J. McCloy.[3] The recommendations for moderate occupation policies that stressed the importance of the retention of the Emperor position along with a three-pronged approach, consisting of disarmament, demilitarization, and democratization, gathered consensus on most important levels of the State Department in 1944.[4] Before the Tribunal was established, there existed a division between the State-War-Navy Coordinating Committee (SWNCC)[5] as to the degree of the US role in the Tribunal's establishment—"the US lead"[6] faction pitched by military members and "the Allied powers" cooperation'[7] faction defended by DoS. In October 1945, in order to avoid the stigma of being exclusively an American tribunal, which would severely undermine its credibility, it was agreed that the Tribunal's international character should be respected but that the US position would prevail in case of disagreement between the Allied powers, a decision that in essence matched the US lead approach. The possibility of trial of the Tōjō cabinet by the American military commission for war crimes was also questioned, but in the face of the IMT, it would harm the consistency of already announced policies for punishing major war criminals.[8] It is important to note that the directive of Joint Chiefs of Staff (JCS) of November 10, 1945, discussed the possibility of organizing exclusively American tribunal to try Hideki Tōjō's cabinet for the Pearl Harbor Attack as they envisioned complications, in the form of delays and disagreements, that could result from the participation of other Allies.[9] The international format of the Tribunal prevailed as it gave the tribunal increased legitimacy, and responsibility for the Tribunal's eventual success or failure would be shared.[10] The stigma of being an American Tribunal was undesirable, and the international character of the tribunal was to be stressed in dealing with the Japanese. The judges were to be appointed by the Supreme Commander upon the recommendation from military and civilian representatives of the Allied powers, while the International Prosecution Section (IPS) within which national teams were formed from each member country with one Chief Counsel was to be under the Supreme Commander for the Allied Powers (SCAP) command. Ultimately, it was also agreed that in case disagreement between the Allies was insurmountable, the US position would prevail. The achieved unified position on October 2, 1945, allowed the US to brace its position so that other powers would not have enough time to considerably challenge its views, especially Australia that had a punitive approach to postwar Japan which stem out of a deep-rooted fear for Japanese invasion and geographical proximity.

The Far Eastern Advisory Commission (FEAC) was the first US attempt to give more voice to other Allies regarding Japanese occupation, including war criminal matters. However, this body was strictly consultative in character and did not allow for any serious joint decision-making. Even its headquarters located in Washington was indicative of the US primus inter pares position in dealing with Japan. The Soviet Union refused to take participation in it as they felt they were not being treated as equal allies,[11] which they perceived as humiliation. Despite these occasional protests against the quasi US monopoly in the occupation of Japan, the Soviet representatives were aware that their stance when it came to Japan did not match the one they enjoyed in German theater.[12]

Another important venue to cherish the international character of the Tribunal was the Far Eastern Commission (FEC)[13] which was instituted in Washington on December 26, 1945, where all the nations represented at the IMTFE were given the opportunity to challenge the US views in formulating and recommending the policies regarding Japanese occupation.[14] FEC directives were translated into concrete policies by the US government and then transferred to the Supreme Commander, while in case of urgent matters regarding policies that were not covered by the FEC directives, the US government was allowed to independently issue interim directives to the SCAP.[15] This institutional mechanism gave the possibility to sideline the Commission and pursue its own policies independently. The authority vested in SCAP to mete out stern justice gave the US a great degree of preeminence regarding the establishment process in comparison to other Allies, thus allowing it to proceed more quickly as it was rushing against the clock to draft the Charter, set the IPS which would prepare the indictment, and select defendants.

On December 1, 1945, Keenan and his legal team left for their mission in Tokyo, and a week later the IPS was established. Mid-January was ambitiously selected by the SWNCC as a target date for the beginning of trials, but their goal proved rather unrealistic.[16] Upon arrival, the American prosecution team started off with drafting the Tokyo Charter, screening suspects and list of incarcerated persons to select key defendants and prepare the indictment. Almost six months into the IMT proceedings, on January 19, 1946, the IMTFE Charter was born, following MacArthur's special proclamation which was grounded in the Instrument of Surrender, the Potsdam Declaration, and the Moscow Conference.[17] From the outset, Dean Acheson, hearing from Jackson of the fastidious London Conference experience, decided to let MacArthur proceed by himself.[18] While it did reflect the IMT constitutive document that was a result of the Allies' consensus, the nature of the IMTFE Charter was not truly contractual. The US amended it on its own while skillfully avoiding to introduce changes proposed by other Allies through FEC Committee No. 5 in charge of war crimes program. For instance, one of the FEC amendments proposed by the British and Australians sought to limit MacArthur's discretion in his power to change the judgement or sentences by introducing an obligation to consult with ACJ members or other powers beforehand. In April 1946, the FEC adopted a document that later amended the Tokyo Charter regarding provisions on the number of judges necessary for establishing the Tribunal, their absence, and the reduced number of judges necessary to constitute a quorum.[19]

The Commonwealth nations, especially Australia, were eager to assert their view of postwar Japan which was different from the US. Australian view clung onto more punitive policies which were rooted in fears of Japanese invasion and a revived militarism. In stark contrast stood the position of Britain, which was preoccupied with its postwar recovery that heavily depended upon its neighbor across the Atlantic for loans. The already fastidious experience of negotiating the IMT Charter at the London Conference made it uninterested for embarking upon another round of endless talks.[20] The punishment of the Japanese was important for the British as it would allow for their vindication of colonies that were indispensable for economic recovery.[21] This transition in the international power structure that saw the US on its top made Britain's rather modest position[22] regarding the occupation of Japan its natural consequence.

The international experience surrounding the IMTFE, other than the official diplomatic channels, was more tangible within the IPS, established in December 1945, where teams from the Allied countries, whose representatives, primed by different legal cultures, expertise, and temperaments, would be compelled to work together in order to satisfy the overall goal of preparing the case against the Japanese leaders. The first to arrive in Tokyo on December 10, 1945, was the American team headed by Joseph B. Keenan, the chief prosecutor at the IMTFE, whose reputation and expertise stood in bas-relief to his counterpart in Nuremberg, prominent Justice Jackson. Keenan's appointment by the executive order of President Truman on November 10, 1945, was not entirely based on his legal prowess. A Harvard University law graduate, Keenan, practiced law in both private offices and government—as assistant to US attorney general and head of the Criminal Division at the Justice Department.[23] Keenan was considered a "second-rate choice"[24] for this prestigious post, intensely scrutinized in international circles, but his strong political connections with the late President Roosevelt and FBI's Director Edgar Hoover were enough to secure him the position.[25] President Truman considered him to be a man who was capable of getting things done; hence he was tasked with prompt and efficient prosecution of Japanese leaders responsible for aggression.[26] Keenan had a successful record in garnering the financial support of the Senate for the executive New Deal projects that were of significance to both Roosevelt and Truman. The Tokyo Tribunal was an example of these executive projects.[27]

Upon arrival, the team was faced with challenging realities on the ground, such as the lack of direct evidentiary documents and the overwhelming mass of documents that needed to be translated, read, and analyzed along with the interrogations that were to be conducted which resulted in acute disorganization and inefficiency until the arrival of the Commonwealth prosecutors. The working groups (A–G) were organized and each in charge of studying a specific phase of Japanese aggression[28]—military, industrial, bureaucratic, and expansionist. But the mission lagged with prosecution's sluggish work, mainly due to chief counsel's lack of sense of organization and clear strategy. On January 19, 1946, responding to an ubiquitous sense of urge to start the trial, MacArthur proclaimed the Charter, but at that time the list of suspects to be selected for the trial was far from being ready.

Keenan did lack leadership skills, but he had a distinctive legal philosophy, based on natural law, that pervaded the work of the prosecution. According to Keenan, the source of law was God from which the spiritual principles were derived to serve the interest of humanity at all times.

Thus, he viewed law as a timeless, ever-"growing thing" that can be easily transformed, independent from written, positive norm and sanction, constrained by time and scope. In a way, the members of the prosecution were aware of their nobler mission of advancing the "cause of peace and right notions of international law"[29]—prohibition of the aggressive war—which went beyond mere punishment of the accused. They might have been convinced in this legalo-moralistic narrative, but it also served as a justification for the proactive, law-making process that took place in 1945. In fact, the Allied powers wanted to preserve the colonial gains that had been established prior to the war and thus been seen as legitimate. In that sense, Japanese behavior was a thorn in the Allied powers' side that would have led to anarchy had it not been punished properly for perturbing the status quo. Far from being inspired by altruism, the Allied powers' approach was a universalistic one that only catered to the interests of states satisfied with the status quo.[30]

The dynamics of prosecutorial work would significantly change when, in early February, associate prosecutors from other Allied nations—British prosecutor A. S. Comyns-Carr, Australian prosecutor Alan J. Mansfield, Brigadier Quilliam from New Zealand, Henry G. Nolan from Canada, and Hsiang Che-Chun from China—arrived in Tokyo. They were appalled at the extremely poor state of affairs. The draft indictment contained charges of all three crimes related to the Pearl Harbor Attack, in which Tōjō figured as the only defendant, whereas the Japanese government was listed among the Allies as the interested party in prosecuting wartime Japanese leaders for aggression. This draft placed the ultimate guilt for war upon the wartime Japanese government, thus confirming the omnipresent view among the Japanese that their leaders deceived them.[31] The newly arrived prosecutors were under the impression that the American version of the indictment was contrary to the Tribunal's goal of cultivating the public sense of responsibility for national policy and were instructed by their respective governments to resist this proposal, after which it was withdrawn. The British speculated that in this way Keenan wanted to cast shadow upon the Emperor and protect him from prosecution.[32] In retrospect, this goal appears as unrealistic given that, in the end, the responsibility for war was narrowed down to a cohort of leaders while the immediate postwar devastation and existential needs, rather than war responsibility, preoccupied the Japanese. Under the lead of Comyns-Carr, the Commonwealth prosecutors would capitalize upon Keenan's bad results and reputation to challenge US preeminence and organize prosecutorial work that would allow for the indictment and list of defendants to be completed as soon as possible. The associate prosecutors' duties were to assist Chief Counsel Keenan in drafting charges, selecting defendants, conducting preliminary interrogations, but every decision was subordinated to the final approval of the Supreme Commander.[33] Above all, they were there to represent and promote national interest of their respective countries.

Contrary to the instructions from Washington, it seemed that the members of the American prosecutorial team were overwhelmed by the load of their task that they seemed to have given up the requirement for expeditious trials. In February 1946, New Zealand Justice Northcroft, one of the two judges with early presence in Tokyo, reported to his government that "[t]he court building itself is only now being planned." By the end of February, Comyns-Carr's memorandum to associate prosecutors called for reorganization of the prosecutorial unit and urged Keenan to select 15 to 20 men for prosecution withstanding the lack of a more conclusive evidence. Comyns-Carr was confident in his proposal as the Commonwealth prosecutor, once united, gained prevalent voting power. As a result, the IPS had new organizational scheme with the Executive Committee and sub-committees, thematically divided into drafting, incidents and treaties, evidence and defendants, whereas Keenan reserved the right to be a member of each. To some members of the American team, these initiatives were displeasing because they saw it as a potential threat to the US leading role in the Tribunal, which they considered was earned by its bore the burden of the Pacific War and Japan's occupation. American Assistant to Chief Counsel Higgins believed that Americans were in a different position and owed to imprisoned suspects a proper investigation of the evidence presented against them. The newly created sense of urgency for speedy trials frustrated the American prosecutors who criticized the British prosecutor for "too much of a tendency to keep an eye on the clock and the other on Nuremberg" is an example of this overwhelming feeling.[34] The reason behind the importance of the time factor was succinctly expressed by almost prophetic words of Comyns-Carr that "from the very day on which the Nuremberg trial is over, world interest, as distinct from the purely Japanese interest, in the whole subject of International Trials, will fall to a vanishing point."[35]

The work on adopting the final indictment was additionally delayed and complicated by the late arrival of French, Soviet, Chinese, and Philippine prosecutorial teams in mid-April.[36] Until then, the Soviets communicated with SCAP through correspondence demanding for clarifications on various points in a manner that gave impression of another London Conference for the IMTFE was taking place.[37] Keenan put high hopes in the arrival of the Soviet representative as he expected that would alleviate "the growing world atmosphere of friction."[38] While the Soviet Prosecutor Sergei A. Golunsky requested the addition of new names to the defendants' lists, other teams asked for amendments of the particulars.[39] All the technical amendments reflected the amalgamation of competing national interests which finally resulted in "the monstrous indictment," detailed and repetitive in character. Its final version was presented to the Tribunal only on April 26, 1946. However, after this moment, the trials would considerably slow down; the presentation of cases in phases, interrogations, and collection of evidence would take toll on the expected expeditious character of the proceedings as prosecutor Quilliam noted in early June that "all the sense of urgency was gone."[40]

Notes

1. UNWCC, SFEC I, "Summary of Recommendations Concerning Japanese War Crimes Atrocities," August 13, 1945, SWNCC 57 in NARA II, RG 353.
2. Ammy Cutter to Green H. Hackworth, Memorandum, August 21, 1945, SWNCC in NARA II, RG 535.
3. Edward D. Beauchamps, ed., *History of Contemporary Japan Since World War II*, New York: Routledge, 2011, 165.
4. *The Occupation of Japan: U.S. Planning Documents 1942–1945*, State Department Draft Policy, Japan: occupation problems: war criminals, Inter-Divisional Area Committee on the Far East, January, 1945, CAC-342 in RG59.
5. The SWNCC was at the origin of the most important directives regarding the occupation policies for the Axis powers representing balanced views between civilian and military officers that were subsequently to be approved by the President. It is a result of an effort to create integrated civilo-military approach to foreign policy which is reminiscent in form to the present-day National Security Council (NSC).
6. Higurashi Yoshinobu, *Tokyo saiban no kokusai kankei: Kokusai seiji ni okeru kenryōku to kihan* (Tokyo: Botakutakusha, 2002), 190–191.
7. Ibid.
8. McCloy to MacArthur, November 17, 1945 in State Department Internal Correspondence (1945–1946) in NARA II, RG 59.
9. JCS to MacArthur, November 10, 1945, State Department Internal Correspondence (1945–1946) in NARA II, RG 59.

10. Ibid., 52.
11. George H. Blakslee, "The Establishment of the Far Eastern Commission," *International Organization 5:3:1951,* 501.
12. Philip R. Piccigallo, *The Japanese on Trial: Allied War Crimes Operations in the East Asia, 1945–1951* (Austin: University of Texas Press, 1979), 145.
13. Far Eastern Advisory Commission (FEAC) was established on October 30, 1945, where other Allied powers were represented (US, Britain, Australia, New Zealand, Canada, the Netherlands, France). As the body was purely advisory in character, Stalin refused to participate. Subsequently, the Soviet Union would join the FEC which had a decision-making role, although a limited one.
14. George H. Blakeslee, "The Establishment of the Far Eastern Commission," *International Organization* 5:3:1951, 503.
15. Ibid.
16. CINCAFPAC Advisor to Joint Chiefs of Staff, December 9, 1945, State Department Internal Correspondence (1945–1946) in NARA II, RG59.
17. Special Proclamation, "The Establishment of the International Military Tribunal for the Far East," January 19, 1945 in Neil Boister and Robert Cryer, *Documents on the Tokyo International Military Tribunal: Charter, Indictment and Judgements* (New York: Oxford University Press, 2008), 5–6.
18. Acheson to Ballatine, Washington, September 6, 1945, in *FRUS, 1945. The British Commonwealth, the Far East,* Vol.6 (Washington DC: Government Printing Office, 1969), 921.
19. FEC 007/7, "Trial of Japanese War Criminals," April 26, 1946 in Makoto Yokibe, ed., Occupation of Japan: US Planning Documents, 1942–1945 (Tokyo: Maruzen), 4A3.
20. Higurashi, *Tokyo saiban no kokusai kankei: Kokusai seiji ni okeru kenryōku to kihan*, 190–191.
21. Ibid.
22. Higurashi, *Tōkyō saiban kokusai kankei*, 190–191.
23. David M. Crowe, "MacArthur, Keenan and the American Quest for Justice at the IMTFE," 77 in Kerstin Von Lingen, *Transcultural Justice at the Tokyo Tribunal* (Leiden: Brill), 2008.
24. B.V.A. Rolling and Antonio Cassese, *The Tokyo Trial and Beyond: Reflections of a Peacemonger* (Cambridge: Polity Press, 1993), 32.
25. Ibid., 263.
26. Patterson to Mac Arthur, November 13, 1945, State Department Internal Correspondence, RG 59.
27. Philip R. Piccigallo, *The Japanese on Trial: Allied War Crimes Operation in the East, 1945–1951* (Austin: Texas University Press, 1979), 10.
28. "Assignment Chart," Preparation of Trial, IPS documents in NARA II, RG331. Group A (July 1930–December 1935) comprising Manchurian

Incident, Kwantung Army activities, assassination in 1932; Group B (January 1936–July 1939) including political intrigues, China Incident, and war; Group C (August 1939–December 1941) studying the Tripartite Pact, Imperial Rule Assistance Association, Japanese-Russian Neutrality Pact, Relations with the US and Britain, Imperial Conferences, Decision to attack the US, Britain, the Netherlands; Group D (Zaibatsu); Group E (Expansionist and Ultranationalist societies); Group F (Army cliques); Group G (Bureaucracy Groups).

29. Joseph B. Keenan and Brendan F. Brown, *Crimes Against International Law* (Washington DC: Public Affairs Press, 1950), 156 In Sellars, *'Crimes against Peace' and International Law*, 207.
30. Judith Shklar, *Legalism: An Essay on Law, Morals, and Politics* (Cambridge: Harvard University Press, 1964), 186–187.
31. Sansom to MacDermont, Telegram, February 26, 1946 in FO262/2047.
32. Ibid.
33. Keenan to Associate Prosecutors, "Responsibility of Associate Prosecutors," February 13, 1946, IPS Documents in NARA II, RG 331.
34. Higgins to Keenan, Confidential Memorandum, February 27, 1946, IPS07–13, "General Policy," in NARA II, RG331.
35. Comyns-Carr to Keenan, Memorandum, February 25, 1946, IPS07–13, "General Policy," RG331.
36. Quilliam to Shanahan, Tokyo, March 11, 1946, Doc.660 in Robin Kay, ed., *Documents on New Zealand External Relations. Volume II: The Surrender and Occupation of Japan* (Wellington: P. D. Hasselberg, Government Printer, 1982), 1532–1538.
37. Donald Cameron Watt, "Historical Introduction," in John R. Pritchard and Sonia M. Zaide, eds. And Donald C. Watt, *The Tokyo War Crimes Trial: The Comprehensive Index and Guide to the Proceedings of the International Military Tribunal for the Far East. Volume I* (New York: Garland, 1981), xvii.
38. Comyns-Carr to Morland, Telegram, March 15, 1946, FO262/2047.
39. Sellars, *'Crimes Against Peace' and International Law*, 202.
40. July 20, 1946, Entry, Quilliam Diary cited in James Burnham Sedgwick, "The Trial Within: Negotiating Justice at the International Military Tribunal for the Far East, 1946–1948," (Phd. Thesis, The University of British Columbia, 2012), 66.

CHAPTER 4

The Hegemonic Narrative of the Pacific War: Japan's Conspired and Aggressive War

The international criminal tribunals tend to make certain choices in producing history; they tend to favor linear, over-determined narratives infused with the views of the Great Powers or sponsoring states—they produce "hegemonic history"[1] as opposed to a more fragmented and ambiguous historical narrative that offers a deeper understanding of forces behind the events. The IPS as a whole, but especially the US legal team, was instrumental not only in editing and adapting the Nuremberg law but also in producing a historical narrative that was supporting the legal structure. The extensive use of historical evidence or narrative to enhance the persuasiveness of the legal argument has been widespread among the prosecution and defense in international criminal trials, although their statutes do not compel them to do so.[2] At the Tokyo Trial as well, the prosecutor and its associate prosecutors held a lot of power when it comes to decision-making process, which charges, historical information will find their place in the indictment, the narrative, the defendants to be put on trial.

After all, law and history are distinct disciplines, interested in different questions and methods for their inquiry. The general character of legal norms clashes with detail-oriented history. What law searches in an event, strictly speaking, is whether actions, circumstances, or individuals can fit into pre-established legal definitions. History on the other hand tries to explain at as many levels as possible why and how the events occurred; in that sense it is not bound by any frameworks. As Chap. 2 has concluded, international law regulating the use of force was created in 1945 at both

A. Babovic, *The Tokyo Trial, Justice, and the Postwar International Order*, New Directions in East Asian History,
https://doi.org/10.1007/978-981-13-3477-1_4

San Francisco and London Conferences—in certain instances, unilateral war and war as a criminal act, respectively, are illegal. This book argues that international law is inextricably tied to politics as it is one of its very expressions. International law is a translation of political decisions, achieved by more or less consensus. International law can be used as a code of conduct providing for restraint or it can be used as a vehicle for enforcement and imposition of policies. In the case of the IMTFE, international rules were created regarding international crimes that dictate a legal narrative or its framework. Crudely put, all events that fit or can be made to fit this legal framework are taken into consideration. In this case, all of the "legal leftovers" belong to history that will aim to reconnect them, with more or less limitations, into a more authentic narrative. This legal framework was used by the dominant powers in a discretionary way, contradicting the presumed sovereign quality of states. Consequently, the law was used to assert hegemony of the Allies, or predominantly the US, which in the case of the IMTs offered a legal framework through which historical narratives were carefully woven to follow its direction. Therefore, this is the main reason why this book concludes that the IMTFE produced, in its indictment and majority judgement, a hegemonic version of history.

With all these legal precedents and an ongoing trial at Nuremberg, the IPS at Tokyo had an important task to prepare the case against Japanese leaders based on the central charge of crime against peace or waging aggressive war. In doing so, the IMTFE was fulfilling another important goal, that is, to confirm the law at Nuremberg.[3] Dean Acheson explicitly put it as "it is most important that the procedure and principles of the Tokyo Tribunal, as well as definitions of crimes, should harmonize with those adopted for the prosecutions in Germany."[4] In other words, the prosecution was supposed to prepare the case that will show how the Japanese war was aggressive in all its instances—starting from January 1, 1928, and concluding with September 2, 1945—and directed against the Allied powers. The nature of the Japanese aggressive war case, meaning including all of the Allied powers' countries, would have been lost had the US organize an exclusively American tribunal to try the Tōjō cabinet for the Pearl Harbor Attack. To put it more succinctly, it would cast a doubt on whether the wars waged by the Japanese Empire were aggressive in their totality.

The "star" charge was the crime against peace, but two other categories of crimes were added as to expand the material jurisdiction of the Tribunal and, at the same time, cherish the interests of nations whose population directly suffered from atrocities at the hands of Japanese soldiers. Had the crime of aggression been prosecuted without war crimes and crimes against humanity, the Tribunal's legitimacy would have been significantly impaired. At Tokyo, three types of international crimes were classified into Class A (crime against peace), Class B (war crimes), and Class C (crimes against humanity) which covered the whole range of Japanese actions in the Asia-Pacific War. The IMTFE defendants were designated as Class A or major war criminals which also indicated the primacy of this charge in the Tribunal's mandate and case presented by the prosecution.

The case was built in a manner to prevent the eventual acquittal of defendants or dismissal of charges. The border clashes or incidents made it to instances of aggression. The *undeclared* war, as written in the IMTFE Charter, was meant to cover the Pearl Harbor Attack and the border clashes or incidents in which war declaration was missing. War was qualified as aggressive independent of these formal requirements. The charges extended over 17 years arguing that the Japanese leaders planned, prepared, and waged war of aggression in the period from January 1, 1928, to September 2, 1945. The act of planning the crime itself was not punishable as a crime under the Common Law tradition whereas the act of preparation had to be particularly advanced and close to the actual commission of a criminal act to be established as a criminal attempt. The indictment started by showing that the Japanese war of aggression started with the invasion of Manchuria, following the Manchurian Incident in 1931, which was qualified as an outright violation of the 1922 Nine-Power Treaty. Interestingly, although one of the draft articles of the IMT Charter at the London Conference regarding the definition of the crime against peace included "invasion or threat of invasion,"[5] this provision was erased as the Soviet delegate thought this would be detrimental as the defense could argue that the Soviets invaded Poland and Finland. The Treaty was a part of the larger Washington Treaty System that offered a principled approach to powers in East Asia.[6] The Nine-Power Treaty vectored the interests of the Great Powers towards the preservation of the status quo in China through the principle of equal opportunity for trade and commerce for all which was also known as the Open Door policy. Following the Manchurian Incident, Japan organized a puppet state, stationed military troops, and built war potential, which the Soviet team qualified as preparation for an attack against the Soviet Union. Thus, the two-week border clash at Lake Khasan in 1938 and the three-month-long clash at Khalkhyn Gol River, on the border between Mongolia and Manchuria, were qualified as "undeclared aggressive wars" by the Soviets, whereas in fact these were mere incidents that ended in armistice. Following these events, the Neutrality Pact was signed between Japan and the Soviet Union on April 13, 1941.[7] The Japanese co-occupation of the northern part of Vichy French Indochina was considered as an instance of invasion. In fact, on September 22, 1940, Japan and France signed an agreement that allowed the Japanese to occupy the northern part of Indochina in order to cut the flow of arms and fuel it was providing to China. This was the result of rounds of negotiations with the French and after the Japanese threats to use force and invade.[8] Contrary to other parts of East Asia where European colonial powers were ousted from power and replaced by the Japanese military domination, Indochina was an exception as it was not placed under their exclusive control. The French kept their military and administrative control over the island together with the Japanese. Few days later, Japan signed the Tripartite Pact with Nazi Germany and Italy in pursuance of the plan to dominate Asia-Pacific which was, in the wording of the indictment, its sphere of influence.[9] According to the indictment, the stronghold in French Indochina was used as a strategic base for Japan to carry out surprise attacks against British Commonwealth nations of Singapore, Malaya, Hong Kong, Shanghai, and then the Philippines, Thailand, and ultimately the US.[10] From these first acts of aggression sprung all subsequent ones which were all conspired, planned, and waged by the Japanese leaders in order to invade its sphere of influence in the Asia-Pacific.

In the words of Japanese historian Akira Iriye, designation of World War II in Japanese literature as a "Fifteen Years War" or "the Asia-Pacific War" created confusion about the nature and scope of the war that took place in that part of the world. Otherwise, the war could be framed as distinct periods and theaters of combat against China, the Commonwealth countries, the US, and the Soviet Union.[11] The minutes of IPS also show that the prosecution had difficulty connecting the aggression in China in the 1930s to other phases of war as they pondered over whether it ought to be distinguished from wars that came in distinct phases.[12] The prosecution was presented with piles of documents consisting of studies, publications, treaties emanating from the wartime period but also reaching into Japanese prewar history. The IPS had difficulty substantiating poorly evidenced claims and building a coherent narrative on Japanese aggression. Sometimes, the prosecution used the prewar Japanese history to establish the origins of Japanese aggression that could help the overall conspiracy argument. This way, the prosecution was writing a highly distorted version of history that was to fulfill a mission of proving the guilt of the defendants, which many prosecutors felt strongly about.[13]

From the outset, the IPS was put in a difficult situation due to the lack of direct evidence against Japanese leaders which would make the burden of proof challenging. Not only was the evidence dispersed all over the former Japanese Empire, but the government documents in Japan were destroyed during the war, in the firebombing of Tokyo, or destroyed by the government in the last days of war in the face of defeat being imminent. On the contrary, the conditions in Germany were friendlier to the prosecutorial efforts. The written record of Nazi plans and evidence of abominable atrocities they committed against ethnic and religious groups were widely available. The fact that these policies came from an easily retrievable and unified command line made the attribution of criminal liability much easier which stood in stark contrast with the political situation in Japan.[14] British prosecutor Comyns-Carr's words are illustrative on this point: "the whole Japanese situation is infinitely more complicated than the German for the purpose of prosecution, as all the politicians, soldiers and sailors were all squabbling and double-crossing one another all the time."[15] The majority of prosecutors in Tokyo were personally convinced of Japan's guilt, and with deep understanding of the grander policies behind the IMTFE, for which many of them considered to be of historical importance, they were committed to build a successful case.

The legal solution that came as a glue to the issue of fast-changing cabinets and dispersed theaters of battle was the doctrine of conspiracy, borrowed from the Anglo-Saxon municipal law. Legally, the conspiracy concept was elastic, as it required only a participation, not necessarily action, of individuals aspiring towards a similar goal.[16] This all-encompassing property made it suitable for the Japanese context of aggression, which consisted of distinct theaters of battle that all fused under the overarching goal of waging an aggressive war.

This "unifying method" was proposed by Colonel Murray C. Bernays, Harvard Law School graduate, who was in charge of drafting legal procedures for the Nuremberg Trial, although his work was further extended to the IMTFE. His idea was that instead of proving the individual criminal responsibility of each member of government, military organs, or party organizations, it sufficed to prove that these institutions conspired to commit international crimes. What mattered was not the individual act but the individual membership to the organ or organization by way of their official position. This legal concept was highly problematic as neither the states practice nor international law recognized the conspiracy as international crime. Its transposition from domestic to international legal order was justified by its effectiveness in dealing with those who violate the stability and integrity of international order.[17] Additionally, the concept of conspiracy, according to Keenan, was universal as it was common to great legal systems of the world, including Japan which incriminated conspiracy against the state.[18] In Tokyo, this method would not only be time-saving for the IPS facing constant pressures for starting the trials but also the acute issue of poor direct evidence against the defendants circumvented. The acts of aggression perpetrated by distinct, often opposing, and fast-changing cabinets' members could fit into the constant, overall conspiracy to plan, initiate, and wage an aggressive war. The defendants' guilt would be established by way of their official rank in the governmental structure and not the actual commission of crimes. In other words, they did not have to give their authorization or consent or commit the actual criminal act; their failure to resign the post or prevent the crime amounted to their implicit consent and, hence, approval of the criminal act. In October 1944, Stimson praised the conspiracy as "it caught everyone in the net, regardless of their actual responsibility for specific acts."[19] This legal category proper to prosecution of "gangs" and carrying the "communal enterprise" was in a way contradictory to the intent of prosecuting the defendants on an individual basis, for which the individual criminal responsibility was introduced. Not all the prosecutors were at first approving of the charge of conspiracy, especially the ones who had training in the Continental legal tradition. The British prosecutor Comyns-Carr, who many times acted as a bridge between warring sides, suggested that putting burden on a single charge of conspiracy would be risky and that it would be prudent to link every conduct to conspiracy in elaborating the narrative of aggressive war.

Conspiracy served as a method for proving guilt of Japanese leaders for all three crimes—aggressive war, war crimes, and crimes against humanity. Article 5 (a) of the IMTFE Charter defined aggression as "planning, preparing, and waging a war of aggression in violation of international law and treaties" or the "participation in common plan or conspiracy for accomplishment of any of the foregoing."[20] Article 5(c) established individual criminal responsibility of leaders who participate "in the formulation and execution of a common plan or conspiracy" to commit war crimes or crimes against humanity or "for all acts performed by any person in execution of such plan."[21]

Aware of the risk of placing the prosecutorial success exclusively on a single charge of conspiracy, the prosecution decided to secure the chances of defendants being prosecuted in case overall or single conspiracy was insufficiently established due to the complexity of the Japanese situation and introduced the additional four counts of conspiracy to be prosecuted as a statutory crime. Legal advisor to Keenan, Brendan Brown, devised the idea that the doctrine of conspiracy considered conspiracy as a crime per se, independent of the criminality of the act itself, distinguishable as "crime of agreement."[22] Each phase of the war in the period between 1931 and 1945 was to be represented by individuals who assumed the key decision-making positions in a cabinet. There were 17 cabinets and 16 prime ministers during the war, whose members were not acting in concert, but often opposed each other while the decision-making process was not a product of a continuous, pre-meditated policy.[23] Illustratively, the first count of the indictment read that the common plan or conspiracy in which Japanese leaders occupying different positions in distinct phases of war took part was meant "to secure military, naval, political, and economic domination of the East Asia and of the Pacific and Indian Oceans and all of countries and islands therein and bordering thereon" and "wage declared or undeclared war or wars."[24] This count, according to prosecutor Solis Horwitz, was meant to establish responsibility of different ministries in the government for the overall conspiracy and then implicitly individuals who participated in it.[25] The second and third counts covered China, while count 4 was encompassing all other Allied powers. The last count of conspiracy went beyond the Asia-Pacific theater to encompass the conspiracy to dominate the whole world with other Axis powers, according to the prosecution, as evidenced by the Tripartite Pact.[26] Counts 2, 3, and 4 came as backup to show that single, geographically focused and thus separate conspiracies existed but that they all institutionally converged into the overall conspiracy presented in count 1. The part where the charge of conspiracy became aberrant is in its count 5 where the Japanese and German leaders joined in their conspiracy for world domination. It could be concluded that the determination and utter pragmatism of the IPS members made sure that at least some of these counts would be supported by the judges.

The IMT prosecuted crimes against humanity as distinct category of crime, unrelated to crime of aggression, given that it matched the specificity of the German context where the Nazis committed crimes against their own population. As the IMT Charter was transplanted to the IMTFE Charter, in crimes against humanity instances, it proved inadequate for the Japanese context and, consequentially, it was merged together with conventional war crimes. Even though certain crimes presented by prosecutorial teams could have entered into the category of crimes against humanity, the prosecution relegated them to serve as evidence to substantiate the main charge of crimes against peace.[27] More precisely, the documented atrocities were used to show patterns of atrocities and their similarity, which would indicate that they were part of a larger policy adopted and ordered at the top level. The crimes against populations in occupied lands such as deportation and enslavement, murder, torture, rape, destruction of private property, and forced labor were only enumerated as to support the supreme crime of crime against peace.[28] The Chinese prosecution team documented the Rape of Nanking which took place in December 1937, but they mostly relied on affidavits. The evidence and interrogation of the defendants pointed at the impossibility of controlling poorly disciplined Japanese troops that engaged in murder, rape, or looting, with support of field commanders. Negative criminality was introduced to compensate for the lack of direct evidence about the Japanese leaders' knowledge regarding the atrocities.[29] The last two counts of the indictment, 53 and 55, established individual criminal responsibility for direct participation in the common plan or conspiracy to "order, permit, or authorize"[30] the entire command chain, from ministers, commanders, to local units to commit atrocities against populations in occupied areas and negative criminality which established responsibility by omission or disregard of duty to prevent the atrocities.

Notes

1. Gerry Simpson, "International Criminal Justice and the Past," 140–141 in Gideon Boas, William A. Schabas, and Michael P. Scharf, eds., *International Criminal Justice: Legitimacy and Coherence* (Northampton: Massachusetts, 2012).
2. Richard Ashby, Wilson, *Writing History in International Criminal Trials* (Cambridge: Cambridge University Press), 2011, 70.
3. Kirsten Sellars, *'Crimes Against Peace' and International Law* (Cambridge: Cambridge University Press), 2013, 185.
4. The Undersecretary of State (Acheson) to the Director of Office of Far Eastern Affairs (Ballantine), Washington, September 6, 1945, FRUS,

1945. The British Commonwealth and the Far East, Vol. 6 (Washington DC: Government Printing Office), 1969, 921.
5. Sellars, *'Crimes Against Peace' and International Law*, 102.
6. Tosh Minohara, ed., *The History of US-Japan Relations: From Perry to Present* (Singapore: Palgrave Macmillan, 2017), 69.
7. Yuma Totani, *The Tokyo War Crimes Trial: The Pursuit of Justice in the Wake of World War II* (Cambridge: Harvard University Press, 2008), 93.
8. Franck Michelin, "L'Indochine française et l'expansion vers le sud du Japon à l'orée de la Guerre du Pacifique. Politique étrangère et processus de décision, 29 juin 1940–8 décembre 1941," (French Indochina and Japan's Expansion in the South Asia at the Beginning of the Pacific War: Foreign Policy and Decision Making Process, June 29, 1940–December 8, 1941) (Doctoral thesis: Université Paris-Sorbonne), 2014, 76; Franck Michelin, "Décider et agir. L'intrusion japonaise en Indochine française (juin 1940)," (Decide and Act. Japanese intrusion into French Indochina (June 1940), *Vingtième Siècle. Revue d'histoire* 83:2004, 75–93.
9. Robert L. Guill, Notes, n.d., RG331, IPS07–13, NDL.
10. Neil Boster and Robert Cryer, *Documents on the Tokyo International Military Tribunal: Charter, Indictment, and Judgement* (New York: Oxford University Press, 2009), 43–45.
11. Akira Iriye and Waren Cohen, ed., *American, Chinese, and Japanese Perspectives on Wartime Asia, 1931–1935*, Wilmington: Scholarly Resources, 1990, 223–234.
12. "Item 2—Minutes of Fourteenth Meeting of Executive Committee," April 5, 1946, Box 1, Folder 3, MSS 93-4, Special Collections, University of Virginia Law School.
13. James Sedgwick, "The trial within: negotiating international justice" 66.
14. Bruno Simma, "The Impact of Nuremberg and Tokyo: Attempts at a Comparison," in Nisuke Ando, ed., Japan and International Law: Past, Present, Future (The Hague: Kluwer Law International, 1999), 83.
15. Comyns Carr to Shawcross, March 19, 1946 cited in Sellars, *'Crimes Against Peace' and International Law*, 190–191.
16. J.B. Keenan and B.F. Brown, *Crimes Against International Law* (Washington: Public Affairs Press, 1950), 89 in *'Crimes Against Peace' and International Law*, 192.
17. State Department to Keenan, "The Crime of Conspiracy," Memorandum, May 23, 1946, 33 in NARA II, RG 84.
18. Ibid.
19. Richard Overy, "The Nuremberg Trials: International Law in the Making," in Philip Sands, ed., *From Nuremberg to The Hague: The Future of the International Criminal Justice* (Cambridge: Cambridge University Press, 2003), 16.

20. "Charter of the IMTFE," April 29, 1946, Article 5(a) in Boister and Cryer, eds., *Documents on the Tokyo International Military Tribunal: Charter, Indictment, and Judgements* (Cambridge: Cambridge University Press, 2008), 8.
21. "Charter of the IMTFE," April 29, 1946, Article 5(a) in Ibid.
22. Sellars, *'Crimes Against Peace' and International Law*, 196.
23. Totani, The Tokyo War Crimes Trials: The Pursuit of Justice in the Wake of World War II, 89.
24. Neil Boster and Robert Cryer, *Documents on the Tokyo International Military Tribunal: Charter, Indictment, and Judgement*, 43–45.
25. Solis Horwitz, "The Tokyo Trial," *International Conciliation* 465 (November 1950): 505.
26. Aleksandra Babovic, "Japan's Share of Responsibility in World War Two Through Legal Lenses: Selective and Exclusive Justice at IMTFE," *Kobe Law Review* 49 (2005), 11.
27. Indictment, Appendix D, Section Thirteen in Neil Boister and Robert Cryer, eds., *Documents on the Tokyo International Military Tribunal: Charter, Indictment and Judgements*, 62.
28. Ibid.
29. Higgins to Fihelly, Weekly Report, January 21, 1946, RG331.
30. Neil Boister and Robert Cryer, *Documents on the Tokyo International Military Tribunal: Charter, Indictment, and Judgement.*

CHAPTER 5

The Partial Interest for Victims and Strategic "Forgetting" at the Tokyo Tribunal

The justice at Tokyo was not designed, and understandably so, to be universal in nature. The newly elaborated laws and principles were not construed as applicable to all parties involved in the conflict—neither victims of colonization nor the Great Powers on the winning side. Crimes committed by the Japanese against the local population in former Japanese colonies and, equally, by the Allied powers against Japan—but also their own colonial subjects—were omitted from the Tribunal's jurisdiction and legal record. These prosecutions, at least when it comes to atrocities committed by the Japanese against population under its colonial rule, were not desirable because of its pragmatic (difficulty of collecting evidence, interviewing victims, and urge for expediency) and strategic aspects as the larger goal of the Tribunal remained to prove the crime of aggression. In addition, it should not be forgotten that many of the Allies had colonies themselves, and, from that point of view, did not want to expose themselves as protectors of colonial subjects whose needs did not rank high on their agenda. Regarding the Allies and the crimes they committed in Japan or against the Japanese, it would have been odd to expect them to stage prosecution for their own crimes; nevertheless it is a point to be addressed because it explains the creation of a hegemonic historical narrative about the Pacific War which naturally aims to "forget" these. The fact that they did not find their place in the Indictment liberated the Allies from assuming any legal responsibility or carrying historical and moral stigma in relation to the war with Japan. The IMT Nuremberg Chief Prosecutor Jackson summarized

A. Babovic, *The Tokyo Trial, Justice, and the Postwar International Order*, New Directions in East Asian History,
https://doi.org/10.1007/978-981-13-3477-1_5

this, in theory, desirable universality of law and its consistent application by saying that "[..]while this law is first applied against German aggressors, the law includes, and if it is to serve a useful purpose it must condemn, aggression by any other nations, including those which sit here now in judgement."[1] In the same address, he recognized that if the Allied powers' leaders might not be judged by the judicial means they crafted for the Germans and Japanese, they would not be able to escape the subsequent judgement of history using as its reference point the very same criteria.

The existence of sexual brothels and the widespread practice of sexual enslavement were evidenced to be the composite part of Japan's war strategy in Southeast Asia as the Australian National Office extensively documented. Victims of sexual enslavement were from the countries that were not represented at the IMTFE bench or that were still looked upon as colonial subjects. In 1945, the Allied powers' governments gave clear instructions on what were the priorities for the war crimes program—to promptly and efficiently prove the charge of aggressive war against the Japanese leaders while all the rest was of lesser priority. These crimes were just brushed off when it came to the Tokyo Tribunal. However, it is to be noted that the trials of the Japanese lesser war criminals, including some high-profile cases such as Tamura and Toyoda, were conducted throughout Asia-Pacific from 1945 to 1952. These trials also brought up charges on behalf of civilians in occupied areas that could be classified within war crimes or crimes against humanity (torture, rape, massacres, forced labor).[2] Since the post-Cold War era, these unprosecuted crimes have constituted, along with Japanese mixed signals about its wartime responsibility as aggravating factor, a combustible issue between Japan and its neighbors, chiefly China and the Republic of Korea.

The knowledge about Unit 731 that carried out human experimentations for the purposes of the development of biological weapons was an open secret in the diplomatic but also prosecutorial circles. The Unit was part of the Kwantung Army's Epidemic Prevention Section that operated in Central China, along the borders of Mongolia, and the USSR under the lead of Colonel Lieutenant Ishii Shiro; this was also known as "the Ishii organization."[3] The military pertaining to the Unit 731 were all acquitted because the US army was eager to acquire scientific and technological findings on the new kind of biological weapon which was object of the GHQ General Staff investigation. Daniel Nelson Sutton and Colonel Thomas H. Morrow, Prosecutor Keenan's assistant, traveled to Chinese cities of Shanghai, Chongqing, and Nanking to gather indispensable evidence which proved to be a frustrating and unfruitful endeavor.[4] When they arrived there, despite the effort, the American Embassy in Nanking failed to provide them with evidence, and persons they deemed "suitable" and "trustworthy" to give court testimony—not Chinese—were scarce.[5] In late April, Morrow briefed Keenan on findings related to chemical warfare in China in the report "General Account of Japanese Poison Warfare in China, 1937–1945,"[6] while Sutton wrote a report on bacterial warfare with recommendation not to pursue these charges against the Japanese as the evidence proved limited. Morrow insisted on the importance of getting Ishii for an interrogation as it could demonstrate that the Japanese leadership used prohibited means of warfare,[7] and, curiously, soon afterward, Morrow's mission in Tokyo was ended as he was reassigned to Washington. When Sutton presented the case of poisonous serum testing on prisoners of war by Unit 1644, also known as the Nanking-Tama Unit, Justice Webb was dismissive, and it was decided that no additional evidence would be adduced.[8] The members of the Organization, including Ishii himself, were interrogated earlier in January 1945 by the GHQ General Staff. They provided scarce information claiming that the experiments were conducted independently from the Imperial Japanese Army leaders or the Emperor. They were committed to remain secretive about the level of authority that ordered and authorized the experimentations, but most of all to shield the Emperor from any connection with it.[9] In the end, they were promised immunity from prosecution in exchange for their scientific findings. The investigation for prosecutorial purposes was nominal in nature, as the higher goal of gathering military intelligence, which would be an important addition to the US biological warfare program started in 1942, was prioritized at the outset. This is one of the many examples where the US betrayed its democratic values—morality and justice—and traded them off for military intelligence information.

The international prosecution section had knowledge and evidence about the systematic and widespread rape of women, as well as enforced prostitution in the former Japanese colonies committed against predominantly Chinese, Korean, Filipino, Thai, and Japanese women. It is noteworthy that rape has been classified as an instance of crime against humanity in Article 5(g) of the ICTY Charter, whereas Article 7(g) of the Rome Statute (the ICC), equally defining crime against humanity, goes further in including "sexual slavery, enforced prostitution, forced pregnancy, enforced sterilization, or any other form of sexual violence of comparable gravity."[10] Nevertheless, in its 16-year practice, for the first time, on March 21, 2016, the ICC handed judgement addressing war crimes and crimes against humanity on counts of rape and sexual violence in the Jean-Pierre Bemba Gombo case. It was also the first case to find the defendant guilty of crimes committed by his subordinates or command responsibility.[11] However, on June 8, 2018, the Appeal Chamber reversed the decision of the Trial Chamber and acquitted Bemba after a ten-year-long trial.[12] Prior to that, both the ICTY and the ICC have been criticized for not prosecuting gender violence as a crime per se despite the presented evidence, but narrowly framing them within the scope of central crimes—the ethnic cleansing or genocide in the case of Yugoslav conflict and enlistment, conscription, and use of child soldiers in the case of the Democratic Republic of the Congo. Gender awareness in the sphere of international relations has been greater than in 1945; nevertheless prosecutions for these crimes by the criminal tribunals remain rather cautious and scarce.

Already in 1919, the Commission of Responsibilities of the Authors of War and on Enforcement of Penalties included "rape" and "abduction of girls and women for the purposes of enforced prostitution" to their definition of war crimes. Before World War II ended, in 1943, the United Nations War Crimes Commission was tasked with making a list of potential war crimes and coordinating with efforts of the national offices that conducted investigations and issued lists of suspected war criminals which would be shared between the Allies for the purpose of their apprehension. Its East Asia branch, the Far Eastern Sub-Commission, hosted in Chunquing, was established in 1944 to perform these same tasks. Although these two commissions were not institutionally linked to the IMTFE, it is significant that their lists and evidence did include rape as a war crime. The IMTFE Indictment indeed included rape as a war crime and crime against humanity charge, but only as evidence for demonstrating the magnitude of Japanese aggression and its cruelty towards local population. Prosecuting the Nanking rape as a separate crime was not considered for prosecution in its own right. The majority judgement at Tokyo concluded that expected instances of occasional rape in military conflicts could be "excused," but when its commission is taking place over an extended period of time in a systematic manner, it is to be considered "barbarous and inexcusable."[13] The sexual enslavement resulting from the widespread presence of sexual brothels throughout the colonies was entirely left out of the Indictment. The Australian National Office possessed abundant evidence on the recurrent rapes and information on the existence of military brothels that testified to forced prostitution as a form of sexual enslavement. For instance, the national offices distributed questionnaires to the Allied soldiers upon their return in order to gather record of crimes committed by the Japanese military. Interestingly, the forms Americans formulated did not inquire about rapes contrary to the Australian ones.[14] The collected information was not exploited at the IMTFE although Alan J. Mansfield, Australian representative to the UNWCC, who was also close to President Webb, became associate prosecutor at the Tokyo Tribunal. As Yuma Totani's research convincingly demonstrated, even documentation prepared by the French and Dutch prosecuting teams at Tokyo during the trial confirmed this and discerned a certain pattern of sexual enslavement in dispersed areas throughout the enormous landmass representing the former Japanese empire.[15] This hinted at the instrumentality of "brothels" in the overall Japanese war strategy.[16] The enslaved women were predominantly from nations that were not represented at the Tribunal while many of these nations were still considered as colonies. After all, at that time, colonial mentality was still the order of the day. The "legal infrastructure" that could have addressed crimes of rape and enforced prostitution existed within the framework of the IMTFE Charter and its Article 5, more precisely under the category of inhumane acts. The prosecution could at least have tried to make the case for crimes against humanity as a separate crime given that considerable evidence had existed. It is uncertain whether the evidence presented would have been enough to establish that these crimes were part of a concerted policy or plan and whether the Japanese top civilian and military leaders could have done something to prevent these given the widely known accounts on troops being difficult to discipline. Given that General Iwane Matsui and Kōki Hirota were tried for Nanking Massacre under conspiracy to commit war crimes and crimes against humanity, it is not excluded that negative criminality could have been applied. What appears, however, as certain is that there was a lack of political will to represent the population of the countries which suffered the most from mass atrocity. Instead, the Tribunal addressed crimes committed against the material interests and population of those nations that stood behind their creation (the US, Britain, France) or, eventually, states they choose to patronize (China). The US that could be considered as the main "judicial entrepreneur" when it came to setting up the trial placed its strongest case for the crime against peace on top of the prosecutorial agenda as that was the charge around which the majority of Allies could certainly be gathered around. "Vilifying Japan for waging aggressive war" sacrificed sexual enslavement for the sake of the dominant narrative alongside with, crudely put, colonial, racial, and gender mentalities of that time.[17]

Ironically, just as the London Conference neared its end on August 2, 1945, the US, which assumed the role of high moral leader in war, used atomic bombs against Japan in Hiroshima and Nagasaki, on August 6 and 9, respectively. The London Agreement posed the judicial framework for prosecuting core crimes—crime against peace, war crimes, crime against humanity—whose nature was so serious that they shocked human consciousness. Hence their prosecution was considered of interest to the international community and humanity as a whole. The use of, at that time, the novel weapon of mass destruction by the US was both morally and legally "excused" by the necessity to bring halt to a protracted war in the Asia-Pacific theater, the qualification of Japan as an illegal belligerent under the 1928 Kellogg-Briand Pact, and the fact that the explicit prohibition to use nuclear weapons in international law did not exist. Nuclear blasts, however, did not have determinant effect upon the end of the Pacific War as the indiscriminate bombing of Japanese cities continued until August 14, 1945. The incendiary bombs used to target industrial complexes that were, contrary to Germany, close to Japanese homes destroyed entire cities and severely harmed Japanese civilians.[18] Second, Japan violated the Pact which virtually made it an outlaw and automatically a non-beneficiary of *jus in bello* rights in war, which in turn liberated other states of the obligation to observe *jus in bello* rules in war against Japan.[19] Unrestricted warfare was, thus, implicitly allowed for the purpose of taming the aggressor. Under the Regulation concerning Laws and Customs of War on Land of 1899, indiscriminate bombing of towns that were not defended was prohibited.[20] In addition, the 1923 Hague Rules of Airfare, although they were in a draft phase, prohibited the use of aerial attacks upon non-military objects. Military powers, however, had already been wired to aircraft in order to accept restrictions to its use.[21] Third, the absence of explicit prohibition of nuclear weapons use did not, however, preclude the application of the 1907 Hague Convention fundamental principle of *unnecessary suffering*[22] caused by indiscriminate use of weapons. This principle is related to the more general principles of proportionality and humanity. In other words, the use of arms is considered to be permissible as long as they are in accordance with the above-presented fundamental principles underlying laws of war. The use of atomic bombs was clearly in contravention to these rules as they caused mass killings and long-term destruction, in the form of radiation and reported worsening health conditions, on a scale incomparable to any other atrocities in the Pacific theater. On August 9, 1945, the Japanese government sent a protest note to the US government, through the Swiss legion, in which they invoked illegality of the use of atomic bombs—indiscriminate choice of means and their disproportionality. The note admittedly stated that Japan employed the prohibited poisonous gas in China but only to point out at the disproportionality and gravity of nuclear weapons.[23] This note is significant as it was the first and the last time that the Japanese government ever protested against the issue of atomic bombs. In his opening speech at the IMTFE Prosecutor Keenan framed the atomic bombing in terms of just war theory: "We admit that great force and violence, including the Hiroshima bomb, have been employed by the Allies, and we make no more apology for that that does a decent, innocent citizen [whose] family employ the use of force to prevent his life being taken by an outlaw." Although Keenan took an unapologetic stance towards the bombings, certain members of the IPS and judicial cohort were deeply disturbed by the judicial silence on it and the scale of devastation they witnessed once they arrived in Japan.

The reverberations the Russo-Japanese war of 1904–1905 had for the two countries' relations were reflected in the extant mutual wariness and the long-felt desire by the Soviets to revenge their loss which they lived as a humiliation.[24] On April 13, 1941, the two nations concluded the Neutrality Pact that was still in vigor and was to expire in April 1946. The Soviets gave assurances to the Japanese that they would not harbor Allied military troops on its soil. Despite these repeated assurances of neutrality, during the Second Moscow Conference in October 1944 the Soviets displayed their mala fides towards cherishing its contractual obligations towards Japan. Earlier that year, the Soviets promised to provide a Siberian base for the US and negotiated conditions for their entry into the war against Japan, which was to take place three months upon the defeat of Germany. Beyond US assistance, they requested for a negotiated agreement with China which would allow the Russians to protect their interests in the region. The Tribunal also had excerpts that showed the reaching agreement during the Yalta Conference between Roosevelt, Churchill, and Stalin, in February 1945, where the Soviets promised to attack Japan in exchange for their interests being recognized in southern Sakhalin, Manchuria, the Kurile Islands, and Mongolia.[25] On April 5, the Soviets notified Japan that they were not interested in renewing the Pact as it lost its raison d'être due to profoundly changed circumstances. On July 13, the Japanese government asked the Soviet Union to mediate the end of war. On August 8, Naotake Satō, Japanese ambassador to Moscow, was informed by Soviet Prime Minister Vyacheslav

Mikhailovich Molotov about the Soviet entry into war against Japan,[26] who made it look like an acceptance of the Allies' request for the Soviets to join the war effort. This decision caused utter shock and desperation among the Japanese elite whose hopes for a negotiated peace agreement were dashed. In the morning of August 9, Soviet troops invaded Manchuria and engaged in indiscriminate warfare against the local population—Korean, Russian, and Japanese civilians—that was subjected to killing and rape while their private property was destroyed. The Kwantung Army received orders from the Emperor to stop the hostilities and negotiate truce with the Soviets on August 16. Although the Kwantung Army officially surrendered on August 19, the Soviet military operation concluded only two weeks later.[27] Japanese forces surrendered southern Sakhalin on August 19 and the attack on the Kuriles came on August 18 after which the Soviets took four islands—known as the Northern territories.[28] After Japan was delivered a crushing defeat by the Soviets, around 600,000 Japanese servicemen and civilians were taken to the Soviet Union, mostly Siberia, where they were imprisoned, exploited for hard labor, and exposed to Marxist-Leninist indoctrination.[29] The Soviets refused to repatriate the Japanese, although they approved the terms of the Communiqué for the Far East, produced at the Cairo Conference in 1943, according to which "Japan will also be expelled from all territories [...] taken by violence and greed."[30] And yet, the repatriation of the Japanese internees would be a wild card skillfully kept by the Soviets who anticipated an almost exclusive US role in the occupation of Japan. The repatriation only took place in 1956, but until then it represented a nexus between Japan and the Soviet Union within larger dynamics of the US-Japan alliance and early Cold War.

The legal premises of the new world order, written in the United Nations Charter, not yet in force, were first tested in legal argumentation given by the Allies regarding the Soviet attack on Japan. The attack could not have been considered as an instance of self-defense, but rather of outright aggression for which the Japanese leaders would face charges. Article 103 of the UN Charter addresses the hierarchy of obligations of the member state when its treaty obligations previously concluded are in conflict with the UN Charter.[31] This Article gives prevalence to the provisions of the Charter over obligations stemming from previously concluded international treaties by the member state in question. Following this line of reasoning, the Soviets had the responsibility—as future member of the Security Council—to join the Allied war effort against Japan, on behalf of the international community, for the purpose of maintaining peace and security. The higher legal status of this goal trumped the Soviet obligation of neutrality towards Japan.

Hence, the attack was legally justified as an instance of collective self-defense, contained in Article 52 of the Charter, against the aggressor, Japan. Soviet entry was justified as the collective military effort against the aggressor under the Covenant.[32] Aron Naumovich Trainin, the Soviet criminal law professor at the prestigious Moscow State University (MGU) and later on state prosecutor, wrote a book *Hitlerite Responsibility Under Criminal Law* in 1943 that would, along with other Allies' influential jurists, impact the development of crime against peace and conspiracy at Nuremberg. The arguments expressed in his book that was edited by Andrei Vichinsky, at that time deputy foreign minister, gained attention and was endorsed by the Soviet government, and almost accepted as its official position, on aggression.[33] Relevant to the instance of the Soviet attack, his distinction between just and unjust wars was instrumental as the former included wars of liberation. In the Soviet view, the attack against Japan was a case of just war, a war aiming to liberate nations exposed to Japan's aggression and domination. Trainin's work, which reflected the Soviet doctrine on international law, made distinction between war of aggression and war in violation of international obligations. At the London Conference, Trainin as the Soviet delegate contended that "war in violation of internal treaties, agreements, and assurances" was rather applying to matters pertaining to bilateral agreements than general international or customary law.[34] As for the IMT Charter, they had in mind the Non-Aggression Pact between Germany and the Soviet Union. Theoretically, this second instance of war could have been applied to the Soviet attack upon Japan, in violation of their 1941 Neutrality Pact, but it was conveniently discarded as an international obligation that became invalid in the face of superior international obligation pursuant to the UN Charter. Later on, Article 5 of the IMTFE Charter used the formulation "war in violation of international law, treaties, agreements, and assurances," in which the world *law* was added as to establish that prohibition of aggressive war did not only follow from contractual law but was an established norm of customary law. Yet, as discussed earlier, this view was legally unsound. The UN Charter came as confirmation that the unilateral use of force in violation of the status quo was an illegal act, with the exception of self-defense, whereas collective military action against nations that violate status quo was permissible with the authorization of the UN Security Council, whose five permanent members were all involved in establishment of the international order. These two instances of the Allied atrocity against Japan further complicated its own understanding of war responsibility in the light of simultaneously being a victim of atomic bombings and what could be qualified as aggression.

Notes

1. Trial of Major War Criminals, Nuremberg, 51; cited in Robert Cryer, *Prosecuting International Crimes: Selectivity and the International Criminal Law Regime* (Cambridge: Cambridge University Press, 2005), 197; 206.
2. For more details on these prosecutions see Yuma Totani, Justice in Asia and the Pacific Region, 1945–1952: Allied War Crimes Prosecutions (Cambridge: Cambridge University Press), 2015; Sandra Wilson, Robert Cribb, Beatrice Trefalt, and Dean Aszkielowicz, *Japanese War Criminals: The Politics of Justice After the Second World War* (New York: Columbia University Press), 2017.
3. Keiichi Tsuneishi, "Reasons for the Failure to Prosecute Unit 731 and its Significance," in Yuki Tanaka, Tim McCormack, and Gerry Simpson, eds., *Beyond Victor's Justice? The Tokyo War Crimes Trial Revisited* (Leiden: Martinus Nijhoff Publishers) 2011.
4. China Press, "Morrow Concludes China Tour, Gathered Evidence for the Trial," April 10, 1946, Section 14, Folder 60, MSS1, Virginia Historical Society. http://imtfe.law.virginia.edu/collections/sutton/14/60/china-press-april-10-1946
5. James Burnham Sedgwick, "The trial within: Negotiating Justice at the International Military Tribunal for the Far East," (Doctoral thesis: The University of British Columbia), 2012, 118–126.
6. Morrow to Keenan, "Evidence of Japanese use of Chemical Warfare Agents in China," Report, April 25, 1946 in RG496, Box 343; Sutton to Keenan, Report on Bacteria Warfare, April 25, 1946, in RG496, Box 343.
7. Sheldon H. Harries, *Factories of Death: Japanese Biological Warfare, 1932–45, and the American Cover-up* (New York: Routledge), 1994.
8. "Item 1 - Trial Transcript, August 29, 1946," Section 8, Folder 39, MSS1, Papers 1919–1965, Virginia Historical Society. http://lib.law.virginia.edu/imtfe/content/item-1-trial-transcript-august-29-1946
9. Keiichi Tsuneishi, "Reasons for the Failure to Prosecute Unit 731 and its Significance," in Yuki Tanaka, Tim McCormack, and Gerry Simpson, *Beyond Victor's Justice? The Tokyo War Crimes Trial Revisited*, 191.
10. "Rome Statute of the International Criminal Court," July 1, 2002, UN General Assembly.
11. Prosecutor v. Bemba, Case No. ICC-01/05–01/08–3343, Judgment Pursuant to Article 74 of the Statute (March 21, 2016), at https://www.icc-cpi.int/CourtRecords/CR2016_02238.PDF
12. For more details on the Appeal Judgement, see Leila N. Sadat, Fiddling While Rome Burns? The Appeals Chamber's Curious Decision in Prosecutor v. Jean-Pierre Bemba Gombo, The EJIL Talk, entry posted on June 12, 2018, https://www.ejiltalk.org/fiddling-while-rome-burns-the-appeals-chambers-curious-decision-in-prosecutor-v-jean-pierre-bemba-gombo/

13. Nicola Henry, "Silence as Collective Memory: Sexual Violence and the Tokyo Tribunal," in Yuki Tanaka, Tim McCormack, and Gerry Simpson, eds., *Beyond Victors' Justice: The Tokyo War Crimes Trial Reappraisal*, 274.
14. Ustinia Dolgopol, "Knowledge and Responsibility: The Ongoing Consequences of Failing to Give Sufficient Attention to the Crimes against the Comfort Women in the Tokyo Trial," in Yuki Tanaka, Tim McCormack, and Gerry Simpson, eds., *Beyond Victors' Justice: The Tokyo War Crimes Trial Reappraisal*, 253.
15. Yuma Totani, *The Tokyo War Crimes Trials: The Pursuit of Justice in the Wake of World War II* (Cambridge: Harvard University Press), 179–180.
16. Ustinia Dolgopol, "Knowledge and Responsibility: The Ongoing Consequences of Failing to Give Sufficient Attention to the Crimes against the Comfort Women in the Tokyo Trial," in Yuki Tanaka, Tim McCormack, and Gerry Simpson, eds., *Beyond Victors' Justice: The Tokyo War Crimes Trial Reappraisal*, 251.
17. Nicola Henry, "Sexual Violence and the Tokyo Trial," in Yuki Tanaka, Timothy L.H. McCormack, and Gerry Simpson, eds., *Beyond Victors' Justice? The Tokyo War Crimes Trials Revisited*, 268.
18. Ian Henderson, "The Firebombing of Tokyo and Other Japanese Cities," in Yuki Tanaka, Tim McCormack, and Gerry Simpson, eds., *Beyond Victors' Justice: The Tokyo War Crimes Trial Reappraisal*, 311–314.
19. Sellars, *'Crimes against Peace' and International Law*, 178.
20. Convention (II) with Respect to the Laws and Customs of War on Land and its annex: Regulations concerning the Laws and Customs of War on Land. The Hague. July 29, 1899. Article 25: "The attack or bombardment of towns, villages, habitations or buildings which are not defended, is prohibited."
21. Heinz Marcus Hanke, "The 1923 Hague Rules of Air Warfare – A contribution to the development of international law protecting civilians from air attack. *International Review of the Red Cross, 33*(292), 12–44.
22. Convention (IV) respecting the Laws and Customs of War on Land and its annex: Regulations concerning the Laws and Customs of War on Land. The Hague. October 18, 1907; in the Annex to the Convention, Article 23 (e) reads that it is forbidden "to employ arms, projectiles, or material calculated to cause unnecessary suffering." https://ihldatabases.icrc.org/applic/ihl/ihl.nsf/Article.xsp?action=openDocument&documentId=61CDD9E446504870C12563CD00516768
23. Yuki Tanaka, "The Atomic Bombing, The Tokyo Tribunal and the Shimoda Case: Lessons for the Anti-Nuclear Movements," in Yuki Tanaka, Tim McCormack and Gerry Simpson, 304–305.
24. William F. Nimmo, *Behind a Curtain of Silence: Japanese in Soviet Custody, 1945–1956* (Westport: Greenwood Press), 1988, 7.

25. Sellars, *'Crimes against Peace' and International Law*, 231.
26. Nimmo, *Behind a Curtain of Silence: Japanese in Soviet Custody, 1945–1956*, 6.
27. Ibid., 12.
28. Ibid., 13.
29. Sherzad Mominov, "'The Siberian Internment' and the Transnational History of the Early Cold War Japan, 1945–56," In Pedro Iacobellu, Danton Leary, and Shinnosuke Takahashi, *Transnational Japan as History: Empire, Migration, and Social Movements* (London: Palgrave Macmillan), 2016, 71.
30. "Final Text of Communiqué," in FRUS, diplomatic papers. *The Conferences at Cairo and Teheran, 1943* (Washington: Government Printing Office, 1961), 448, 556.
31. Richard Minear, Victors' Justice, 97.
32. Aron Trainin, Russian legal scholar, whose work infused the legal philosophy of Justice Jackson, author of *Hitlerite Responsibility Under International Law* explained the Soviet view on the aggression by making distinction between just and unjust wars. Wars of liberation fit the category of collective self-defense in terms of assistance to the state prejudiced by the aggressor.
33. For more on Trainin's work and significance when it comes to international criminal law, see Kirsten Sellars, 'Crime against Peace' and International Law (Cambridge: Cambridge University Press, 2014); Francine Hirsch; The Soviets at Nuremberg: International Law, Propaganda, and the Making of the Postwar Order, *The American Historical Review*, Volume 113, Issue 3, 1 June 2008, Pages 701–730; Penn, Michelle Jean, "The Extermination of Peaceful Soviet Citizens: Aron Trainin and International Law" (2017). *History Graduate Theses & Dissertations*. 39.
34. Roger S. Clark, "Nuremberg and the Crime Against Peace," *Washington University Global Studies Law Review* 6:3 (2007), 534. https://openscholarship.wustl.edu/cgi/viewcontent.cgi?article=1148&context=law_globalstudies

CHAPTER 6

Emperor Hirohito as the Japanese Kaiser and Selection of the IMTFE Defendants

The Divinity Shielded from the Trial

Emperor Shōwa was the only constant in the complex interplay of fast-changing cabinets whose leaders were often reactive and confrontational which was spoiling the linearity desperately needed by the prosecution section to establish a strong case. Under the Emperor's divine authority, the treaties had been signed, wars declared, and the army directly controlled. And yet, he remained out of reach of international criminal justice. Not because of his divinity, which he had to renounce as part of the unconditional surrender, but because the throne was of strategic value to the occupation authorities. His importance was illustrated by the words of the Supreme Commander MacArthur who wrote that if the Emperor had been destroyed, the Japanese nation would have disintegrated.[1] Kaiser Wilhelm II might have had to find refuge in Holland in 1919, but Emperor Hirohito remained in the comfort of the Imperial palace in Tokyo, without facing any responsibility for the Pacific War. The Emperor has not, nevertheless, escaped the judgement of history. *The New York Times* article from 2014 by Herbert Bix, a historian who has extensively written on the Emperor, describes him as a "string puller," who played the decisive role in the invasion of China and the Pearl Harbor Attack, which contrasts the prosecution's little convincing defense of the Emperor as a "puppet."[2]

At the outset of the occupation, it was clear to those involved in the occupation of Japan that Emperor Hirohito was not immune from

A. Babovic, *The Tokyo Trial, Justice, and the Postwar International Order*, New Directions in East Asian History,
https://doi.org/10.1007/978-981-13-3477-1_6

prosecution—his arrest, trial, and punishment as a war criminal were a viable option.[3] During the war, the fate of the Emperor was recognized as a unique feature of the Japanese state that should be resolved at a later date. The already mentioned tactic, employed by the US and Britain during the war to issue low-key war declarations with warnings to the Japanese regarding their criminal punishment in order to ameliorate the sort of their POWs, was also applied to the Emperor who was victimized as being a puppet in the hands of the militarist.[4] This served to postpone decision-making to a later date when his reputation was damaged by the full disclosure of mass atrocity, committed under his approval. The understanding was that the institution of the Emperor in Japan was the source of authority and cherished as "sacred and inviolable," which, if removed, would hinder the occupation as Japanese officials would resist cooperating with occupation authorities.[5] In addition, the anticipated opposition of the other Allies regarding the Emperor and his wartime responsibility made this matter open-ended, to be resolved at a later date, depending on conjuncture.[6] On February 1, 1944, *The New York Times* published an interview given by the former American Ambassador in Tokyo Joseph Grew in which he expressed his view that saw the Emperor as being in control of the military and his importance in postwar Japan for the coherence of the Japanese nation. In Grew's words, in the postwar context, the Emperor would be "an asset."[7] Given the already mounting anti-Japanese sentiment, following the publication of reports on Japanese atrocity, this insightful and farsighted interview was out of place. Two years later, these words would make much more sense, once the occupation authorities were on the ground.

The Potsdam Declaration of July 1945 did not contain any concrete reference to the status of the Emperor. As already noted earlier, the internal lack of consensus on views regarding the status of the Emperor reemerged again in this period, opposing those who, like Grew, advocated preservation of the throne, and those who considered it was better to remain vague on the topic, like Secretary of State Byrnes.[8] Finally, the latter view prevailed and the text of the Declaration remained vague on the future of the dynasty in stating that the Japanese people reserve the right to choose their system of government. This created a considerable unrest and uneasiness among Japanese leaders, especially from November 1945, when the first wave of arrests started, including the most sensational one of Hideki Tōjō.[9] According to Bix's account, from September 1945 to March 1946, Brigadier General Bonner Fellers pursued his mission of "saving the Emperor" with other government officials. He asked Tōjō to assume responsibility for the war and represent the Emperor as a puppet in the hands of the militarists.[10] It appeared that many forces, besides Japanese leaders, were working towards the goal of saving the Emperor as a cohesive force that would preserve the unity of the polity or ***kokutai***. However, there were some more vocal attempts to gain President Truman's approval for putting Hirohito on trial. For instance, Senator Richard Russell Jr. from Georgia thought that Hirohito was a "superaggressor" responsible for the crime against peace and atrocities towards the American soldiers and prisoners of war. He was behind a joint resolution in Congress that argued that the Emperor should be tried as a war criminal. Keeping him on the throne would lead to another war. With all the fervor, he went on saying that the Japanese people should be made conscious about their total defeat in a radical way, by removing the throne. Although he was widely supported, press and public opinion included, his efforts remained in vain. The Emperor's immunity was quasi decided. The excuse was coated with naiveté of depicting an emperor almost as a stranger to the decision-making process and completely unaware of the plans that had been plotted by the Japanese Army and Navy.[11]

In the ranks of the other Allies, there were those who were acting as "spoilers" regarding this vindicating policy towards the criminal responsibility of the Emperor. Britain, itself a monarchy, was sensitive to the question of prosecution of a head of imperial family and adopted a hostile attitude. China and Australia were staunch supporters of his inclusion on the Class A defendants' list. The Australians would frenetically try to use all available institutional venues to get their views through, starting with the UNWCC which was presided by Lord Wright from Australia. The Australians made a long list of major war crimes which comprised 61 individuals. Besides civilian, military, and navy officials, it also included industrial and bureaucratic circles and the Emperor, who was charged with crimes against peace and crimes against humanity. The said list was complemented with an extensive memorandum describing the specificities of a century-long Japanese historical and political development that detailed the Japanese militaristic nature in support of the charges against the Emperor.[12] The list provoked a turmoil among the members on the suitability of dealing with the fate of the Emperor that was a highly political question within the Commission which was the institution deprived of decision-making power. The controversial list was further transmitted to the IPS and the Allied Council for Japan, but nothing budged.

On April 3, 1946, at its fifth meeting, the members of the FEC voted the American directive that would become the official document of the Allied powers to be transferred to the Supreme Commander for the Allied Powers (SCAP). The voted SWNCC document in its paragraph 17 prohibited any action against the Emperor without further instructions. A member from New Zealand, Sir Carl Berendsen, considered that Hirohito was "unquestionably a war criminal and at the appropriate circumstances should be treated accordingly," but expressed adherence to the view that the time was not ripe for publicizing the issue when the Emperor was instrumental in occupation.[13] The adopted document by the FEC was following the same line of the SWNCC in remaining idle with respect to the Emperor as a war criminal.[14] Few days later, on April 8, 1946, at the meeting of the IPS Executive Committee, Alan Mansfield, the associate prosecutor from Australia, initiated a vote for the inclusion of the Emperor to the indictment. His initiative did not gain the support of Keenan and other counsels who considered themselves incompetent to discuss the matter, which was to be decided at "the higher political levels,"[15] thus following the reasoning of the SWNCC and FEC. The wandering list reached into the hands of the Supreme Commander who transmitted it to JCS that reiterated the inconvenience of the policy change in the absence of new evidence, staying standardly vague on the topic.[16]

The fact that the Emperor was not the part of the final version of the indictment in 1946 did not imply that the US completely abandoned the possibility of him being added at later stages. Assistant Secretary of War Robert A. Lovett suggested that policy alterations would call for the recommendations of the Supreme Commander and analysis of the available evidence to be submitted to SWNCC and JCS.[17] On January 24, 1946, MacArthur warned that the trial of the Emperor would require colossal changes in the occupation plans at military and civilian levels and a priori meticulous preparation. The Emperor was the unifying agent for Japanese people and his removal would cause a tremendous popular upheaval calling for stationing more troops indefinitely, as well as additional import of civilian personnel as the Japanese officials might refuse to cooperate with the SCAP. In this scenario, the occupation would not only be costly, but a failure to introduce democracy in Japan could give way to revanchism and represent a fertile ground for Communist ideas to spread among the disillusioned masses.[18] This, however, was contrary to the account in MacArthur's memoir that he was instrumental in removing the Emperor from the list.[19]

At the prosecutorial level, Keenan was not preoccupied with the responsibility of the throne but was minding about the fabrication of the story that would make the Emperor appear like a mere tool in the hands of the militarists. He gave a task to his staff to find a witness whose testimony would reveal that he was coerced to accept the decisions pre-made at the Cabinet level for traditional, practical, and constitutional reasons.[20] Under these pretexts, on June 18, 1946, Keenan announced that the Emperor would not be tried.[21] It is noteworthy that in this case, the insistence on the passivity of the Emperor was, in fact, not exculpatory according to the conspiracy doctrine according to which remaining on the official position was enough for establishing guilt. This narrative was highly contradictory.

The unilateral character of the Potsdam Declaration, which embedded the unconditional surrender, made the Allied powers unbound regarding the preservation of the Emperor. What saved the Emperor was the conjuncture, with him becoming an asset that would render occupation smoother, as Joseph Grew correctly observed in 1944. The final indictment of the war criminals, presented on April 29, 1946, was a part of the *demilitarization* goal of the occupation, whereas the preservation of the throne had added value for the *democratization* goal. These two objectives were coherent with the overarching goal of creating a new international order, preserved by law, in which aggressive war was prohibited. Yet, this overarching goal proved shortsighted as the challenges brought by the Cold War would heavily test and invalidate these lofty premises.

On January 24, 1946, MacArthur warned that the Emperor was the instrument for effective governing of Japanese people, that his removal threatened popular upheaval which would call for not only more troops to keep the order but also setting civil service members as they might lose the support of Japanese officials. This, he contended, would be not only costly, but it might halt the democratic reforms and give way to Communist ideas, which desperate masses would be receptive of. On June 18, 1946, Chief Prosecutor Keenan announced that the Emperor would not be tried and instructed his staff to fabricate a story and find evidence indicating his passive role in the decision-making to which he was coerced by the pre-made Cabinet decisions. However, this was not consistent with the conspiracy charge which disposed that as long as the defendant did not withdraw from the position of power covering the 17-year period, he was considered guilty. The non-prosecution of the Emperor relieved the Japanese, but at the same time "it sent out ambiguous messages to the Japanese understanding of war responsibility, indicating paradoxically that it rested with both everybody and nobody."[22]

The IPS was pressured to select 30 defendants from 50 Class A suspects faced with lack of evidence in case of which they used all sorts of documents to establish some sort of evidence. US intelligence reports, studies on Japanese history, militarism, politics, secret and industrial societies, diaries, hearsay evidence would be all admissible. Slow and inefficient work under Keenan prompted Comyns-Carr to organize the Executive Committee which would select the defendants by a majority vote of associate prosecutors. The war criminal suspects' files were in competition which further rendered the process painful, but the new criterion was based on how representative the individuals were of the key phases of aggression, their membership in the key agencies in the Imperial government, and the degree of their cooperation with the IPS. Some defendants were discretionary included at the special request of the Allies. For example, as it will be shown later, few defendants against whom no evidence was available were added to the list at the request of the prosecutors from China and the USSR with the promise that their teams would provide the evidence against them at a later date, which had never happened.

A great number of civilian and military leaders (listed as military officers of high and low rank, members of ultra-nationalistic organizations, members of the Imperial Rule Assistance Association, and industrial conglomerates who gave their support to the war effort) were considered to be detrimental to the process of democratization and were removed from public office by SCAP directives in January 1946.

Frying the Big Fish: The Main Defendants at the Tokyo Trial and the Process of Establishing Major War Criminals List

The individuals tried at the Tokyo Tribunal were the Japanese elite civilian and military leaders, also known as Class A war criminals, primarily charged with crime against peace. As noted in earlier chapters, 17 cabinets and 16 prime ministers represented the Japanese political elite during the Pacific War. Only 28 made it to the indictment. The process of their selection is important in that it reveals the quality of criteria that distinguished the suspects and ultimately made them defendants. Equally important, it shows pragmatism of the prosecutors in the face of technical and logistical difficulties which constantly plagued the Tribunal and hindered the quality of international criminal justice in Tokyo.

The work of the prosecutor within an international tribunal is, above all, rendered difficult by the transnational character of evidence as well as political and societal pressures. Interests of justice are not the only driver behind their choices, but they are rather inclined to include political and security imperatives at the same time. To give an example from present-day international criminal justice, at the International Criminal Court (ICC), the United Nations Security Council can interfere into the work of the prosecutor. Namely, by way of a resolution, the Security Council can suspend any investigation or prosecution, for 12 months renewable, if it deems it necessary to the conflict resolution or peace process in a specific country.[23]

In postwar Japan, the problem of evidence would be exacerbated by the lack of documentary evidence, destroyed in firebombing of Tokyo during the war and deliberate destruction of incriminating documents by the Japanese government following the surrender. Beyond Japan, the evidence of Japanese aggression and atrocities in colonized nations was dispersed throughout the vast former Japanese empire. The evidence required investigators to travel abroad in search for witnesses or documents for which they had to ask for cooperation of local authorities or local representatives of their respective governments. That exercise required, above everything, time that the prosecution simply did not have as well as good willingness of counterparts abroad which often was not the case. The drafters of the IMTFE Charter anticipated these challenges and lowered the bar regarding the quality of evidence as to meet the requirement of expediency. The Court was not bound by technical rules of evidence which meant that affidavits, political, medical, or intelligence reports, unsigned official documents, diary entries, letters, secondary evidence were all admissible if they appeared to have probative value.[24]

Keenan and his staff, as earlier noted the first to reach Tokyo in December 1945, had to get their hands on selecting defendants from four main lists that had been prepared by the War Crimes Office, created in 1944 within the Office of the Judge Advocate General. The American team was not unified, it was divided into two groups: the first group comprised excellent lawyers and interrogators from the Department of Justice that was cohesive and the second group comprised sound names who found their way to the IPS as Keenan's acquaintances.[25] John Darsey, excellent lawyer and main rival to Keenan, in tandem with John Fihelly, lawyer and interrogator, both distinguished members on the American team, instructed the team to filter those who bore the most important responsibility for the Japanese aggression. Without direct evidence at hand, they immersed themselves into piling up and studying US intelligence and reports, special studies about Japanese history, militarism, political organizations, suspects' activities, and secret militarist and industrialist societies. Another major logistical issue in Tokyo that further complicated the preparation of the indictment was the Japanese language and translation service. Even some of the captured Japanese government documents had to be translated which required time and personnel. The number of translators the US provided was not sufficient to meet the amount of task at hand, so the Japanese government provided additional translators whose integrity was highly questioned.

The first approach to selecting the defendants was to form key groups—civilian, military, diplomatic, economic, and ideological—which include a wide range of official duties which were expected to be involved in planning, preparing, initiating, or waging the war of aggression or general conspiracy to do the aforementioned. Keenan insisted that the choice of defendants should reflect the legal narrative of the indictment—encompassing the responsibility of all defendants to set in motion worldwide acts of aggression leading to the creation of the Great East Asian Co-Prosperity Sphere.[26] In the beginning of January 1946, the only clear-cut case, amidst dossiers of hundreds of potential war criminals who were being studied, was against the 39 individuals from the Tōjō Cabinet, also considered for trial en bloc.[27] These were also among the first 39 individuals to be arrested on September 11, 1945. As had already been predicted during the war, many of them attempted suicide, but not all ended up successfully, including Tōjō. The goal was to narrow down the list to utmost 30 names to appear as defendants before the Tribunal, a task hardly to be completed by the prosecution section overwhelmed with a secondary information and trapped into making a long-winded account on the origins of Japanese militarism. The main candidates scrutinized for defendants were individuals who held key ministerial positions (prime minister, foreign minister, home minister, army and navy ministers). Additionally, the American team was also considering members of ultra-nationalist and secret societies who supposedly instigated aggressive war policies behind the curtain.

The arrival of the Commonwealth prosecutors in February would galvanize the prosecution into effective action regarding the list of defendants. Under the initiative of Comyns-Carr, investigators and prosecutors were instructed to draw up several lists of the Japanese who could be charged under the crime against peace, war crimes, and crimes against humanity. From these lists, a maximum of 20 defendants who were chosen by different teams would be singled out for discussion and then investigated on a personal basis.[28] Comyns-Carr knew that a minimal number of defendants would speed things up as longer lists would require gathering new evidence and further complicate the already delayed procedure that risked to make the IMTFE a protracted trial. Other associate prosecutors wanted to avoid the Sisyphean labor of trying to establish guilt of every individual held into custody. They had in mind the overarching goal of the Trial that was charging a few Japanese leaders with crime of aggression. Other concerns of the American team included the non-punishment of arrested Class A war criminal suspects and their fate once they were dropped from the list.[29] For British prosecutors these were trivialities. On February 25, Comyns-Carr proposed the selection based on official capacity or position held by the suspect at the time of the pre-determined important phases of the Japanese aggression (Manchurian Incident, Pearl Harbor Attack, etc.).[30] Simply put, the criterion that made the prosecutorial machine finally grind was based on the official position at the time of the crucial phases of the Japanese aggression.

And yet, the selection remained a difficult task and required adding up further criteria. The dossiers of suspects were in competition; their suitability for trial was being measured in degrees. Those who represented more than one important phase had priority over others. For instance, Kōichi Kido served as minister of education and welfare in 1937–1938, home minister in 1939, and lord keeper of the privy seal in 1941–1945 which positioned him to the place of the closest confidant to the Emperor to whom he recommended Tōjō for the prime minister. Tōjō was also the head of several important positions, starting as a member of moderate Control Faction in the Army, dispatch to Kwantung Army Headquarters in 1936, vice-minister in the war ministry, army minister in 1940–1941, and ultimately both army and prime minister during the Pacific War.[31]

The existence of multiple selection criteria did not prevent erroneous assessments of guilt. Another decisive criterion was the suspects' membership to the key agencies that were in a position to conspire and plan the aggressive war. This criterion matched the crime of conspiracy, in depth developed in Chap. 3, which required only a participation in the overall plan or policy, without a suspect having to act or do something. Just the fact that he did not withdraw from the organization amounts to tacit support for the criminal action. The Imperial Conference, Liaison Conference, Cabinet, Supreme Command, and Privy Council were listed as key institutions that fabricated the aggressive war plans and actions. Kōki Hirota who assumed positions of foreign minister in 1933–1936 and 1937–1938 and prime minister in 1936–1937 was included for his participation at the ministerial conference in 1936 where the expansionist policies were concocted.[32] The prosecution lacked the direct evidence for establishing his responsibility for instigation of the war, participation in conspiracy, and support for the army's aggressive and expansionist policy. After all, they included him because he did not resign, thus tacitly condoning the army's policies. In his letter to Sir Hartley Shawcross, British chief counsel at the IMT at Nuremberg, Comyns-Carr lamented that in Japan, due to diffuse command lines[33] and erratic relations between politicians and soldiers, it was considerably more difficult to pick the right defendants.[34]

The final cuts and selections by the Executive Committee that gave the list with 29 defendants were done from mid-March to the beginning of April. The minutes of the Committee show that another decisive tool for dilemmas that it had due to few suspects whose cases were in competition was the reference to Marquis Kidō's diary entries, Imperial Conferences, and Fumimaro Konoe's Memoirs.[35] Kidō, who was the Emperor's closest advisor, kept a diary that covered the temporal jurisdiction (*rationae temporis)* of the Court.[36] The diary had almost played role of manual that was uncritically exploited by the prosecution which was constantly checking the entries about the relevant individuals.[37]

In the immediate postwar Japan, factionalism reigned among and within Japanese military and civilian bureaucracies where officials were pointing at each other for the war responsibility.[38] Some individuals were constant providers of insider information that was precious to the IPS which did not heed to critical assessment or verification; they needed that kind of information and fast. For instance, Major General Ryukichi Tanaka, a former chief of the Department of Military Affairs, served as another substantial source of evidence, for his exhaustive insider information about army level decision-making, involvement in China, and opium-trafficking.[39] Also known under the nickname "the Monster," Tanaka appeared vengeful and resentful against the defendants. Nevertheless, his word was taken for granted without any reserves taken.[40] Hidenari Terasaki, who was the Emperor's interpreter and liaison with the prosecution and general headquarters, was another informer who provided the prosecution with a list of 44 individuals responsible for war with extensive notes about each.[41]

On April 13, the Russian Associate Prosecutor Golunsky arrived in Tokyo, being presented for the first time with the list of defendants, crafted in his absence, without raising any objections, to other prosecutors' relief.

Contrary to monolingual Soviet Judge Zaryanov, Golunsky was proficient in English, both diplomat and jurist, sent as a protégé of Soviet Foreign Minister Vishinsky.[42] Golunsky did not care about who had been included into the indictment, except for individuals the Soviet government wanted to see on the list. Therefore, he requested the inclusion of four or five additional suspects to the final list. On April 17, at the meeting of associate prosecutors, after the consideration of Soviet proposals, it was agreed that Yoshijiro Umezu, Kwantung army commander near Soviet border, and Mamoru Shigemitsu, former Japanese diplomat to USSR, would be added to the list, thus making it complete with 28 defendants. Initially, they were left out from the list, as they appeared less guilty when the available evidence against them was compared with other dossiers. Finally, Umezu and Mamoru were blindly added for their pronounced anti-Soviet stance, under the Soviet assurances that they allegedly possessed strong probative evidence against the two. The discretionary inclusion was seen as an acceptable recompense for non-consultation of Soviets in the pre-trial preparation process.[43] Doihara Kenji was included at the insistence of the Chinese prosecution claiming that the evidence, at that time inexistent, would be adduced from China. The list was complete, but the evidence still had to be collected which made French, Chinese, and Dutch prosecutors leave on April 21, 1946, for Indochina, China, and the Dutch East Indies[44] a few days prior to the presentation of the indictment to the Tribunal.

The importance of piling up multiple criteria proved necessary for building an overpowering case against each individual that would reduce any possibility for the acquittal, of primary importance for demonstrating crime against peace committed by Japanese militarists. In addition, the promotion of national interests, by states' representatives in the prosecution section, made the selection criteria for alleged crimes mainly rely on deduction that, in many cases, appeared ill-founded and unconvincing. A pressure to place certain individuals into the indictment justified the use of scarce or sometimes inexistent evidence and other methods of establishing guilt.[45]

Notes

1. MacArthur to JCS, "Enclosure B," January 24, 1946, JCS 1512/10 in Makoto Iokibe, ed., Occupation of Japan: US Planning Documents, 1942–1945 (Tokyo: Maruzen, 1987), 2-A-120.
2. Herbert P. Bix, "Hirohito: String Puller, Not Puppet," *New York Times*, September 29, 2014.

3. War Department to SWNCC, "Apprehension and Punishment of War Criminals in the Far East," Memorandum, September 29, 1945, in Makoto Iokibe, ed., *The Occupation of Japan, Part 2: US and Allied Policy, 1945–1952*, microfiche, 2A105.
4. Parliamentary question, Sir Geoffrey Shakespeare, February 2, 1946, F.O. 371/41788. The question was addressed to Mr. Eden, the Secretary of State for Foreign Affairs, on whether the formal warning would be issued, along with the US, against Japan that the procedure agreed at Moscow for Germany will be imposed upon Japan as well. In his reply on February 8, he stated that the punishment of war criminals will follow German scenario.
5. IDACFE, "Political Problems: Institution of the Emperor," CAC-93a, May 9, 1944, in Makoto Iokibe, ed., *Occupation of Japan: U.S. Planning Documents, 1942–1945* (Tokyo: Maruzen, 1987), microfiche, 2-A-7, NDL.
6. Ibid.
7. Foreign Office Minutes, Sir Ashley Clarke, April 23,1944, F.O. 371/41; Bertram D. Hulen, "Tokyo War Lords Guilty, says Grew", *The New York Times*, February 1, 1944, FO371/41.
8. Stimson Diaries, Entry from July 24, 1945 in Henry Lewis Stimson. *Diaries*. Vol. 52 (New Heaven: Yale University Library, 1973).
9. Herbert Bix, *Hirohito and the Making of Modern Japan* (New York: Harper Collins, 2000), 543–589.
10. Ibid.
11. Sellars, *"Crimes against Peace" and International Law*, 191.
12. Joint Chiefs of Staff to MacArthur, "Australian First List of Major War Criminals," JCS 1512/10, January 22, 1946, in Makoto Iokibe, ed., *The Occupation of Japan, Part 2: US and Allied Policy, 1945–1952* (Maruzen: Tokyo, 1989), 2-A-120.
13. Berendsen to Fraser, January 18, 1946, Doc. 651 in Robin Kay, ed., *Documents on New Zealand External Relations Volume II: The Surrender and Occupation of Japan*, 1508–1509.
14. Johnson to Byrnes, "Letter of transmittal", SWNCC 57/12, April 4, 1946, in Makoto Iokibe, ed., *The Occupation of Japan, Part 2: US and Allied Policy, 1945–1952*, 2-A-118.
15. Quilliam to Shahanan, Tokyo, April 9, 1946, Doc. 667 in Robin Kay, ed., *Documents on New Zealand External Relations Volume II: The Surrender and Occupation of Japan*, 1554–1556.
16. "Australian List of Major Japanese War Criminals (JCS 1512/10)", Memorandum by the State Member, SWNCC 57/13, August 16, 1946, in Makoto Iokibe, ed., *The Occupation of Japan, Part 2: US and Allied Policy, 1945–1952*, 2-A-120; 2-A-121.
17. Lovett to SWNCC/SFE, "Apprehension and Punishment of War Criminals (Japan)," Memorandum, October 10, 1945 in Makoto Iokibe, ed., *The Occupation of Japan, Part 2: US and Allied Policy, 1945–1952*, 2-A-110.

18. MacArthur to Joint Chief of Staff, "Enclosure B," January 24, 1946, JCS 1512/10 in Makoto Iokibe, ed., *Occupation of Japan: U.S. Planning Documents, 1942–1945*, 2-A-120.
19. Totani, *The Tokyo War Crimes Trials: The Pursuit of Justice in the Wake of World War II*, 57.
20. "Method of presentation", April 26, 1946, IPS Documents in NARA II, RG331. Washington to Foreign Office, Telegram, June 18, 1946, F.O. 262/2047.
21. Washington to Foreign Office, Telegram, June 18, 1946, F.O. 262/2047.
22. Gerry Simpson, 137.
23. Article 16, "The Rome Statute," July 28, 2002.
24. Article 13, "The IMTFE Charter," April 24, 1946.
25. James Burnham Sedgwick, "The trial within: Negotiating Justice at the International Military Tribunal for the Far East, 1946–1948" (The University of British Columbia, 2012), 63.
26. Joseph Keenan to Tom Clark, January 2, 1946, IPS Documents in NARA II, RG331.
27. Foreign Office to Tokyo, Telegram, January 5, 1946, F.O. 262/2041.
28. Comyns-Carr to Keenan, Memorandum, February 11, 1946, International Prosecution Section Documents in NARA II, RG331.
29. Higgins to Keenan, "General Policy," Confidential Memorandum, February 27, 1946, IPS Documents in NARA II, RG 331.
30. Yuma Totani, *The Tokyo War Crimes Trials: The Pursuit of Justice in the Wake of World War II* (Cambridge: Harvard University Press), 66.
31. Awaya Kentarō, *Tōkyō Saiban e no Michi*, Vol.1 (Tokyo: Kodansha, 2006), 193–194.
32. Awaya Kentarō, "Selecting Defendants for the Trial," 56 in Neil Boister and Robert Cryer, eds., *The Tokyo Military Tribunal: A Reappraisal* (Leiden: Brill, 2011).
33. John W. Dower, *Embracing Defeat: Japan in the Wake of World War II* (New York: W.W. Norton and Co., 1999), 481.
34. Sellars, *"Crimes against Peace" and International Law*, 190–191.
35. Awaya Kentarō, "Selecting Defendants for the Trial," 52 in Boister and Cryer, *The Tokyo Military Tribunal: A Reappraisal.*
36. Ibid.
37. Solis Horwitz, "The Tokyo Trial," *International Conciliation 465* (November 1950), 494.
38. Dower, *Embracing Defeat*, 480–481.
39. Ibid., 482–483.
40. Awaya Kentarō, "Selecting Defendants for the Trial," 52 in Boister and Cryer, *The Tokyo Military Tribunal: A Reappraisal*, 52.
41. Dower, *Embracing Defeat*, 482.

42. Watt, "Historical Introduction," xvii.
43. Quilliam to McIntosh, Tokyo, April 24, 1946, Doc. 669 in Robin Kay, ed., *Documents on New Zealand External Relations Volume II: The Surrender and Occupation of Japan*, 1559–1564.
44. Ibid., 1562.
45. Lyal S. Sunga, *The Emerging System of International Criminal Law: Developments in Codification and Implementation* (The Hague: Kluwer Law International, 1997), 7.

PART II

CHAPTER 7

Towards the Post-institutional Phase of the Tokyo Tribunal: Narratives, Sentences, Detentions

The majority judgement did mark the institutional death of the Tokyo Tribunal, but the process of the administration of justice entered a new phase—that of the execution of sentences, an equally relevant and valuable piece of the puzzle for assessing the justice meted out by the Tribunal. After the judgement was rendered, the window of opportunity opened for the review of the sentences which provoked the controversy regarding the international character of the Tribunal. Already in 1948, the US foreign policy towards Japan started to shift, but it failed to be reflected in the looser policies regarding war criminals. Ultimately, the negotiations leading to the San Francisco Peace Treaty between the Allied powers and Japan failed to reflect its changing status.

The Institutional Apogee of the Tribunal: The Dissipating Legal, Historical, and Political Narratives

The IMTFE judgement or the majority judgement represents the dominant legal, political, philosophical, and historical narrative produced by the judicial body that was mainly driven by Anglo-American forces. This cohort of politicians, lawyers, and judges was uncompromisingly committed to pragmatism that corresponded to the larger strategic objectives, formulated through law, in the context of postwar expediency. Yet, the

A. Babovic, *The Tokyo Trial, Justice, and the Postwar International Order*, New Directions in East Asian History,
https://doi.org/10.1007/978-981-13-3477-1_7

dissenting and separate opinions lodged by the five justices within the Tribunal revealed the plurality of reasoning when it came to legal, political, and historical narratives which would not be possible in reference to the majority judgement exclusively. This also opened the door to more ambiguous and fragmented views of Japanese aggression and war responsibility, although these views did not share the spotlight with the "star" majority judgement. This chapter starts by observing the fragmentation of views within the judgement, also related to the harsh sentencing of the accused, because it is illustrative of constant disagreements between the Allies and their representatives, as well as the start of dissipating narratives around the meaning of the Tribunal. This would be the starting point of constant reframing of both legality and legitimacy of the Tokyo Tribunal in the face of Cold War power reconfiguration.

Contrary to the initial post-surrender political context of urgency and high expectations put on the Tribunal to expediently deliver its judgement, the members of the Tribunal and defendants "enjoyed the luxury of time."[1] After two years, on February 10, 1948, the IMTFE brought its hearings to a close. From November 9 to 12, 1948, the Tribunal read the majority judgement and sentences. The IMTFE President Justice William Webb said that the judgement was not reached unanimously by the 11-member tribunal but that Justice Pal dissented from the majority opinion, while Justices Röling and Bernard dissented in part, and Justice Jaranilla and Webb lodged their separate opinions, although they concurred with the majority judgement.[2] The dissenting and separate opinions were not read in the courtroom, but the President promised that they would be incorporated in the official trial record. Dissenting and separate opinions are important for the Tokyo Tribunal in particular for a few reasons. First, they show a certain degree of transparency and openness in judicial decision-making and deliberations.[3] Second, in the context of the Tokyo Tribunal, these indicate the presence of a degree of judicial independence from the views of the majority. In their work, the members of tribunals should keep in mind that their verdicts or jurisprudence is likely to exert considerable influence upon the future cases rendered by similar jurisdictions which in practice tend to base their decisions on these precedents. Although the IMTFE was established on an ad hoc basis and had a precise set of goals to fulfill, these judges felt compelled to also question the law or determine its legality before its being applied which corresponds to legislative and judicial functions fulfilled by the courts. Furthermore, these dissenting opinions are a "safety valve"[4] that offer a psychological relief for the losing party and assurances that the Tribunal had given attention to all the arguments presented in the case.

More importantly, they are instrumental for avoiding the "misleading of the public" for thinking that the decision had been reached unanimously or by the majority of judges. In that sense, the majority judgement along with dissenting and separate opinions represented an outlet for all the parties to sift and sort out the parts that would fit their version of events—hence leading to dissipating narratives.

Justice Pal's dissenting opinion is instrumental in offering a diametrically opposed view of the Pacific War and the Japanese leaders' criminal responsibility framed through the lenses of anti-imperialism. In essence, although the majority judgement had the final authority, together with separate and dissenting opinions it represents a fragmented view of the case at hand. In postwar Japan, and not surprisingly, Pal's dissenting opinion gained such authority that it is referred to as *Pāru hanketsushō* or Pal's judgement,[5] instead of dissenting opinion. His dissenting opinion has been extrapolated and distorted by revisionists to refute the responsibility of not only Japanese leaders for waging the aggressive war but the Japanese nation more generally. Justice Pal was a respected judge at the Calcutta High Court, interestingly without delivering a single dissenting opinion in his practice and well-versed in Hindi and Anglo-Saxon law. Prior to his appointment at the Tokyo Tribunal, Pal did not have any background in international law; his international judicial career started in 1952 with his appointment to the UN International Law Commission.[6] Since he joined the Tribunal, he did not hide his inclination towards dissent. His dissent was particularly indignant to Indian Prime Minister Jawaharlal Nehru who considered Justice Pal's opinion divergent with one of the Indian governments and informed the other Allies about his disapproval.[7]

His dissenting opinion is relevant on a few points. First, he criticized the crime of aggression and crimes against humanity as instances of *ex post facto law*.[8] Rather than preventing wars and securing peace, he wrote, these rules would encourage aggression. It can be argued that his point has been valid as law only prohibited unilateral use of force as instrument of national policy, but all other variants and exceptions to that were permitted. The wars that broke out in the post-World War II period tested this law and failed. For instance, the concept of self-defense has been constantly stretched to justify instances of use of force such as wars in Afghanistan and Iraq that were justified as acts of pre-emptive self-defense. Second, his overly expansive view of self-defense comes as a contradiction to the previous point as he contended that states had arbitrary right to decide on the circumstances under which they could exercise their right to self-defense as long as such decision was animated by a genuine belief or bona fide.[9] In his view, this entailed that valid justifications for triggering right to self-defense, even proactively, could be "inhospitable international environment,"[10] economic, political, and ideological threats.[11] Under these premises, the Japanese invasion of Manchuria was not an instance of aggression but self-defense due to the spread of communism, boycott of Japanese goods, harsh sanctions the US and Britain imposed upon Japan, their support for Chiang Kai-shek, which fell within ideological and economic motives,[12] although he did not imply that Japan was under a threat of imminent attack. As noted in Chaps. 2 and 3, this was the view of many states that lodged their reservations to the Kellogg-Briand Pact. Third, he partially refuted the Yamashita standard or command responsibility doctrine of military commanders on the grounds of negligence or omission for the actions of troops on the field; he rather considered that the liability stem from acts that the superior "could reasonably have prevented."[13] The leaders, including Japanese leaders, could not have been responsible for acts committed by lower military ranks and their superiors upon which the stern justice had already been meted out by the Allies' under Class BC crimes. Hence, he refuted counts of war crimes on which the defendants were accused. Furthermore, Pal refuted the concept of conspiracy as a non-existent category of crime in international law. Japan's decision to attack the US, according to the evidence adduced, was part of an overall conspiracy, but according to Pal political decision was a reaction to the failed diplomatic negotiations and the receipt of the Hull note which as he says "cornered Japan"[14] Pal's convoluted dissent was profoundly anti-Western and anti-imperialist in his proposals as he assigned the guilt for "Japan's aggression" in Manchuria to the colonial practices of the Western Powers, which it was trying to mimic, and whose policies propelled Japan to defend itself, which was consistent with international practices at the time, alluding to the long-time practiced Western imperialism. In this respect, Pal's view somewhat deviates from the legalistic and flows into political discussion that goes along the reasoning of classical realism.[15] Pal thought the Allies' motives for creating the new charge were highly suspect, especially considering their own history of violence towards the non-Western nations. In essence, nations disapproving of status quo, on whatever basis, are prohibited from settling these differences by force.[16] Ironically, colonialism per se was not illegal, but efforts of colonized nations to gain independence by force were illegal and potentially a criminal act. Crudely put, the legal reasoning of the majority was condoning unrestrained domination for the sake of peace.[17] Pal's 1235-pages-long dissent, against the 1444-pages-long majority opinion, meshed his anti-colonial bias with some sound legal conclusions which reflected legal philosophy of positivism in opposition to natural law legalism that dominated the majority of IMTFE members. His conclusions were not that Japanese leaders were morally or politically innocent but innocent from the point of view of international law in force at the time of its establishment. Equally, Japanese atrocities, "devilish and fiendish,"[18] were not refuted, but the evidence adduced was judged as non-probative. It can be concluded that Pal's dissent, primarily directed against the European powers which pioneered colonialism, somewhat toned down Japan's expansion, although it did imply that it shared the moral responsibility for colonialism, but not a criminal one.[19]

On the other hand, French Justice Bernard and Dutch Justice Röling who lodged their partial dissent to the majority judgement did not side with Pal on colonial remarks as they "accepted the assumptions of European superiority engendered by colonial rule."[20] The French Justice was a colonial magistrate, and his appointment was motivated by the cautiousness of the French government to control the information regarding French atrocities in Indochina from appearing before the Tribunal— it was important to "rectify their image to appear more worthy of the era that came to its end."[21] While Justice Bernard was more sensitive to procedural and probative rules,[22] in his dissent he agreed to the legality of crime against peace, but on entirely different legal grounds than the majority judgement group.[23] Justice Röling dissented from the finding that interwar pacts and resolutions, specifically the Pact of Paris, outlawed war, in the sense that waging illegal war was criminal. In his role of judge, he first established that the provisions of the Charter were ex post facto *law*, and thus he felt compelled to disagree with the majority of judges who, fervent to confirm the Nuremberg law, came to different conclusions.[24] Nevertheless, he considered that wars ought to be prevented in the future by incrementally codifying the precedents.[25] Another important point, later found in the separate opinion of Justice Webb, was the critique of legal immunity of the Emperor whom he considered to be the main instigator of the Pacific War, while the defendants at the dock were his subordinates.[26] The three dissenters remained unswayed in their formalism, personal convictions, and ideologies.[27] They had to cohabit with the majority group which was more pragmatic in that its judges completely acquiesced to the natural law-infused indictment prepared by the prosecution.[28]

The majority judgement cohort of justices came to Tokyo imbued with a deep sense of pragmatism, postwar urgency, and conviction that the IMTFE had an important role to play not only in exercising retribution against the Japanese but also for the future, by confirming the new law. It could have been expected that in the last institutional stages of the IMTFE, the floor would be given to the impartial justices, yet this was another group of legalists with a sense for pragmatism. British Justice Patrick dogmatically assented to the idea that the Tribunal had a momentous significance for declaring criminality of aggressive war.[29] The bench's "triumvirate"[30] represented by British Justice Patrick, US Justice Cramer, and New Zealand Justice Northcroft was the pragmatists who tried to reconcile the discrepancies between legal philosophies and commitments to justice as they considered the IMTFE as a valuable project which merited transcending the differences for the sake of punishment in the context of postwar exigency. The Commonwealth faction railed against the justices who questioned or disagreed with the legality of the Charter; their obligation as judges was to follow the law.[31] Justice Northcroft was anxious that the divisions of the bench would be a setback for the outlawry of war and talked about potential dissent from Nuremberg in terms of disaster.[32]

IMTFE President Justice Webb was notorious for his arrogance, inflexibility, and authoritarian behavior towards other justices as he believed that he ought to be the one to write the majority judgement, while others were supposed to agree or disagree with him. Even in his interactions with the Supreme Commander, Webb was very protective of the judicial body from outside incursions; he insisted that the judges should be left to act independently in their interpretation of the Charter or any other activity pertaining to their duties.[33] Besides bad temper, Justice Webb's previous post of the President of Australian War Crimes Commission in 1943 was problematic in respect to integrity and impartiality. The Commission, set up to investigate Japanese war crimes in New Guinea, Burma, and Thailand, produced numerous reports he had authored which certainly gave him solid pre-conceptions on Japanese leaders' war guilt. Philippine Justice Jaranilla was survivor of Bataan Death March and prisoner of war in Japanese hands. In his separate opinion, he lamented the leniency of the sentences which were disproportional to the gravity of the crimes committed, thus marring the deterrent effect of the Tribunal.[34] Soviet Justice Zaryanov was a member of the USSR Supreme Court and had a poor conduct of English despite which he managed to become quite engaged in the work of the Bench, contrary to the dominant views in the literature,[35] by being committed to the IMTFE objectives and exercising a great degree of flexibility. Given the Cold War tensions, ironically, "he proved instrumental in cementing the majority in Tokyo."[36] The fact that the majority judgement sentenced seven IMTFE defendants to death by hanging has been often invoked as one of the manifestations of victors' justice at Tokyo. And yet, not all of the judges were in favor of the gallows out of fear it might be seen as vindictive. American Justice Cramer unwaveringly defended the idea that punishing criminals by death following the law was "a matter of justice, plain and simple."[37]

The judicial process was primarily led by Anglo-American jurists who were prepared to exercise a strong sense of pragmatism and commitment to the IMTFE project which was based on natural law legal tradition. These individuals performed the role of "jurist-politicians" as they were involved in matters not only pertaining to international law but also international politics. The case of British who were ready to disregard the impartiality of the judicial body, in order to avoid ridicule for failing to prosecute Japanese militarism or meet the prestige of Nuremberg, is exemplary on the point. The knowledge that other judges were questioning the law of the Charter was unsettling to Alvary Gascoigne, British political representative to Tokyo, who was ready to go as far as to appeal to MacArthur and Webb for help. In the end, Justice Patrick discouraged him to the effect that it would be inappropriate to expose differences between the judges publicly, and took the initiative upon himself to persuade his fellow judges to converge to the vital goal of confirming the Nuremberg conclusions.[38] Although they exercised a considerable degree of independence, justices went along the lines of ideas forged by the lawyer-statesmen.

No Mercy for Class A War Criminals: Sentenced Without Appeal and Review

The last moment before the post-institutional phase of the Tribunal started was when the harsh sentences imposed upon the accused could have been reviewed. This was an opportunity to rectify the eventual errors of justice and respond to already changing geopolitical configuration of East Asia in which Japan started to emerge as a friend.

The majority judgement sentenced seven defendants (Kenji Doihara, Kōki Hirota, Seishirō Itagaki, Heitarō Kimura, Matsui Iwane, Akira Mutō, Hideki Tōjō) to *death sentence* by hanging. Twelve defendants received *life sentences*, Shigenori Tōgō received *20-year sentence*, and Mamoru Shigemitsu received *7-year sentence*. In their separate opinions, four justices expressed their opinion that the sentences should have been more lenient. Justice Pal found all defendants non-guilty, Justice Röling uphold the death sentences of all defendants, except for Hirota—he was opposed to the aggression and personally negotiated the cessation of atrocities with War Minister Hajime Sugiyama. Instead of him, he recommended Shimada who had violated laws of war, while Hata, Hirota, Kidō, Shigemitsu, and Tōgō should all have been acquitted as their guilt had not been proven.[39] President Webb considered death sentences to be a harsh punishment in view that "the main leader" in crime, the Emperor, had been granted immunity and suggested commutation of death sentences to life imprisonment. Webb observed that the accused were old and no longer impressive and that "it may prove revolting to hang or shoot such old men."[40] Justice Bernard found them all not guilty due to the defective procedure, not because he believed that crime of aggression was not criminally punishable.[41]

The Tribunal did not have an appellate body, but the IMTFE Charter, unilaterally proclaimed by MacArthur, did contain a provision, Article 17, according to which the Supreme Commander for the Allied Powers had the authority to "at any time reduce or otherwise alter the sentence except to increase its severity." Later, however, the FEC adopted a policy directive, drafted by the British and Australian delegations, which was meant to amend Article 17, more precisely to limit the Supreme Commander's discretion for review by imposing an obligation of prior consultation with members of the Allied Council for Japan (ACJ)[42] or representatives of other powers in Japan prior to adopting any such decision.[43] The idea behind was to cherish the international nature of the institution and keep MacArthur's authority preponderance in check. The final version of the amended IMTFE Charter of April 26, 1946, ignored the FEC amendment leaving Article 17 intact. Aside from the above-mentioned justices' opinion that certain sentences should be reduced, the IMTFE defense counsels appealed to MacArthur to exercise his authority of judicial review urging him to prevent "atrocities against the law and justice."[44] Beverley Coleman, defense counsel who resigned in mid-1946, personally pleaded that MacArthur should consider the possibility of consulting the United Nations International Court of Justice which could provide an advisory opinion on the criminality of aggressive war prior to committing any injustices regarding the sentencing of the defendants.[45] Three days after the petitions were filed, the ACJ hurriedly set the meeting between MacArthur and diplomats from the countries represented at the IMTFE. Naturally, diplomats' positions almost entirely reflected legal positions of their justices. France proposed clemency, India proposed commutation of death sentences, while Australia left it to the discretion of the Supreme Commander.[46] In his pompous speech MacArthur decided to keep his deferential stance towards the judicial work and decided to uphold all the sentences. Although he did not believe in criminal punishments for war of aggression, he had probably decided to maintain the sentences given the postwar idealism and ubiquitous sentiment that authors of aggressive wars should be sacrificed for a better world.[47]

Before the seven defendants were sent to gallows, they appealed before the US Supreme Court for a writ of habeas corpus. The idea was instigated by the defense counsel which claimed the IMTFE to be an "enterprise" of the US executive and military authorities.[48] By defying the international character to the IMTFE and bypassing the SCAP, the action on behalf of the IMTFE defendants provoked responses from the nations represented at the Tribunal which came to justify and save its "international" appeal. When the case got before the Supreme Court, its justices were evenly divided between a group of four who believed that the Japanese war criminals should get their case heard, and another group of four who believed that, based on the Constitution, the Court had no jurisdiction to decide on the matter. Justice Robert Jackson, former chief prosecutor at Nuremberg and, at that time, judge at the Supreme Court, decided to cast a tie-breaking vote in favor of the Court deciding whether it could hear the case.[49] On December 20, 1948, the Supreme Court decision refuted its jurisdiction to "review, affirm, set aside, or annul" the IMTFE judgement and sentences imposed upon Japanese citizens.[50] Justice William O. Douglas who was in the group that refused the petitioners to file for a writ observed that this new type of military tribunals was out of judicial scrutiny, leaving them with an absolute power, while the prisoners did not benefit from the right of appeal for which they had to appeal to the mercy of the executive.[51] Justice Douglas observed that the Tokyo Tribunal is not a judicial but a political question, describing it as instrument of military power of the executive.[52] The Supreme Court episode touched upon the extant delicacy and ambiguity surrounding the question whether the Tokyo Tribunal was an American tribunal or international tribunal given its unilateral proclamation by MacArthur. The defense counsel saw that as a loophole to be exploited in order to try to change the sort of the IMTFE defendants. However, the IMTFE was rooted in international instruments such as the Cairo Declaration of December 1, 1943, the Potsdam Declaration of July 26, 1945, the Instrument of Surrender of

September 2, 1945, and the Moscow Declaration of December 26, 1945.[53] The Tribunal practically gained its "internationality" with the power granted to the FEC to adopt policy resolutions, although of an arguable reach, as discussed earlier, and with the arrival of other countries' prosecutors, judges, defenses who will try to challenge the US leading role. The refusal by the Supreme Court to sit in judgement on the IMTFE case was a show of awareness that such an interference would play havoc with the Allied war criminal program in the Far East. Notwithstanding its international character, "the chain of command from the US government to SCAP was unbroken," held the Court. In this way, the Supreme Court affirmed that there was "no serious doubt [...] that the tribunal is dominated by American influence."[54] MacArthur's decision to suspend the execution of sentences waiting for the decision, after he had initially decided to uphold the sentences, further exacerbated the issue of American dominance in the IMTFE.

The participation of the Allies countries, other than the US, to the IMTFE was adding to their prestige and power which the US unilateralism sometimes tended to jeopardize but for which they were ready to unite and assert throughout all stages of the IMTFE. The Commonwealth countries, in particular New Zealand, framed the defendants' appeal to the US Supreme Court as a "threat" to all the countries represented at the IMTFE.[55] The British were more confident in dealing with this unpleasant matter. To them, the Supreme Commander was embodying the medium to carry out the decisions on behalf of the Allied powers enshrined in international instruments establishing the Tribunal. Douglas MacArthur was not an American in Japan, but the "embodiment of the Allied cooperation,"[56] concluded the British. The Russian representatives at the FEC displayed anger at MacArthur's decision to suspend the execution of sentence and wait for the Court's decision on the admissibility of the case which amounted to violation of the US commitments pursuant to the Potsdam Declaration and the IMTFE Charter.[57]

With MacArthur's order given to the US Eight Army to execute the seven Class A war criminals, the window of opportunity to rectify and balance out the majority judgement's sentences which represented the views of 7 judges out of 11 came to a closure. MacArthur reluctantly used his prerogative to make sure that the IMTFE did not suffer from further delays. From that moment, more precisely, from 1949 onward, the IMTFE entered into its post-institutional phase that would last until the very last Class A war criminal was released in 1956.

Lustration for the Class A War Criminals Suspects

On January 8, 1948, the US started the Trial of Ministries Case in West Germany which is specific for its prosecution of diplomats, bureaucratic leaders, and fifth columnists on counts of crimes against peace. And that was not the only one. The Farben Trial, involving the industrialist charged with crime of aggression, ended in July 1948 rejecting the charges and arguing that those who merely followed orders of leaders who led the nation into an aggressive war could not be guilty of such crime.[58] Not only was this a narrow interpretation of the superior orders defense, but it was also contrary to the logic of the doctrine of conspiracy, extensively used at the Tokyo Tribunal, although industrialists were not in its indictment. It is noteworthy that in the same case, the defense counsel argued that those guilty of crime against peace under international law should have been first determined as responsible for waging war under domestic law, by way of their political authority under the Constitution.[59] In the 1950s, in the trials organized by Germans the international legal categories were abandoned and the above approach was adopted.[60] It was the first time since the IMT rendered its judgement on October 1, 1946, that the US undertook the task up to prosecute individuals for crimes against peace in a series of trials which are also known as the subsequent Nuremberg Military Trials (NMTs).[61] More importantly, given the changing diplomatic and geopolitical outlook, it was the last chance to get prosecutions for "the supreme crime." The judgement rendered in the Ministries case, which almost coincided with the IMTFE judgement, was handed down on October 7, 1948, convicting five individuals for crime against peace.[62] Telford Taylor, former chief counsel at IMT Nuremberg, commended the reached consistency in the judgement observing that "the judgement is more important than those which ended nearly four years ago [...] it proves that we still mean in 1949 what we meant in 1945."[63]

After the Tokyo judgement was rendered, the question of Class A war criminal suspects who had been held in confinement for almost three years without a trial became a pressing issue, although there had been some preliminary discussions in various venues. In 1947, Keenan urged his team to prepare files on the 50 Class A war criminals still in confinement in which British prosecutors also took part, somewhat hesitantly, as they did not want to support the policies of protracted detention without a trial. In September 1947, about half of that number was released. At this time, Britain also voiced its intention not to take part in any subsequent international criminal tribunals in the Far East and anticipated that the US would take a similar position. The older FEC policy directive FEC 007/3 required that individuals suspected of crime against peace be prosecuted by an international tribunal which pointed at the need of amending the said policy decision by an international agreement. The revision entailed putting the amendment before the FEC which would give space to the USSR delegate to oppose it and uncompromisingly call for international trials which both British and Americans thought was to be avoided at all cost.[64] An alternative explored was to place some of the Class A war criminals for trials under the Class BC war criminals which was one of the programs under the jurisdiction of Alva Carpenter, chief of the GHQ Legal Section.[65]

In March 1948, Chief Prosecutor Keenan appeared before the FEC recommending the release of Class A war criminal suspects where he touched upon the purpose of the IMTFE, political and financial arguments against subsequent trials, and the general unwillingness of the IMTFE members to sit for another round of international trials. The war crimes trials program was funded by the Department of Army that was faced with considerable financial restrictions.[66] The IMTFE project was time-consuming, costly, and required immense effort due to difficulty of finding probative evidence, obtaining cooperation from the parties involved, and the need to study a massive number of documents.[67] In case the FEC governments wanted to organize subsequent international trials, they would have to organize them independently and appoint a new prosecutor and panel of judges which might result in lack of uniformity with the IMTFE, as the German case had shown. In short, Keenan strongly advocated the closure of the institutional basis for the prosecution of Class A war criminal suspects, to the effect that the IMTFE prosecution had been exemplary.[68]

The chief prosecutors' stance ought to be placed in a broader context of shifting policies which moved from their emphasis on occupation and punishment towards democratization and conclusion of a peace treaty. In 1948, Washington decided to bring a halt to harsh occupation policies imposed by GHQ, including the protracted IMTFE trials which, in precarious economic and political conditions in Japan, threatened to turn public opinion against the Allies which could potentially represent a fertile ground for the Communist cause.[69] George F. Kennan, director of Policy Planning Staff, repudiated the IMTFE trials as "the hocus-pocus of a judicial procedure," a completely inadequate form of punishment that should have taken "place as an act of war, not justice."[70] In other words, it would have been more efficient and effective to have shot the captured Japanese leaders than to organize political trials, well suited for historians and international politicians, not lawyers which rather endangered the US image and had nothing to do with domestic legalism. Kennan believed that the trials lost the attention of the public opinion which started to observe the defendants as victims enduring "humiliating ordeals."[71]

In October 1948, the New Zealand delegation proposed draft directive FEC 314 which would constitute a basic document open for discussion to other members with the main goal of releasing Class A war criminal suspects under investigation for crime against peace. The target date for the cessation of war criminal trials for all classes of war criminals was June 30, 1949.[72] While the released Class A war suspects would be able to engage in public life, resume office, and have their property restored, their eventual trial for lesser crimes would not be precluded.[73] The document was proposed in view that the two years were sufficient to fulfill general goals of the trial and punish a representative number of individuals in both classes,[74] after which "justice would take its natural course."[75] This raised a few objections among the FEC members as they considered that the target dates outside of Japan would scrutinize the pace of investigations and prosecutions of national courts which would be stigmatized for eventual delays. For example, the Australian government in particular worried about its capacity to meet the target date. The representatives of the Netherlands and the Philippines worried that rushing to terminate the trials would give impression to their public opinion, still inflamed over Japanese aggression, that the war criminals would escape the punishment.[76] The Chinese proposed that FEC 314 should take the form of recommendation as it would imply that the member states have a moral obligation to terminate their trials by the target date, whereas in case of policy decision, a dissent or abstinence from it would imply no obligation at all.[77]

In December 1948, the SCAP released 17 Class A war criminal suspects upon the recommendation received from the IPS in accordance with directive FEC 007/3. Among the released were Nobusuke Kishi, minister of commerce and industry (1941–1943), and Andō Kisaburō, minister of home affairs (1943–1944), who both had served in the Tōjō cabinet. In 1950, the Soviets urged the US Secretary of State Dean Acheson to organize new international trials which would try Emperor Hirohito and high military ranks for the most serious crimes against humanity. The Khabarovsk trials were held on December 25–30, 1949, by the USSR to try 12 Japanese military and physicians on counts of preparing and using bacteriological weapons in pursuing their aggressive war against the Soviet Union, in particular the Nomonhan Incident in 1939, and China. These trials were meant to correct the IMTFE trials,[78] in which the Soviets exercised limited influence, for not developing a strong case for crime against peace against the USSR, non-prosecution of the Emperor, and biological warfare. The Soviet justice served as a supportive platform for its Cold War diplomacy by using propaganda and geopolitics.[79] The Allies used lustration to deal with individuals who could have equally been prosecuted at the Tribunal, given the selection process analyzed in Chap. 6. Class A criminal suspects were detained for two years without trial which is problematic from a legal and humanitarian point of view. Many of these individuals would return to public and political life and use their influence to help the cause of their colleagues who were behind the bars at Sugamo Prison. This was also the time when the fate of convicted Class A war criminals was discussed in view of the coming negotiations for the conclusion of the Peace Treaty or San Francisco Peace Treaty.

Notes

1. Sandra Wilson, *Japanese War Criminals: The Pursuit of Justice After Second World War* (New York: Columbia University Press) 2017, 84.
2. Neil Boister and Robert Cryer, eds., *Documents on the Tokyo International Military Tribunal: Charter, Indictment, and Judgements* (Oxford: Oxford University Press: 2008), 626.
3. Edward Dumbauld, "Dissenting Opinions in International Adjudication," *University of Pennsylvania Law Review* (1942), 934.
4. Ibid.
5. Yuma Totani, *The Tokyo War Crimes Trial: The Pursuit of Justice in the Wake of World War II* (Cambridge: Harvard University Press, 2008), 233.
6. Yuma Totani, "Japanese Receptions of Separate Opinions at the Tokyo Trial," The Council on East Asian Studies, Yale, April 7, 2015, 17.
7. Totani, *The Tokyo War Crimes Trial*, 223.
8. John Pritchard, ed. *The Tokyo Major War Crimes Trial: With an Authoritative Commentary and Comprehensive Guide*, Vol 105 (New York: Edwin Mellen Press, 1998), 35–73.
9. Pritchard, *The Tokyo Major War Crimes Trial: With an Authoritative Commentary and Comprehensive Guide*, Vol 106, 473.
10. Totani, *The Tokyo War Crimes Trial*, 219.
11. Ibid.

12. John Pritchard, ed. *The Tokyo Major War Crimes Trial: With an Authoritative Commentary and Comprehensive Guide*, Vol 105, 123–131.
13. Pritchard, *The Tokyo Major War Crimes Trial: With an Authoritative Commentary and Comprehensive Guide*, Vol 108, 1111.
14. Pritchard, *The Tokyo Major War Crimes Trial: With an Authoritative Commentary and Comprehensive Guide*, Vol 108, 1038–1039.
15. Yoshinobu Higurashi, *Tōkyō saiban* (Kodansha: Tokyo, 2008), 272.
16. Kirsten Sellars, *"Crime Against Peace" and International Law* (Cambridge: Cambridge University Press, 2015), 235.
17. Ibid.
18. Pritchard, *The Tokyo Major War Crimes Trial: With an Authoritative Commentary and Comprehensive Guide*, Vol 106, 609.
19. Pritchard, *The Tokyo Major War Crimes Trial: With an Authoritative Commentary and Comprehensive Guide*, Vol 106, 483.
20. James Burnham Sedgwick, "The Trial Within: Negotiating Justice at the International Military Tribunal for the Far East, 1946–1948," (PhD diss., University of British Columbia, 2012), 259. https://open.library.ubc.ca/cIRcle/collections/ubctheses/24/items/1.0072876 (accessed November 14, 2017).
21. Esmein, "Le juge Henry Bernard au Procès de Tokyo," *Vingtième Siècle* 59 (Juliet–Septembre 1998): 4.
22. Sedgwick," The Trial Within," 211.
23. Totani, "Japanese Receptions of Separate Opinions at the Tokyo Trial," 210.
24. Ibid., 210.
25. Ibid.
26. Higurashi, *Tōkyō saiban*, 267.
27. Sedgwick," The Trial Within," 208.
28. Ibid.
29. Sellars, *"Crime Against Peace" and International Law*, 235.
30. Sedgwick," The Trial Within," 208.
31. Justice Northcroft's words, March 18, 1947, cited in Sellars, *'Crime Against Peace" and International Law*, 235.
32. Ibid.
33. Nortcroft to Nash, March 5, 1946, in Robin Kay, ed., *Documents on New Zealand External Relations Volume II: The Surrender and Occupation of Japan* (Wellington: Historical Publications Branch Department of Internal Affairs, 1982), 1531.
34. Sedgwick, "The Trial Within," 203.
35. Ibid., 199–201.
36. Ibid.
37. Ibid., 207.

38. Sellars, *"Crime Against Peace" and International Law*, 235.
39. Higurashi, *Tōkyō saiban*, 266.
40. Richard H. Minear, *Victors' Justice: The Tokyo War Crimes Trial* (Princeton: Princeton University Press, 1971), 162.
41. Ibid., 163.
42. The Allied Council for Japan (ACJ) was established in Tokyo to allow the US, Britain, the Soviet Union, and China to consult the Supreme Commander, however devoid of any decisive power, and with meetings scheduled for every two weeks.
43. FEC 007/7, "The Trial of Japanese War Criminals," April 26, 1946, in Makoto Iokibe, ed., *Occupation of Japan: Planning Documents, 1942–1945* (Tokyo: Maruzen), microfiche, 4-A-3.
44. Minear, *Victors' Justice: The Tokyo War Crimes Trial*, 161.
45. FEC, Letter from Beverly M. Coleman to General Douglas MacArthur, November 11, 1948 in NARA II, RG 43, General Records, March 1946–1949, Box 1.
46. Minear, *Victors' Justice: The Tokyo War Crimes Trial*, 160–161.
47. Ibid., 168–169.
48. FEC, Minutes, Committee No. 5, War Criminals, Minutes, 13th Meeting, December 10, 1948 in RG 43, General Records, March 1946–1949, Box 1.
49. Minear, *Victors' Justice: The Tokyo War Crimes Trial*, 170.
50. Ibid.
51. Ibid.
52. Ibid., 171.
53. Sedgwick, "The Trial Within," 280.
54. US Supreme Court, *Hirota v. MacArthur*, 338 US 197 (1948), https://supreme.justia.com/cases/federal/us/338/197/case.html (accessed on September 20, 2017).
55. Sedgwick, "The Trial Within," 281.
56. Ibid., 280.
57. Ibid.; 282–283; FEC, Minutes, Committee No. 5, War Criminals, Minutes, 13th Meeting, December 10, 1948 in RG 43, General Records, March 1946–1949, Box 1.
58. Kim C. Priemel and Alexa Stiller, eds., *Reassessing the Nuremberg Military Trials: Transitional Justice, Trial Narratives, and Historiography* (New York: Berghahn Books, 2014), 254.
59. Ibid., 256.
60. Ibid.
61. For extensive analysis of NMTs see Peter Maguire, *Law and War: An American Story* (New York: Columbia University Press, 2001); Kim C. Priemel and Alexa Stiller, eds., *Reassessing the Nuremberg Military*

Trials: Transitional Justice, Trial Narratives, and Historiography (New York: Berghahn Books, 2014).
62. Peter Maguire, *Law and War: An American Story* (New York: Columbia University Press, 2001), 163.
63. Ibid.
64. Memorandum of Conversation, by Miss Katherine B. Fite of the Office of the Legal Advisor (Fahy), Washington, August 6, 1947, in FRUS, *Far East*, Volume VI (Washington: US Government Printing Office, 1972), 279–280.
65. Ibid.
66. Awaya Kentarō, "Selecting Defendants at the Tokyo Trial," in Yuki Tanaka, Tim McCormack, and Gerry Simpson, eds., *Beyond Victors' Justice: The Tokyo War Crimes Trials Revisited* (Martinus Leiden: Nijhoff, 2011), 57.
67. FEC, Transcript of Minutes, Committee No. 5, War Criminals, Minutes, 9th Meeting, March 31, 1948, in RG 43, General Records, March 1946–1949, Box 1.
68. Ibid.
69. "Explanatory Notes by Mr. George F. Keenan," March 25, 1948 in FRUS, 1948. The Far East and Australasia, 1948, 717–719.
70. Ibid.
71. Ibid.
72. FEC, Minutes, Committee No. 5, War Criminals, Minutes, 10th Meeting, October 11, 1948 in RG 43, General Records, March 1946–1949, Box 1.
73. Ibid.
74. Ibid.
75. FEC, Transcript of Minutes, FEC, 146th Meeting, March 31, 1949 in RG 43, General Records, March 1946–1949, Box 1.
76. Ibid.
77. Ibid.
78. Valentyna Polunina, "From Tokyo to Khabarovsk: Soviet War Crimes Trials in Asia as Cold War Battlefields." In Kerstin von Lingen, eds., *War Crimes Trials in the Wake of Decolonization and Cold War in Asia, 1945–1956* (London: Palgrave Macmillan, 2016).
79. Ibid.

CHAPTER 8

Forgiveness by Law and Dilemmas on the Nature of the War Criminal Program in Japan

SCAP Parole System and War Criminal Policies

The intensifying Cold War rivalry only meant one thing—that the US could no longer act on behalf of the Allied powers in the same way it did in the immediate postwar period which only led to provocations and extended debates mainly by the Soviet Union. With its refusal to sign the Peace Treaty with Japan in 1952, the USSR lost voice in the clemency and parole process of Class A war criminals, and yet, as will be shown in later chapters, it found a way to exert considerable influence over the process.

Before the occupation ended, the SCAP Legal Section established the SCAP Clemency System by means of Circular No. 5 on March 7, 1950, which was based on the US Federal system. Prisoners were able to earn "good time" credit for observing prison rules and regulations and pre-trial detention credit, thus allowing them to reduce their sentences and become eligible for parole, after serving one-third of the sentence or 15 years in case of life sentence and sentence exceeding 45 years. This mechanism will serve as a model for clemency and parole system established in post-occupation Japan. Not only did the Circular not mention any institutional link with the FEC or ACJ, but it also did not make a distinction between the classes of war criminals which implied that the IMTFE defendants could be paroled under the newly established system without consultation with the representatives of other countries. Again, the SCAP was exercising the sole authority for the execution of the IMTFE sentences on behalf

A. Babovic, *The Tokyo Trial, Justice, and the Postwar International Order*, New Directions in East Asian History,
https://doi.org/10.1007/978-981-13-3477-1_8

of the Allied powers[1] to the effect that China and the Soviet Union would protest the inability to influence the process.

The Chinese mission in Japan was suspicious about the SCAP parole system as it contended that it amounted to the modification or alternation of the original sentence, thus requiring consultation of the Allies.[2] They invoked MacArthur's speech in which he announced his decision to retain sentences established by the Tribunal which was now altered by the SCAP parole system. The US did not heed as the parole system was an administrative method, widely practiced in democratic societies, which only represented the change of the manner in which the sentence was executed.[3] Along similar lines, the USSR dissatisfaction revolved around the fact that the measure was unilateral, that the SCAP ought to consult and obtain agreement of other nations as the IMTFE was an international tribunal and requested the revocation of Circular No. 5.[4] Article 17 of the IMTFE Charter did not allow for the premature release of Class A war criminals. Already in the 1950s, it became evident that the issue of war criminals could potentially become fastidious and that, as such, it should be left to the past as soon as possible. Just before the outbreak of the Korean War, U. Alexis Johnson from State Department Far Eastern Bureau expressed this idea as follows: "I hope that one of these days we may be able to relegate questions concerning war criminals into the historical past where it so well belongs, particularly at this moment when we are looking toward the re-instatement of Japan into the family of nations."[5] Mamoru Shigemitsu, who was included to the indictment at the Soviet request and received seven-year sentence, was the first Class A war criminal to be paroled by the SCAP parole system and ready to go back to public life.

The San Francisco Peace Treaty and Relics of War

In the first two years, the initial occupation policies towards Japan were almost exclusively delegated to General MacArthur, a highly authoritative persona, who wanted to play the central role in rebuilding Japan. As part of intensive demilitarization process, former Japanese leaders were prosecuted within the IMTFE. Another measure was purge of around 210,000 wartime officials by the directive for the removal of undesirable personnel from public office of January 4, 1946,[6] while the military structure was dissolved. This latter measure of lustration was based on assumption of wrongdoing due to the official rank or simply by way of occupying post within the government apparatus. The "guilt" was not established on a case-by-case basis. In 1946, the GHQ Government Section, headed by Courtney Whitney, pushed for more radical reforms that were imposed to the Japanese government and often out of touch with Japan's peculiar geopolitical environment. As part of these reforms, Japan adopted an amendment to Article 9 of the Constitution in 1946 that was originally construed to eliminate the right to both aggressive and defensive wars. Only during Prime Minister Yoshida's second term would Japan be allowed to interpret the Constitution as to allow for the right of self-defense.

With Premier Yoshida in office, the main focus of the occupation was economic development and integration within the global market and concluding peace treaty in view of restoring Japan's independence. Comprehensive economic reforms—agricultural land reform, removal of zaibatsu, the Anti-Monopoly act, growth of entrepreneurs and economic groups—gave impetus to much needed efficiency and growth. The advance of Communists in Chinese civil war and the increasing rivalry with the USSR made the US slowly pivot towards Japan as reflected in NSC-13/2 which included Japan within George F. Kennan's "containment" policy whereby the US committed to building a thriving economy in Japan. In 1949, the political and geostrategic outlook of East Asia profoundly changed. The Chinese Communists took power and the Nationalist Government almost completely moved to Taiwan; the USSR performed its first nuclear test which triggered the arms race with the US, whereas the Sino-Soviet Treaty of Amity and Cooperation was signed in February 1950. This increased the awareness of President Truman of Japan's strategic value and importance of its place within the Western camp once it regained its sovereignty. Furthermore, the outbreak of the Korean War on June 25, 1950, swayed Truman from Kennan's economic containment strategy towards Paul H. Nitze's costly "military containment" which entailed increases in the US defense budget and military buildup. This placed US military bases in Japan at the heart of the US Cold War strategy and Yoshida decided to allow their presence as he saw value in Japan belonging to the "US nuclear umbrella" and having its security guaranteed while Japan could focus on rebuilding its economy. Japan reaped the economic benefits from the Korean War by way of special procurements contracts. At the same time, due to the decline in the number of US forces which were now deployed in Korea, MacArthur requested Japan to establish the National Police Reserve (NPR) in 1950 for both domestic security purposes and future Japanese rearmament. Many politicians in Yoshida's entourage advocated rearmament, but Yoshida decided to go another way around—prioritize stable political system, recover economy, regain independence, and, only then, rearm.

In 1947, US officials had already started pondering about the type of a peace treaty that should be concluded with Japan. One of the questions put before the drafters, other than burning questions related to security and reparations, was what would be the fate of Japanese war criminals once the occupation came to an end. During the occupation, Sugamo Prison was under the control of the US military which meant that after Japan regained its independence there would be institutional void related to the management of war criminals. The Americans knew that there was a widespread belief among the Japanese that once the Peace Treaty was concluded, the war criminals would be released as their sentences would have expired as the trials were part of occupation that thereby ended.[7] However, the IMTFE was also a post-occupational project or better said having reach into the post-occupation era by way of the execution of sentences. Automatic release after the occupation was not an option as the Allies wanted to validate the legal character of war crimes program that had been completed and justify the costly and fastidious prosecution process. Otherwise, automatic release would damage the legal basis of the trials, proceedings, sentences, and be embarrassing to the Allies. The war crimes program validation was of the utmost importance. Countries such as the Netherlands, Australia, and the Philippines which bore the brunt of Japanese atrocities feared that their public opinion would be unsettling if their government allowed for the outright release of Japanese war criminals. The negotiations leading towards the conclusion of the Peace Treaty were of multilateral character which brought into perspective the Allies' disparate and competing visions on what kind of peace should be concluded with Japan.

The Allies were well aware that the lack of a clear clause regulating the conditions for the execution of the sentences imposed by the tribunals by the Japanese government after the occupation might end up in an Italian war criminal scenario.[8] The fate of Italian war criminals prosecuted by the American and British military tribunals was not taken into account by the provisions of the Peace Treaty that was signed between the two Allies and Italy in 1947. Despite the oral assurances given by the Italian government that it would ensure that the war criminals would carry out the full term of their sentences or will not be released earlier without the Allies' approval, Italy ended up releasing its war criminals in violation of the informal agreement that existed.

In 1947, Allies could somewhat agree that the provisions of the Peace Treaty with Japan should be harsh and restrictive. Hugh Borton, Japan hands from the State Department's Far Eastern Affairs Bureau, drafted a peace treaty with provisions on war criminals that obliged Japan to fully carry out the sentences imposed by the tribunals and gave no power to it over clemency process. Interestingly, Borton's draft envisaged that the issue of clemency could be settled by an independently established diplomatic body which would be composed of representatives from the FEC. This implied that the issue of clemency would be settled within a diplomatic framework rather than a legal one which would turn the end of the war crimes program into a "political solution." The British Commonwealth nations, the Philippines, and China all feared the resurgence of Japanese militarism and thus advocated a hard line approach towards Japan and their peace settlement.[9]

As noted earlier, one of the main forces behind the change in US foreign policy towards Japan in 1948 was George Kennan who argued that the only way to prevent Japan's fall into the Communist orbit was to build a strong economy and assure political stability. This meant that the initial harsh and disruptive occupation policies had to be terminated in favor of economic assistance to Japan to which President Truman acquiesced and which NSC 12/3 reflected as a part of the economic containment policies. From 1949, the evidence of Soviet military dominance, the defeat of Chinese Nationalist Government, the Chinese entry into the Korean War in addition to precarious social and economic situation in Japan swayed the key decision-makers in Washington towards a more liberal and tolerant policies towards Japan and the upcoming negotiations of the Peace Treaty.[10] The draft treaties produced in 1950 evidenced this change in its draft Article 14 that accorded to the Japanese government the power to vary sentences subject to the prior approval of the interested governments.[11]

The progress towards finding a common ground between the Allies came with Truman's appointment of John Foster Dulles as the main person in charge of negotiations. The main obstructers to the liberal peace treaty terms and minimal limitations were Australia and New Zealand which were fearing Japan more than they feared the Soviet Union.[12] The main issue for them was the absence of restrictions upon Japan's rearmament. John Foster Dulles who was the US representative at the Versailles Peace Conference, as noted earlier, was deeply marked by the lessons of punitive peace and insisted that peace ought to be generous and with minimal restrictions.[13] Dulles achieved breakthrough with the Commonwealth nations a week prior to the Peace Conference with the conclusion of Australia, New Zealand, and the US Security Pact (ANZUS) which alleviated their fears of Japanese militarism.[14] Another point of contention was the war guilt clause whose introduction to the treaty was sought by Australia and New Zealand. Dulles considered that public denouncement of Japan's war guilt for waging aggressive war, especially in view of their cooperation under the occupation and the Korean War, would be contrary to the aim "to turn Japan into a viable and peace-loving nation"[15] and met with general dissatisfaction in Japan. The final compromise was achieved by introducing the clause whereby the Japanese government accepts the judgements, thus tacitly accepting the war guilt.[16] In relation to the Japanese government role in the clemency and parole process, Article 10 granted to it the faculty to recommend, but the final decision rested with the Allied powers or interested country contrary to earlier drafts in which Japan and the Allied powers had a "joint" decision in deciding the variation of sentences.

The Japanese government also authored its versions of the Peace Treaty starting from 1950, and later on, as the negotiations progressed, they were asked to participate more actively in the drafting process by expressing their opinions or seeking amendments. The most extreme demand was to grant a general amnesty to the Japanese war criminals which was unacceptable to the Allies. Amnesty as a well-established legal measure of pardoning the wrongdoer for the committed crimes by restoring its rights and privileges is usually used as an expression of compassion and mercifulness on behalf of the powers.[17] Although it might have been too high of an expectation on the part of the Japanese for unconditional amnesty, the Allies had an option of conditional amnesty that could have served their strategic interests better by allowing them to employ carrot and stick method. The magnanimity on the part of the Allies might have resulted in a more solid peace.[18] Many Japanese officials, especially the ones from the Foreign Ministry Treaty Bureau, aware of the tough stance taken mainly by the Commonwealth countries, mistakenly believed that the US would exert influence upon all other countries regarding their decisions as well as be expeditious in their efforts to clear the prison. As the system of clemency and parole mentioned earlier had already existed during the occupation, it was only expected that the end of occupation would considerably speed the matter up.

The San Francisco Peace Treaty was meant to close the chapter of the Fifteen Years War (1931–1945). However, another war almost immediately started, the Cold War (1946–1987) that altered the dynamics between the powers. Japan concluded the Peace Treaty with some of the Allied powers which were now fighting other wars. However, that peace did not resolve many chapters that would haunt the Japanese regional relations to the present day—territorial issues, historical issues, security issues (US bases in Okinawa, rearmament). China and Korea, the two countries that suffered the most from Japanese expansionism, were not included, and neither was the war responsibility clause. In a certain way, the San Francisco System determined the postwar regional order in East Asia, but at the same time contributed to the quick forgetting of the past on the part of Japan to which the US also contributed. This amnesia gave birth to policies and actions by the Japanese government which only further exacerbated the already sensitive historical issues and prevented regional reconciliation.[19]

Behind the Clemency and Parole: Forgiveness by Law

Before delving into the clemency and parole mechanism that was created to deal with the Japanese war criminals, both Classes A and BC, it is important to understand their use and meaning they are assigned to. Clemency and parole in the international criminal sphere are legal categories that are borrowed from domestic judicial systems. The Allied powers were already familiar with mimicking domestic law in their legal undertakings as it had been demonstrated in an earlier chapter treating the introduction of the crime of conspiracy into the IMTFE Charter. The early release in domestic law prioritizes reducing costs and preventing recidivism; international criminal tribunals are rather concerned with retribution for the most serious international crimes and reconciliation between enemy parties after or during the conflict.[20] The transposition of these domestic legal practices into the practice of international criminal tribunals can have perverse effects—mitigation of guilt and dissatisfaction of victims—for their lack of transparency and dilution of the original illegal act.[21]

Parole is an encouragement for prisoners to show good behavior and participate in rehabilitative programs, its main goal being rehabilitation. In the practice of modern international criminal tribunals, war criminals found themselves automatically released to unconditional, unsupervised parole after they have completed two-thirds of their sentence, contrary to domestic parole where they are under conditional release and supervision. In contrast, clemency is rarely used in domestic law; it exercises an "error-correcting" role,[22] allowing for sentence adjustment in the light of changed circumstances, and is often politically motivated.[23] The main criterion for early release in international criminal tribunals is not primarily based on newfound evidence that mitigates the guilt or cooperation after sentencing, but rather repentance, the gravity of crimes committed, or the probability of recidivism.[24]

The importance of discussing the aim of clemency and parole, extensively used in the stage of execution of the IMTFE sentences, lies in pointing out at the meaning that this process had for its key stakeholders—the Allied governments, postwar Japan, and victims. Clemency and parole do not emanate from the realm of interpersonal forgiveness, it is a public institutionalized form by which officials accord "forgiveness" to the wrongdoer.[25] The prerogative to grant clemency and parole pertains to the executive, veiled in monarchical privilege,[26] exercised in a discretionary manner almost "disregarding the declared law," and it becomes "a form of legally sanctioned alegality."[27] Thus, the subject of these revisionary practices is different—"in forgiveness, it is the victim; in clemency it is the official; in repentance it is the wrongdoer."[28] The clemency and parole system as such represents an institutional forgiveness, forgiveness by law, where the main actors were high-level officials, and hence without any repercussions regarding forgiveness originating from the victims of war. This lack of forgiveness became one of the valuable political assets for elites in Beijing and Seoul to exploit when it comes to Japan's war responsibility as much as institutional punishment and forgiveness for its war criminals became an excuse for Japanese not to sincerely apologize to the victims of their imperialism.

Legalism Until the Very End: War Criminal Program and the Clemency and Parole Board

After the Peace Treaty came into effect in April 1952, the SCAP parole system was abolished. Contrary to the high expectations of the Japanese elite, populace, and prisoners themselves, the release of Sugamo inmates based on clemency and parole process started to stagnate. Procedurally speaking, the fate of Class A war criminals appeared more complicated as it was in the hands of the majority governments represented at the IMTFE. The release of Class BC war criminals who were subjected to decisions of a respective government that prosecuted them in their national courts promised a less burdensome path.

Months into Japan gaining its independence, no specific procedure or framework was set forth to harbor the decision-making process of the majority governments represented on the IMTFE regarding Class A war criminals. The SCAP Legal Section strongly advised the State Department officials to establish a venue for informal coordination between the representatives of interested governments, requiring them to assure the preservation of the judicial and legal character of the process.[29] More precisely, the British proposal that the Committee should be exclusively composed of ambassadors was rejected as it threatened to stain the legal character of deliberations with its political and diplomatic outlook. The stubborn attitude of extending the legal character to all ensuing stages of sentence execution and at every level of decision-making, dominant among the legal staff of Department of State (DoS), had been already discernable. The legality and legitimacy of the war crimes programs in both Germany and Japan had to live up to the unified foundation of legal standards until the very end.

At the outset, the Allied powers decided that individual positions of the Allied powers regarding the Japanese recommendations related to the release of Class A war criminals should not be directly communicated to Japan[30] in order to maintain unity and avoid displaying any potential disagreements.

In May 1952, the State Department Assistant Legal Advisor for Far Eastern Affairs, General Conrad E. Snow, discussed the modus operandi to be devised for reaching US decisions regarding the Japanese recommendations for clemency and parole for war criminals. It was of the utmost importance to make decisions that were in accordance with the words of the Potsdam Declaration of July 26, 1945, related to Japanese war criminals that "stern justice should be meted out to all war criminals." Any disregard of this principle threatened to enflame public opinion, especially of those who were personally or indirectly aggrieved by Japanese cruelties inflicted upon the POWs. More generally, the lofty ideal that animated the American architects who led the Allied powers' war crimes program back in 1945—that was to ensure that the quality of American justice in the war criminal tribunals would be preserved—was as relevant in the closing phase of the program.[31] General Snow had a distinguishing career as a military and a lawyer. He was a member of Justice Owen J. Roberts Advisory Board for Clemency established after the war to mitigate the sentences of court-martialed soldiers which had been considered too harsh in the light of new geopolitical developments.[32] His experience in clemency and parole matters was further boosted by his appointment as one of the prominent figures of the Loyalty Security Board which dealt with Senator Joseph R. McCarthy's accusations of the Communists' infiltration into, among other pores of American political establishment, State Department. Later on, he sat on the Advisory Board on War Criminals in Germany in 1950, appointed by John J. McCloy, High Commissioner for Germany.[33] This board was granting the reduction of sentences that were considered "excessive" and thus required some dose of leniency, on a strictly legal basis, for German minor war criminals convicted by subsequent Nuremberg Military Trials organized under the US aegis.[34] This extensive legal expertise made him rank high among the candidates for the position of the chair of Clemency Parole Board that had been envisioned. Furthermore, his professional link to East Asia was established as he had served as a legal counsel to the American representative on the FEC which was formulating policy decisions to General MacArthur until its dismantlement in 1951. According to his legal advice, clemency as a judicial solution would address the cases in which sentences are inappropriate to the crimes committed (unfairness of the sentence, mitigating circumstances, health, family conditions of the prisoner, or his conduct) while the parole would serve to end confinement that no longer served its purpose (good conduct of the prisoner or nature of his crime).[35]

A few months before the establishment of the Clemency and Parole Board (hereafter CPB), the US Embassy in Tokyo proposed to the Secretary of State[36] the initiative to undertake the clemency and parole process. The embassy-level process would allow for the clemency and parole process, which had previously started under the now disbanded SCAP Legal Section, to be overturned smoothly to an unofficial board of senior embassy officers that would put recommendations before the ambassador. American Ambassador Robert Murphy considered that the proposed setting would spare the release process of unnecessary public attention and avoid this issue becoming of great magnitude, which appeared likely to ensue should the President be involved in the process. After the State Department gave a consideration to this idea, Dean Acheson rejected it out of concern that it might be received with criticism among the Japanese for being reminiscent of the "pattern of occupation"[37] as well as the complication it would introduce to a necessary coordination of procedures related to the treatment of war criminals in Japan and Germany.

On September 4, 1952, President Truman established the CPB for war criminals by Executive Order 10393.[38] The Board was meant to operate independently from the State Department. It consisted of three members designated from the Department of State, the Department of Defense, and the Department of Justice—Conrad Snow, Roger Kent, and James V. Bennett, respectively—each appointed by the president. The composition was meant to reflect a delicate balance between different aspects that the CPB activity touched upon—related to foreign policy, international law, and treaty commitments (State Department), authority over the military courts which tried the war criminals (Ministry of Defense), and legal expertise in criminal law and matters related to clemency and parole (Ministry of Justice).[39] The CPB would become one of the main bodies in the decentralized decision-making process for the release of war criminals that was to investigate cases for which the Japanese government requested clemency or parole via the US Embassy in Tokyo. The IMTFE war criminals were also a part of deliberations of the CPB.

In October 1952, Ambassador Murphy, reputed as "a skillful troubleshooter,"[40] indicated that the CPB should proceed swiftly with processing the eligible cases in order to somewhat appease the war criminals issue fraught with danger of turning public opinion against the US.[41] He warned that the emotional heights and Japan's diplomatic animosity against the Soviet Union, for illegally retaining Japanese POWs, should serve as an indicator of how sour can US-Japan relations possibly turn. Although these two situations were of a different nature, humanitarian concerns were their common point. Indeed, the US, along with other Allies, had already taken risks that made them gamble larger diplomatic goals for the sake of a successful solution of what they considered a judicial problem. For the Japanese, in turn, it was considered to be an emotional one.

Similar dangers were voiced in other venues, including the CPB. Few months into its mandate, on January 8, 1953, Roger Kent, general counsel of the Department of Defense, wrote in his resignation letter to the President that the "program [was] in fact a political one involving clemency and release rather than parole, because [they] have delegated vital elements of the parole system to the Japanese."[42] In his opinion, the program was detrimental to US interests but also impractical and ill designed to fulfill "political considerations [that] dictate that Japanese war criminals should be released within a short time—possibly a year."[43] He lamented that the US had already abandoned its commitment to justice when it decided to commute death sentences of the war criminals who committed the most heinous crimes and abandoned further prosecutions after June 25, 1950, thus showing "the Japanese that we [the US] respect the realities of international relations."[44] Kent warned, and correctly so, that the protracted detention of Japanese war criminals carried risks to seriously turn the Japanese against the US and to the advantage of the Russians, given that the Japanese Communists heavily capitalized on the existence of the war criminals issue. As long as this matter remained unresolved, the US would not be able to benefit from the situation and its relations with Japan would suffer, as he put it, "while the issue of prisoners held by Russia somewhere in Siberia may get cooler, it is certain that the issue of war criminals held by Japanese jailers in Japanese prisons will get hotter."[45] Kent's final advice offered the unpopular solution in the form of general amnesty, a strategic move that would efficiently eliminate the war criminal program in Japan before things get highly publicized and out of hand like in Germany.[46]

Forever Unified by Legal Foundation: Last Phase of the War Criminal Program in Nuremberg and Tokyo

Although, the IMFTE and IMT were not institutionally linked in a direct way, their connectedness was visible in the political goals they were aiming to fulfill—this bond will not fade away until the dismantlement of both programs. In the same period, decisions of the Allies in Japan had to be carefully weighed against their possible repercussions for the war crimes program in Germany and vice versa.

In 1952, West Germany was preparing to ratify the Bonn Agreements which were the equivalent of the Peace Treaty in Japan. On March 10, 1952, Joseph Stalin tried to prevent the rearmament of West Germany by proposing the reunification of Germany and organizing free elections.[47] These attempts failed, but they benefited the West German government by increasing their confidence in negotiations leading to the ratification of the Bonn Agreements with the US. Contrary to Article 11 of the Peace Treaty that clearly states that Japan accepts the judgement and sentences imposed by the IMTFE, Article 6 and Article 7 of the contract restoring German sovereignty were formulated in a way that they devised a way for the West German government to contest the legal validity of judgements delivered in the Allied war crimes program. Article 6 set the basis for the establishment of the clemency and parole board, composed of not only the Allied powers' representatives, but also Germans, which in its activities should refrain from "calling into question the validity of the convictions."[48] Article 7 imposed an obligation upon Germany and its legal and judicial institutions, in explicit terms, to endorse legal validity and authority of the Allied powers' criminal tribunals. Curiously, Article 6 contained a clause limiting the application of the provisions of Article 7 for the matters it dealt with—in other words, the board did not have to accept legal validity of court's judgements.[49] Prior to the ratification, Heidelberg Jurists Circle,[50] a powerful lobby group promoting rejection of legal authority and verdicts delivered by all the Allied powers' tribunals, recommended that the war crimes tribunals should not be recognized, a policy line that was endorsed by both the Bundestag and German Chancellor Konrad Adenauer.[51] From the outset, the US talks about German rearmament did not sit well with the idea of top ranking military being held as war criminals in German prisons. As early as 1952, by linking the German defense contribution to the release of German war criminals as pre-condition,[52] Germans gained a wild card they could use in their negotiations with the Allied powers. However, the Mixed Parole Board planned for Germany would be put on hold as the ratification of the contractuals by the French National Assembly dragged on which heavily frustrated both Americans and Germans. This highly crystalized contestation of the tribunals at all levels, both political, intellectual, and societal, was not present in Japan right at the outset which is discussed in detail in Chap. 9.

Meanwhile, waiting for the conditions to be fulfilled for the Mixed Parole Board to come to life, and in the face of Bundestag elections in the fall of 1953 that threatened to punish Adenauer and his coalition partners given that the war criminal questions did not budge, Secretary of State John Foster Dulles proposed appeasement in the form of an interim parole board.[53] The US military authorities could use that time to shift their stance to adopt a more liberal policy towards the war criminals. In Germany, the US organized the War Crimes Modification Board in 1949 and the Advisory Clemency Board, the so-called Peck Panel, that granted clemency in cases where such grounds existed and harmonized the differences in sentencing existent between the subsequent Nuremberg Military Trials.[54] In 1954, the Japanese government complained that German war criminals had been released much quicker than the Japanese without taking into consideration that such system had already existed prior to the establishment of the Mixed Clemency Board in late 1953. The official stance of the US government was that the clemency and parole systems in both countries would be treated equally and without any discrimination.[55] However, both Germany and Japan would keep an eye on the developments regarding the release of war criminals in their theaters and would try to play on the differences in the release pace against the US.

The election of President Dwight Eisenhower in November 1952 placed rearmament on the top policy agenda, a policy shift that supported more liberal views towards the treatment of war criminals held by his Secretary of State, John Foster Dulles, who belonged to the third generation of *lawyer-statesmen*.[56] This shift was endorsed by officers from the Political Affairs of the State Department who promoted expediency and greater leniency of the clemency and parole system as they observed "the problem as political one, and not as juridical or moral one."[57] However, over time President Eisenhower's hardened stance regarding the issue will pose an additional hurdle which will obstruct the initiatives to release war criminals.[58] As a result, State Department officers, especially the ones from political and legal affairs, were divided by an internal struggle regarding which course of action would be the most appropriate for the final phase of war crimes program. In a similar manner, institutional rivalry was also dividing the US administration in 1945 when the deliberations on the war crimes tribunals establishment took place—the State Department and the Department of Treasury were in fierce competition for advancing policies of war crimes trials and summary executions of war criminals, respectively. The State Department memo summarized the general amnesty policies for Japanese Class BC war criminals that had been recommended by Ambassador Allison and were scheduled to be further discussed by the Department's legal and political officers for the Far East and Europe for the purpose of coordination between the two clemency programs. The note observed that the State Department's German officers displayed opposition to any form of amnesty given that they tried to implement a proper judicial system for clemency and parole. Those arguing for amnesty thought that consultations would be detrimental to the desired fast solution to the "war criminal business"[59] which they considered "an unnecessary exacerbation in US-Japan relations."[60] Prior to the meeting convened to discuss amnesty for Japanese war criminals, John Auchincloss, State Department legal advisor, discussed the detrimental repercussions of Allison's proposal in a secret memo he sent to the US Embassy in Bonn. He highlighted that political solution would "undermine, in retrospect, the entire war crimes program,"[61] while it would boost the far right in Germany, raise questions before the US Congress, and agitate public opinion. He thought that the uneasy questions of principle should be raised and bluntly pondered his view: "The men now serving sentences for war crimes are doing so because we believed at one time that they deserved to be punished for what they did. Do we still believe this, or do we not? If we do not, then we should release the men as soon as possible [...] If we believe it, we should stick to it, for to act against it would be cynical, if our purpose were to gain a political advantage, or weak, if our purpose were to avoid political pressure."[62]

Ambassador Allison met State Department representatives on February 16, 1954, to discuss his proposal regarding the US policy towards the war criminals in view of granting amnesty or "take some action less than amnesty"[63] in case of Japanese war criminals as he was conscious of the repercussions this policy shift might have in German theater. Mr. Herman Phleger, the legal advisor, Mr. John M. Raymond, German officer, and Mr. James Bonbright, deputy assistant secretary for European Affairs, refused the proposal for an amnesty as it would be observed as giving concessions under the pressure of Germans.[64] They also pointed out that the Department of Army which held the German war criminals in custody had conservative views regarding the parole system and would not be willing to go as far as Allison's proposal. It was generally agreed that the liquidation of war criminals question would be beneficial but that the decision should be weighed against public opinion and overall policy needs towards Germany and Japan.[65] It was concluded that speeding up the release within the CPB would not be acceptable to German officers in DoS.

Interestingly, the German counterparts to Class A war criminals in Germany—seven prisoners convicted by the IMT at Nuremberg, detained in Spandau Prison in Berlin, under the four Allied powers' authority—were not included in the parole program in Germany and served their sentences until the very end, with two exceptions. The subsequent Nuremberg Military Trials organized independently by the US and judged by their national judges did have a few cases based on crime against peace charges. All the rest were war criminals prosecuted by national military courts. However, given the level of publicity that the issue reached in German society this distinction between Class A and Class BC that had existed in Japan was irrelevant to Germany. The next chapter discusses the position of the Japanese government regarding the release of its war criminals after the occupation and the evolving position of the Allied powers on the topic of the release of Class A war criminals.

Notes

1. FEC, Minutes of Meeting, FEC, 191st Meeting, April 20, 1950 in RG 43, Records Related to FEC, Minutes of Meetings, February 1946–1949, Box 3.
2. FEC, Minutes of Meeting, FEC, 193rd Meeting, May 18, 1950 in RG 43, Records Related to FEC, Minutes of Meetings, February 1946–1949, Box 3.
3. Ibid.
4. Message, Acheson, State Department to SCAP, August 30, 1950 in NARA, RG 84, Japanese War Crimes Cases, Box 26.
5. Letter, U. Alexis Johnson, Department of State, Far Eastern Bureau to William J. Sebald, US Political Advisor to Japan, June 23, 1950, in NARA, RG 84, Japanese War Criminals, Box 1.
6. Tosh Minohara, ed., *The History of US-Japan Relations: From Perry to Present* (Singapore: Palgrave Macmillan, 2017), 116.
7. Draft Basic Civil Affairs/Military Government Criteria Among Those to be Encompassed in a Japanese Peace Treaty, War Department, August 29, 1947, FRUS, *Far East*, Volume VI, Washington: US Government Printing Office, 1972.
8. "The Effect of Blanket Clemency for Italian War Criminals on NA's Position Regarding Post-Treaty Clemency for Japanese War Criminals," April 5, 1950, in NARA, RG 59.
9. Sandra Wilson, Robert Cribb, Beatrice Trefalt, and Dean Aszkielowicz, *Japanese War Criminals: The Politics of Justice After the Second World War* (New York: Columbia University Press, 2017), 155.
10. Frederick S. Dunn, *Peace Making and the Settlement with Japan* (Princeton: Princeton University Press, 2016), 59–62, 172–188; Michael Schaller, *The American Occupation of Japan: The Origins of the Cold War in Asia* (Oxford: Oxford University Press, 1985), 122–140.
11. "Commentary of Draft Treaty of Peace with Japan," in NARA II, RG59.
12. Dunn, *Peace Making and the Settlement with Japan*, 125.
13. Wilson et al., *Japanese War Criminals*, 159–160.
14. Ibid.
15. Ibid., 161.
16. Higurashi, *Tōkyō saiban*, 337.
17. Zachary D. Kaufman, *United States Law and Policy on Transitional Justice: Principles, Politics, and Pragmatics* (New York: Oxford University Press, 2016), 27–28.
18. Minutes, October 27, 1952, in NARA II, RG 220, Box 1, Folder: Minutes, M-6.
19. Kimie Hara, ed., *The San Francisco and Its Legacies: Continuation, Transformation and Historical Reconciliation in the Asia-Pacific* (London: Routledge, 2014).

20. Jonathan H. Choi, "Early Release in International Criminal Law," *The Yale Law Journal* 432 (2014), 1789.
21. Ibid.
22. Ibid., 1801.
23. Ibid., 1802.
24. Ibid. The author discusses early release in international criminal law that has started with the IMT at Nuremberg and IMTFE, to become more refined with the practice in modern international criminal tribunals—ICTY, ICTR, and ICC. Although he makes distinction between historical cases of criminal justice in Nuremberg and Tokyo as solely based on political and geopolitical grounds, his discussion is relevant as similar dilemmas could be traced in the parole system applied in the respective cases.
25. Kathleen Dean Moore, *Pardons: Justice, Mercy, and the Public Interest*, Oxford: Oxford University Press, 1989 cited in Austin Sarat and Nasser Husain, eds., *Forgiveness, Mercy, and Clemency, Mercy, and Clemency* (Stanford: Stanford University Press, 2007), 5.
26. Austin Sarat and Nasser Husain, eds., *Forgiveness, Mercy, and Clemency*, 6.
27. Austin Sarat and Nasser Husain, eds., *Forgiveness*, 7.
28. Ibid., 11.
29. Note, SCAP, Legal Section to Department of State, March 27, 1952 in NARA, RG84, Japanese War Criminals, General Files, Box 26.
30. Ibid.
31. Working Papers, A Board of Clemency and Parole for War Criminals, From Conrad Snow to the Legal Advisor, May 9, 1952, NARA, RG220, Box 1.
32. Harry S. Truman Presidential Library & Museum, Transcript of Oral History Interview with Conrad E. Snow, Richard D. McKinzie, July 2, 1973, 6–7. https://www.trumanlibrary.org/oralhist/snowce.htm#transcript (accessed on August 14, 2017).
33. Ibid., 11.
34. Ibid., 15–16. According to the interview transcript, the Advisory Board for Clemency in Germany or the Peck Board had 40 days to review thousands of pages of transcripts of the trials and other legal documents in order to examine the suitability of the sentence.
35. Working Papers, A Board of Clemency and Parole for War Criminals, From Conrad Snow to the Legal Advisor, May 9, 1952, NARA, RG220, Box 1.
36. Telegram, Murphy, American Embassy, Tokyo to Secretary of State, July 31, 1952, in NARA, RG84, Japanese War Criminals, Box 1.
37. Telegram, Secretary of State to American Embassy, Tokyo, August 23, 1952 in NARA, RG84, Japanese War Criminals, Box 1.
38. Working Papers, CPB, NARA, RG220, Box 1.
39. Report of the Clemency and Parole Board for War Criminals, Minutes, January 15, 1953, NARA, RG220, Box 1, folder: Minutes CPB, M-12.

40. Martin Weil, "Robert D. Murphy, Diplomat, Advisor to Presidents, Dies," Washington Post, January 11, 1978. https://www.washingtonpost.com/archive/local/1978/01/11/robert-d-murphy-diplomat-adviser-to-presidents-dies/ca989305-de2d-457d-be31-2bf2f12391be/?utm_term=.e8f5bb4de395 (accessed on March 3, 2017).
41. Foreign Service Dispatch No. 654, US Embassy Tokyo to the Department of State, October 2, 1952, NARA, RG220, Box 1.
42. Repercussions on the German problem? Enclosed Letter of Resignation from Roger Kent to the President, Minutes, January 14, 1953, NARA, RG 220, Box 1, folder: Minutes CPB, M-12.
43. Ibid.
44. Ibid.
45. Ibid.
46. Ibid.
47. Peter Maguire, *Law and War: An American Story* (New York: Columbia University Press, 2001), 238.
48. Ibid., 239.
49. Ibid.
50. Ibid., 235. Otto Kranzbühler, defense counsel at Nuremberg, was one of the prominent figures behind this plan.
51. Ibid., 238.
52. Ibid.
53. Telegram, Department of State to Tokyo, April 10, 1953, in NARA, RG84, War Criminals—General, Box 28.
54. Peter Maguire, *Law and War*, 213.
55. Telegram, David K. E. Bruce, American Embassy, Paris to HICOG Bonn, August 26, 1952 in NARA, RG84, War Criminals—General Files, Box 28.
56. Peter Maguire, *Law and War*, 243.
57. Ibid., 242–244.
58. Memorandum of Telephone Conversation, Department of State, November 10, 1954, in *FRUS*, 1952–1954, China and Japan, Vol IV, Part 2.
59. The Weekly Notes for Tokyo, December 5, 1953, in NARA, RG 84, Japanese War Criminals, Box 1.
60. Ibid.
61. State Department legal advisor John Auchincloss to Geoffrey Lewis at the US Embassy in Bonn, January 28, 1954, RG59, Box 16 cited in Peter Maguire, *Law and War: An American Story*, 253–254.
62. Ibid., 254.
63. Memorandum, "General Amnesty for Japanese War Criminals," February 16, 1954 in NARA, RG84, War Criminals—General Files, Box 28.
64. Ibid.
65. Wilson et al., *The Japanese War Criminals: The Politics of Justice After the Second World War*, 187.

CHAPTER 9

Stagnation and Confusion: The Incoherencies of the War Criminal Program in Japan

The SCAP Legal Section sought to assure that in serving their sentence Sugamo inmates would receive "no better or no worse" treatment than ordinary domestic felons and in accordance with minimally accepted international standards.[1] In addition, they wanted to secure that the power to grant clemency, parole, or reduction of sentence would stay with the governments concerned.[2] And yet, the Japanese, well before the independence date, used SCAP's Circular No. 5 to draft several versions of law that would allow for a domestic legal basis for managing various aspects of the clemency and parole process for all categories of war criminals—authority accorded to the Japanese government by Article 11 of the Treaty of Peace. In crafting the text of the law, the Japanese interpretation of Article 11 opted for the most general terms possible which meant that there was no obligation upon Japan regarding the manner in which the sentences were to be executed, thereby giving them free hands to implement their own general prison laws in instances that were not prescribed in the provisions of the special law on war criminals. Bothered by the fact that the Peace Treaty retained wartime victors' formulation "war criminals," in newly independent Japan, the drafters tried to remove the war stigma by intentionally using terms such as "inmates" over "prisoners"[3] or "detention house" over "prison."[4] The goal was to get over with the issue as soon as possible while maintaining large room for maneuver. The final version of Japanese Law No. 103 of 1952 that was deemed acceptable by

A. Babovic, *The Tokyo Trial, Justice, and the Postwar International Order*, New Directions in East Asian History,
https://doi.org/10.1007/978-981-13-3477-1_9

the US government served as the main guideline for the National Offenders' Prevention and Rehabilitation Commission (hereafter NOPAR) or *Chūō kōsei hogo shinsa kai*, established within the Ministry of Justice (hereafter MOJ), in presenting its recommendations for the release of war criminals to the interested governments via the Ministry of Foreign Affairs. This made the whole process of decision-making regarding the parole institutionally fragmented and burdensome.

The release of Class A war criminals, although they were procedurally displaced from the IMTFE, was still subjected to the majority of the Allied powers involved in this stage of the process. For instance, Communist China, the USSR, and India lost their right to participate in the clemency and parole process as they did not sign the Peace Treaty. Once presented to the CPB, recommendations made by the Japanese government for Class A war criminals via the US Embassy in Tokyo were to be discussed among the legal representatives of interested governments in Washington.

At first the Japanese government was institutionally divided when it came to the pace regarding the release of war criminals. The Ministry of Foreign Affairs adopted a cautious approach in dealing with war criminals; they sought for Japan to appear as a country that cherishes its international obligations and accordingly did not object to the Peace Treaty provisions under which it accepted the tribunals' judgements or had only a faculty to recommend the release of war criminals instead of sharing the decision-making power with the Allies.[5] On the other hand, the Ministry of Justice believed that the process of clemency would be accelerated following the formalities around the signature and ratification of the Peace Treaty or that the Allies would simply accept the recommendations from the Japanese government for the release.

On October 6, 1952, Mr. Saito, Chief of Japanese Protection Bureau for Judicial Affairs, visited the CPB in Washington to convey the seriousness of the state of affairs regarding the war criminals in Japan by raising several points. First, that the public opinion had been gaining strength as the main driving force behind the requests for general clemency for all war criminals which formed into a solid movement. In the light of the overall "spirit of trust and reconciliation" that the Peace Treaty exuded, it was expected that the recommendation by the Japanese government would lead to an automatic acceptance of general clemency by the interested governments having in mind that the sentences imposed immediately upon surrender were harsh. The financial and moral hardship of war criminals' families added up further drama and exacerbated the emotional aspects of the issue. Second, stagnation of the process further discouraged and frustrated the prisoners who thought that they endured harsh sentences only for obeying superiors' orders and committing acts whose criminal nature they were not aware of. Mr. Saito inadvertently discredited the war crimes program by pointing out that as the purpose of punishment was accomplished, the detention of war criminals who had already served seven years was no longer justifiable, and contrary to humanitarian considerations.[6] Mr. Hagen, former Chair of SCAP's Parole Board, considered the popular movement for release of war criminals to be contrary to the Peace Treaty, while his general impression was that the Japanese passed well beyond war and war guilt.

In October 1952, the NOPAR recommended clemency and parole for Class A war criminals urging for their release by invoking the key points of Prime Minister Churchill's "Two Freedoms" speech, delivered in Dover in 1951 to legitimize their cause—"[...] it is in our interest and duty [...] to bolt out and sweep away the hatred and vengeances of the past." From the NOPAR perspective, the protracted detention of Class A war criminals, who personified the main actors behind the war, lost its meaning and no longer had contribution to make. On the occasion of the entry into force of the Peace Treaty, the Ministry of Justice granted amnesty and reduction of sentence to some minor Japanese criminals to celebrate Japan's newly gained independence but also to send a strong signal to the Allies that the war era was officially behind Japan. The Commission believed that there should be no discrimination against war criminals in the words of National Offenders' Prevention and Rehabilitation Commission's Chairman Matsusuke Shirane.[7]

In the Commission's document, Shirane specified that the sympathies of the public opinion in Japan were not exclusively directed towards Class BC war criminals but were also shifting towards Class A war criminals. The new story that the responsibility for war should not rest only upon their shoulders but be shared "by the Japanese nation as a whole" was gaining acceptance and momentum.[8] For different reasons, the US and other Allies were not quite ready to give a follow-up to the Japan's government requests for a special treatment, in the form of amnesty, clemency, or parole, for 12 Class A war criminals.[9] The CPB was aware of the difficulties that any action on behalf of Class A war criminals at that moment would create diplomatic difficulties for the Allies in reaching a majority decision, agitate their constituencies, and potentially have negative repercussions for the war crimes program in Germany. Most importantly, it would compromise the whole effort for retribution and wipe out the seriousness of crimes prosecuted. Hence, the Class A war criminal file was left to lie dormant.[10]

The Japanese government displayed a rather disparate interest in the release of war criminals. The Ministry of Foreign Affairs was a defender of the "gradual release" view regarding war criminals. Their interaction with foreign governments' representatives resulted in a greater level of awareness about certain governments' adamant opposition to the release of war criminals.[11] The MOJ was advocating the "urgent release" approach of war criminals. Japan was an independent, sovereign nation again which came back into the international arena and that was profoundly incoherent with keeping its own citizens, labeled as "war criminals," imprisoned in Sugamo. As there were many other sensitive issues to deal with in the immediate post-occupation period, Yoshida chose to exercise prudence in not provoking agitation both at home and abroad over the issue of war criminals that were not regarded as ordinary felons, but were accused of the most heinous crimes.[12] In the atmosphere of political uncertainty brought by the political comeback of influential politicians, previously purged under the occupation, such as Hayato Ikeda, Prime Minister Yoshida dissolved the Diet on August 28, 1952, and organized general elections in October 1952. This opportune political move was motivated by Yoshida's awareness of his little coordinated opposition consisting of political figures who wanted to oust him from power. In such a precarious political atmosphere and to appeal to the growing demands of public opinion for the release of war criminals, Chief Cabinet Secretary Hori Shigeru announced that recommendations for release would be sent to various governments. In addition, the pressures from the Diet for the release of war criminals were intensifying. In August 1952, Foreign Minister Katsuo Okazaki tried to elicit the release of war criminals[13] by linking it to the anniversary of Japan's acceptance of the Potsdam Declaration which defined the terms of Japan's surrender and posed the legal basis for the establishment of the war crimes program. Given the occasion, he requested the grant of general clemency or amnesty release of all BC Class criminals, with the exclusion of Class A war criminals who were linked to the Tokyo Tribunal.[14]

U. Alexis Johnson from the State Department's Far Eastern Bureau considered the demand unfortunate in that it could escalate into a political issue and be negatively received by the American press and public opinion which believed that justice had been done in Tokyo.[15] The decision-makers in the US refused to readjust their legalistic policies when it came to the war crimes program. In November 1952, on the occasion of the investiture of the Crown Prince, the Japanese government sent telegrams to all concerned governments asking for the general release of Class A war criminals and expressing concern that the public pressure placed upon Yoshida could also be targeting the US. A few lines in the telegram displayed the Japanese government's assertiveness in stating that Class A war criminals "had been imprisoned for seven years and the purpose of punishment was accomplished,"[16] hence openly questioning the sentences imposed by the IMTFE. In the same way the Japanese seized every occasion to stress the domestic aspects of the issue,[17] the US also decided to instrumentalize its own public opinion which would "not tolerate indiscriminate mass releases,"[18] and insisted that Japanese demands perturbed the parole system, which was based on examining cases on an individual basis with low-level publicity.[19] Another line of defense used was that if Class A war criminals were released, it would have repercussions for all Class BC war criminals.

In December 1952, Justice Minister Takeru Inukai appeared before the plenary session of the Lower House—the day the resolution for the release of the war criminals was passed—and presented the government's efforts for parole or amnesty of Class A war criminals, to which governments of China and India consented which was received with applause from Diet members.[20] Ambassador Murphy warned the State Department that the continuous incarceration of war criminals could lead to constant pressures from Japan for their release. To support this belief, he drew attention to Mamoru Shigemitsu, a member of the Lower House of Representatives who was expected to become one of the leading figures in Japanese politics and who openly opposed the clemency and parole system and argued for general amnesty as he considered trials were "defective and committed injustices."[21] Shigemitsu, and not erroneously, predicted that judicial solutions due to their "tediousness" would have negative repercussions for US-Japan relations and that resentment because of the incarceration was widespread.[22]

On December 24, 1952, the Japanese Diet approved the amendments to Law No. 103, Article 24, which allowed prisoners to be released for "provisional parole" for unspecified special circumstances up to 15 days, renewable for an additional 15 days, and without reference to the consultation with the interested governments. In other words, as there were no limits set for the number of renewals a prisoner could apply for under "provisional parole," war criminals could stay outside indefinitely. The US saw these vague provisions as highly problematic from the point of view of Article 11 of the Peace Treaty and questioned Japanese good faith in carrying out its terms.[23] Ambassador Murphy warned that "[t]his Japanese Amendment [...] opens door to wide-spread release of war criminals under guise of emergency conditions in violation of Article 11 of the Peace Treaty."[24] In this sense, the measure was oblivious to negative consequences it could produce for the Allied powers' countries, and most importantly the US which aimed to base the program on careful judicial review of each case and prevent its further politicization. In response, the US pressed the Japanese government to ensure that no extension of provisional parole beyond five days that had been already granted should be approved without referral to the interested government,[25] while in case of emergency provisional paroles, the US Embassy would have authority to grant the final approval.

Another reason for Yoshida's prudence was the erroneous understanding that Class A war criminals represented a benchmark for the whole war criminals release issue, as these were the most notorious cases that, if liquidated, would set in motion the final settlement on the war criminal question.

Regional Powerplay Outside of the IMTFE

The clemency and parole process similar to the IMTFE establishment process, which involved coordination between the Allied powers, was not immune from their inter-relational dynamics and geopolitical considerations. Although the IMTFE has often been portrayed as an American Tribunal, in reality it was an international experience where other interested countries tried to challenge the US lead. The US outnumbered other countries when it came to the war criminals tried under US authority and held in Sugamo Prison. Hence, it was the expectation of the Japanese government that the release pace set by the US would be followed by other countries.[26] However, despite occasional considerations for speeding up the process of release by granting clemency or amnesty mentioned earlier, the US was attached to the preservation of the judicial character of the procedure, hoping that it would not become a political one, in a manner that did not really help the process. Ironically, the Tokyo Trial had never been immune to politics. In the immediate geopolitical vicinity dictated by the Cold War mentality and the Korean War, the outlook upon the Tokyo Trial was reconfigured as the premises of the immediate postwar international order failed to perform in preserving peace. Japan became a US ally, an integral part of its security umbrella, the nation that was proactively pursuing its international comeback.

The first point of contention between the original group of the Allied powers was the participation of governments that did not sign and ratify the Peace Treaty with Japan. The participation of governments represented on the Tribunal in reaching the majority decision for the release of war criminals was stipulated by Article 11 of the Peace Treaty on the basis of their representation on the Tribunal. Article 25 was, however, formulated to preclude the application of the Peace Treaty terms onto non-signatories and hence implied their inability to vote in the decision-making process regarding the release of war criminals. In the initial deliberations, the British proposed that the fate of major war criminals, as Class A war criminals were otherwise called, whose actions were predominately related to the USSR and China, should not be settled by majority governments in Washington, but rather dealt with on a bilateral basis between Japan and the respective countries. Britain pondered whether China might be included in the majority governments' decision-making as Japan signed the Peace Treaty with the Nationalist Government of China or whether China, USSR, and India should be left out as they were not signatories of the Peace Treaty with Japan.[27]

In November 1952, the Japanese government approached India to support the clemency for 12 Class A war criminals, which India accepted. In the spring of 1953, the Japanese Foreign Ministry informed India that as it was a non-signatory of the Peace Treaty, its right to vote should be transferred to Pakistan which was the successor state to British India. India was not really interested in Japan's major war criminals issue but rather in using this occasion to give a vent to its frustration and dissatisfaction over Britain excluding it from consultations to the advantage of Pakistan which was included in the majority deliberations.[28] The State Department saw the inclusion of Pakistan, previously not represented at the Tribunal, as unwise, whereas it saw a strategic value in including the three other governments, especially the USSR. The Soviet negative stance towards the release could not affect the majority decision but could generate a more valuable result of increasing resentment towards the Soviets among the Japanese.[29] In their note to the secretary of state, the Indian government explained that it reserved its right of participation in the clemency process based on its representation at the IMTFE even after its independence in

1947. The note stressed that both Britain and Pakistan agreed that after the partition India was solely entitled to assume memberships to international organizations and treaties.[30] The US decided to comply with the British request in its reply to the Indian government in asserting that Article 25 of the Treaty precluded India from participating, while Pakistan, according to international law, was entitled to be granted rights and obligations that belonged to British India that participated on the Allied side in the war against Japan.[31] The advanced legal explanations were ambiguous and not quite correct but truly reflected the Cold War and postcolonial mentalities.[32] Prime Minister Nehru was infuriated at the ill treatment of India and the fact that Britain agreed with other countries that Pakistan could also pretend to be legal successor of British India which it qualified as outright violation of international law.[33] The real concern was that the language of the reply would have repercussions on other diplomatic questions where the argument that Pakistan was a successor state to British India could be advanced to India's disadvantage.[34]

Differences in diplomatic outlooks on postwar Japan and domestic factors in respective countries were factors that introduced complications in terms of pace and method of releasing war criminals. The Commonwealth countries and the Dutch held particularly conservative positions. The British considered the Japanese government tactic in demanding general amnesty imprudent in view of the British sailors' incident that stressed Anglo-Japanese relations in the second half of 1952. The officials in London were livid at the harsh sentences that the Japanese authorities imposed upon two drunk British sailors who were convicted for robbery and violence against a taxi driver, who had his money returned.[35] Initially sentenced to two and a half years of imprisonment, the British sailors were eventually released in November 1952. In the negotiations for Japan's accession to the GATT, the British decided not to offer their support despite pressures coming from Washington. The British did recognize the status of Japan as an important and significant partner; however it kept a suspicious eye on its rearmament and frustratingly searched for a way to engage with it, especially since its preponderance in the Asia-Pacific region had been challenged by Pax Americana.[36] Such British attitudes ought to be placed within the larger context of its position being relegated to a secondary role in the postwar international order where it no longer belonged to the premier league in which the US and the USSR dominated. Hitherto, the British were bothered by the US-sponsored Japanese rearmament and US-Japan "unhealthily intimate bonds."[37] Furthermore, the signing of the ANZUS Treaty in 1951 resulting in Australia and New Zealand exclusive military alliance with the US was regarded as international indignation to the Britain.[38] Lord Hankey, the UK cabinet secretary throughout the world wars, and author of *Politics, Trials and Errors*, published in 1950, emerged as a vocal critic of the post-World War II war crimes trials in both Japan and Germany. On July 31, 1952, he wrote to the editor of *The Times* that "the war crimes trials now proposed by the Chinese" are just "poisoning peace with no benefit to anyone."[39] In an unapologetic style, he insisted that "[t]he allies should admit that Nuremberg and Tokyo had not fulfilled the hopes of their originators, and should adopt a policy of liquidation."[40] He proposed that general amnesty be given to German and Japanese war criminals and that exclusive authority over the release process should be transferred to their respective governments. He further pointed out to the fact that Britain had never tried any of its military for crimes against peace and crimes against humanity which implied that it did consider them to be punishable crimes.

Australia was one of the Commonwealth countries that was slow to readjust to the view of Japan as a Cold War ally of the West. The war memories and Japan's colonial past continued to play a significant role in feeding feelings of suspicion in Canberra which led to its unwillingness to allow any form of clemency or a major concession for Japanese war criminals. The domestic hatred against Japan was running high which gave the Australian government a powerful pretext not to initiate or agree to any breakthroughs on the war criminal question. Justice William F. Webb of Australia, the presiding judge at the Tribunal appointed by General MacArthur, notorious for his domineering posture and his previous involvement into war crimes investigations in Australia, made sure that Australian and British interests were imposed at the courtroom. Upon his return to Australia, he gave an interview which reflected his racial bias and suspicious stance towards Japan. In a nutshell, the statement showed his deprecation for Japanese democracy and conviction that the security of "White Australia" rested upon its close relations with powerful states and neighbors.[41]

The Netherlands government's position was mainly dominated by stagnation in Japan's compensations towards the Dutch internees, the popular anti-Japanese sentiment, and the general dissatisfaction with the way in which the worst atrocities were prosecuted. These determined the degree of Dutch responsiveness towards the evolution of the clemency and parole program.[42] Regarding Class A war criminals, the Dutch government first considered that they should not receive better treatment than Class BC war criminals,[43] a position that would soon change. The French government was ready to grant parole or clemency to all Class A war criminals who were over 70 years old or in consideration of the extent of their contribution to the aggressive policies in the desire to bring a quick solution to the problem which was objectionable to the CPB which was concerned with considering each case on its merits.[44]

The method of notifying the Japanese government on the decisions regarding Class A war criminals brought into focus among the Allies' representatives in Washington the question to what degree should the Japanese government be informed about their individual positions or deliberations leading to the final decision. The US wanted to preserve the right to include its government's individual position in each case, after stating the majority decision, in order to be able to distinguish itself from other governments in case of a negative majority decision. Britain, on the other hand, argued that the decisions reached by the majority of governments should be communicated to Japan en bloc, in reference to consultation among its participants, "thus relieving the governments in minority of the onus attached to their position."[45] It was of the utmost importance that the Allied powers' deliberation process remain secret for the Japanese government, more precisely reasons behind the majority decision regarding the Japanese government applications for clemency and parole.[46] The notes regarding the release of Class A war criminals were to be kept low profile and not publicized in the Allied powers' capitals as it risked to provoke public clamor. The UK, the Netherlands, and New Zealand decided they would not use the faculty of individual decision,[47] and the British decided to press the US to rectify its position as "the US going alone" would complicate other countries' relations with Japan, and consequently make the respective governments less willing to support the US policies towards Japan, such as rearmament.[48] The British wanted to further muddle up the decision-making process by adopting a code of standard to use in preliminary consultations in order to reach a unanimous position, a proposal that the US and Commonwealth countries opposed. The US was of the view that such technicalities would be an unnecessary waste of time that would "leave a problem involving delicate political relations with the Japanese in a state of continued irresolution."[49] For the US it was obvious that as the whole process would be confidential "the Japanese would [not] be able to play politics"[50] in manipulating Allied governments' opposing views.

At the same time when the Allied powers were deciding on the basic framework for decision-making and interacting with the Japanese government in 1953, the Japanese press carried headlines such as "12 Class A War Felons May Be Paroled" by *Mainichi* and "US Offers Plan to Secure Release of 12 War Criminals" by *Nippon Times* which offered the garbled account of the conversation General Snow had with Jun Tsuchiya from the Japanese Embassy in Washington on the matter even before the Japanese government's press release. Snow did promise that, once received, Class A war criminals' applications would be given priority but that only after the president's approval would they be discussed with other governments concerned.[51] The Japanese press enthusiastically reported that the US would be glad to assure the release of Class A war criminals and that it was representing the views of the other eight governments. In order to remedy the confusion that was created among other representatives in Tokyo, the US Embassy sent assurances to other governments that the news was false.[52]

Impossible to Ignore: The Public Sphere and the War Criminal Cause

The Peace Treaty gave impetus to Japanese public opinion and private, religious, and municipal organizations to ask for the release of Japanese war criminals. The associations of war criminals' families and relatives were the first to mobilize and gain the support of the press and media for their cause. The media will become one of the main driving forces "in the war criminals' rise to prominence as a political and social issue."[53] Contrary to the case of Germany where the government's interest in war criminals fate came organically as the elites had never really accepted the authority and judgement of the IMT at Nuremberg which was the widespread belief among the population, in Japan it was the popular movement that propelled the government's action for the release, especially in the first months after the occupation. The general view of the Japanese people was that the ongoing detention of war criminals was not consistent with the newly signed Peace Treaty. This issue represented "relics of the defeat" that ought to be eliminated. It is important to note that the Allied powers were well aware of the possibility of this outcome in 1945 when they urged for the expedite prosecution of the major war criminals who could start gaining reputation of martyrs as the passions of war cooled down. It could be said that the same concerns were shared from 1952 by the Allies, especially the US which needed rearmed Japan as its ally in the Cold War. What's more, the perception of collective war guilt to be shared on a national level rather than individual guilt established by the military tribunals started to emerge. The social and emotional dimension of the issue made headlines in editorials that diffused a narrative of *Japan* paying its debt to the world community, not only the *war criminals*.

The relaxation of press censorship gave space to new stories to be told about war criminals and war experience.[54] At the beginning, this freedom was scarcely explored as the articles questioning the quality of justice and the legality of the military tribunals under the rubric of victors' justice were rather occasional and articles related to atomic bombings and related crimes against humanity were seldom.[55] In the words of John M. Steeves, political counselor at the US Embassy in Tokyo, the press was extensively reporting on vociferous criticism towards the legal principles, sentences, and authority of the military tribunals coming from Class BC war criminals in Sugamo Prison.[56] Unrepentantly, press accounts expressed their belief that they should have never been prosecuted, "that they were taking responsibility for Japan's defeat on behalf of the Japanese people,"[57] and urged for their immediate release. Invoking "superior orders" to advocate for their innocence, and expressing strong disillusionment with the military organization, they reportedly sent letters to young officers from the Public Security Force to discourage them from enlisting.[58]

In the first years of occupation, Class A prisoners were rather left out of the press as they refused to be interviewed, according to the Embassy dispatch. They remained peaceful and confident in that before Class BC war criminals were released, their cases could not be considered.[59] A more credible reason can be found in a rather ambiguous popular position towards them. First and foremost, they were the main characters behind planning and waging war of aggression, thus bringing Japanese people to the brink of misery and poverty for which they deserved to be punished. This view rooted in the Tokyo Tribunal version of events and enshrined in the majority judgement, remained unchallenged by the harsh censure during the occupation. The fact that there were classes of war criminals and that those tried at Tokyo were Class A was self-explicatory; they were the worst kind of criminals.[60]

This differentiation between war criminals was visible in the Diet debates. On July 30, 1953, Naruse Banji, the representative of the Socialist Party, during his talk regarding the amendment to the Pension Law, said that he had sympathy for Class BC war criminals while he stressed that it should be made clear that Class A war criminals were the responsible ones for the

Pacific War, although they were not prosecuted domestically.[61] Later in 1954, the same amendment was debated regarding the possibility that the families of executed war criminals and those who died in prison could benefit from the same financial support that the families of war dead had received.[62] Considerable portion of the Japanese society was concerned about the rise in prominence of war criminals, their victimization, which cast a shade onto Japan's war guilt, and was potentially dangerous for postwar Japan.[63] The social aspect of the war criminal problem, various forms of discrimination they suffered or difficulties in finding employment, the families of deceased or executed war criminals who remained without financial support, and the financial misery of families of Sugamo prisoners were underreported by the press and representatives of these less empathetic parts of the society.[64] The general empathy for war criminals' suffering and families that was gaining powerful momentum throughout 1953 had slowly started having a spillover effect upon the views of Class A war criminals as well. Thousands of petitions that were sent to foreign representatives and governments by private associations, prefectural assemblies, and war criminal families mainly asking for the release of Class BC war criminals also started including the 13 Class A war criminals into their demands.

One of the postwar pioneers of historical revisionism was Tanaka Masaaki, who was editor of the paper of the Great East Asian Association, the organization whose chairman was General Matsui Iwane, the IMTFE defendant sentenced to death in 1948.[65] In his book, which had a misleading title, *On Japan's Innocence: The Truth on Trial*, published right after the media censure was terminated, he accurately summarized Justice Pal's dissenting opinion.[66] However, the title was highly problematic as it implied Japan's innocence. Pal's opinion was not applicable to all Japanese war criminals, but was applicable to Class A war criminals. In his dissent, he did find that Class BC war criminals bore criminal responsibility for atrocities they had committed. The term "innocence" related to Class A war criminals was established from the point of view of the international law in force at that time which did not strip them of their moral responsibility.[67]

In early 1953, there was a general feeling that the government did not do enough for the war criminals which encouraged various associations and influential public figures to appeal stronger for their release not only within Japan, but also extended their demands to foreign embassies, and governments, including Presidents Truman and Eisenhower. The end of the occupation removed restrictions that SCAP purge directives placed upon the public and military officials in Imperial Japan which brought them back into political life. Many of these figures had a personal or institutional link to the Tokyo Tribunal and other military tribunals which made for a foundation of their commitment to the war criminals' release cause. Some among them felt guilt as they were not the ones prosecuted, purged, or incarcerated which made them feel as they ought to return a favor to their fellow, less fortunate colleagues.[68] Furthermore, what made others bandwagon was that the political, social, and emotional aspect of the war criminals question made it a fertile ground for gathering political votes. Mamoru Shigemitsu, former Class A war criminal convicted by the IMTFE and released in 1950 by the SCAP Parole System, became the chairman of the Progressive Party or Kaishintō in 1952. Among the released Class A war criminal suspects were Nobusuke Kishi, member of the Liberal Party elected to the Diet in 1953, Genki Abe, a candidate for general elections for Lower House in 1952, Ryōichi Sasakawa, who was indirectly involved in Japan's postwar politics by helping political parties and businesses as a highly influential and wealthy businessman. From persons institutionally related to the work of the IMTFE was Ichirō Kiyose, General Tōjō's defense attorney, formerly purged by SCAP, who returned to politics as a secretary-general of Kaishintō.[69]

On December 16, 1952, the National Convention for the immediate release of the war criminals was held and attended by many of the abovementioned public figures and others, such as Shūmei Ōkawa, the Class A defendant dismissed during the Trial as mentally unfit, and later released from the mental hospital in 1948. They provided support for the Declaration which openly challenged the Trial.[70] The Declaration rejected the legal grounds of the Tribunal as contrary to international law and treaties, "unilateral judgements as revengeful,"[71] and based on flawed investigations which only brought indignation and sorrow to the Japanese. The detained war criminals represented an impediment to Japan's reintegration to postwar international relations read the concluding paragraph of the Declaration.[72]

One of the most influential private groups that worked on behalf of the war criminals was the Association for Relief of War Criminals, whose director was Chūichi "King Kong" Hara, an admiral in Japanese Imperial Navy, who was prosecuted for war crimes in an American military tribunal in Guam and released from Sugamo on April 19, 1951.[73] In 1953, he was appointed by the Ministry of Justice as an advisor to the chief of the Rehabilitation Bureau, his functions mainly consisting of preparing parole applications of war criminals for the Allied powers' governments and helping rehabilitation of the released war criminals. At the same time the Ministry of Justice decided to organize vocational guidance program for war criminals in Sugamo Prison which aimed to be a way for them to earn money, made available from the Ministry of Finance funds, which was promised to be given to them as a reward after their release.[74]

Other than many Americans of Japanese descent who used their influence to promote the resolution of the Japanese war criminal issue, among influential Americans who traveled to Japan was E. Stanley Jones, Methodist Christian Missionary. In his letter to General Snow, he rightly observed that "the whole affair has spilled over from judicial to the political and to the human […] This can no longer be looked as a merely judicial affair and confined to that area."[75]

By the end of 1953, while the sympathy for war criminals reached new peaks, the situation in Sugamo was becoming critical with loose discipline and threats of mass escape.[76] In September 1953, the Sugamo Prison Committee concluded that there was a lack of understanding among people regarding the distinction between Class A and Class BC war criminals which had been hindering the release movement. The petitions were no longer enough in order for the movement to finally transition from social to political one in order to gain vigor. Despite this public outcry and political engagement around the war criminals release, Yoshida kept his conservative stance towards this issue. The Committee expressed frustration at the "stubborn" war criminal problem in relation to the US and Britain, which were linking the release of war criminals with the Korean War and Japanese rearmament. The report suggested that Japan should exploit its renewed and strengthened international stance under the peaceful offensive by the USSR and Communist China in order to make the US and Britain speed up and settle the war criminal problem.[77] Although the issue of war criminals had not yet reached its peak on the political agenda, both Japan and the US were, in their own way, using the war criminals release as a trump card in dealing with each other with more or less success.

Notes

1. Ibid.
2. Background Information Re Japanese Law 103 of 1952 "Concerning the Enforcement of Sentences, the Granting of Clemency Etc. In Accordance with the Provisions of Article 11 of the Treaty of Peace." In Records of CPB in NARA II, RG220, Box 1.
3. Ibid.

4. Ibid.
5. Ibid., 347–348.
6. Minutes, October 6, 1952, NARA, RG 220, Box 1, folder: Minutes CPB, M-1 through M-30.
7. Ibid.
8. Matsusuke Shirane, "Decision on Recommendation on Release by Clemency of A Class War Criminals," October 20, 1952 in NARA, RG84, Japanese War Criminals, Box 1.
9. Minutes, November 20, 1952, NARA, RG 220, Box 1, folder: Minutes CPB, M-8.
10. Minutes, December 11, 1952, NARA, RG 220, Box 1, folder: Minutes CPB, M-10.
11. Higurashi Yoshinobu, *Tōkyō saiban* (Kodansha: Tokyo, 2008), 359.
12. Ibid.
13. Telegram, Murphy, American Embassy, Tokyo to Secretary of State, August 21, 1952 in NARA, RG84, Japanese War Criminals, Box 1.
14. Memorandum, "Japanese War Criminals," Mr. Hawley, August 14, 1952 in NARA, RG84, War Criminals – General Files, Box 28.
15. Ibid.
16. Memorandum, "Japanese Embassy Requests for Special Clemency to War Criminals on Occasion of Investiture of Crown Prince Akihito," November 7, 1952 in NARA, RG84, War Criminals – General Files, Box 28.
17. Telegram, Secretary of State to American Embassy, Tokyo, November 10, 1952 in NARA, RG84, Box 1.
18. Telegram, Mr. Robert D. Murphy to Secretary of State, November 10, 1952 in NARA, RG84, Japanese War Criminals, Box 1.
19. Ibid.
20. Dai-15 Kokkai Honkaigi Dai-11, December 9, 1952. http://kokkai.ndl.go.jp/SENTAKU/syugiin/015/0512/01512090512011a.html (accessed on September 4, 2017).
21. Letter of Robert Murphy from the American Embassy in Tokyo to Conrad Snow, October 27, 1952, NARA, RG220, Box 9.
22. Ibid.
23. Deptel, Murphy, American Embassy, Tokyo to Secretary of State, January 6, 1953, in NARA, RG84, War Criminals – General, Box 28.
24. Telegram, Murphy to Secretary of State, December 30, 1952 in NARA, RG84, Japanese War Criminals, Box 1.
25. Ibid.
26. Dispatch, John M. Steeves, American Embassy, Tokyo to State Department, October 2, 1952 in NARA, RG84, Japanese War Criminals, Box 1.
27. Memorandum of Conversation, "Implementation of Article XI of the Peace Treaty with Respect to War Criminals Sentenced by the IMTFE, June 15, 1952, in NARA, RG84, Japanese War Criminals, General Files, Box 26.

28. Telegram from Murphy of American Embassy Tokyo to Secretary of State, April 15, 1953, NARA, RG220, Box 1.
29. Memorandum, Department of State, "Governments Entitled to Participate Under Article 11 of the Peace Treaty in Decision with Respect to War Criminals Sentenced by the IMTFE," April 29, 1952, in NARA, RG84, Japanese War Criminals, Box 1.
30. Telegram from Mills of American Embassy, New Delhi to Secretary of State, April 28, 1953, NARA, RG220, Box 1.
31. Working Papers Reg A, B, + C War Criminals, Folder 1, Dispatch from Robert W. Zimmermann, American Embassy to London to State Department, July 28, 1953 in NARA, RG220, Box 1.
32. James Burnham Sedgwick, "The Trial Within: Negotiating Justice at the International Military Tribunal for the Far East, 1946–1948," (PhD diss., University of British Columbia, 2012), 334. https://open.library.ubc.ca/cIRcle/collections/ubctheses/24/items/1.0072876 (accessed November 14, 2017)
33. General Working Files, Robert Trumbull, "War crimes issue still irks Nehru," *The New York Times*, October 5, 1954, NARA, RG220, Box 5.
34. G. D. Anderson, Commonwealth Relations Office, London to L. Cole, New Delhi (5 August 1954), NZ Archives, EA W2619 54,106–3-39 Part. Cited in James Burnham Sedgwick, "The trial within: negotiating justice at the International Military Tribunal for the Far East, 1946–1948," 334.
35. Sandra Wilson, Robert Cribb, Beatrice Trefalt, Dean Aszkielowic, *Japanese War Criminals: The Politics of Justice After the Second World War* (New York: Columbia University Press, 2017), 185.
36. Makoto Iokibe, Caroline Rose, Tomaru Junko, and John Weste, eds., *Japanese Diplomacy in the 1950s: From Isolation to Integration* (Abingdon: Routledge, 2011), 35.
37. Iokibe et al., eds., *Japanese Diplomacy in the 1950s*, 36.
38. Ibid., 36.
39. The CPB, Minutes, October 27, 1952, folder: Minutes, M-6 in NARA, RG 220, Box 1.
40. Ibid.
41. "Warning on Japan," *Sidney Morning Herald*, December 7, 1948, cited in Sedgwick, *"The Trial Within,"* 316.
42. Dispatch, John M. Steeves, American Embassy, Tokyo to State Department, October 2, 1952, in NARA, RG84, Japanese War Criminals, Box 1.
43. Summary of Meeting, November 5, 1953, of Representatives of IMTFE Governments with Respect to Class A War Criminals in NARA, RG84, War Criminals – General, Box 28.
44. Memorandum for the Record, Mr. Pelletier, French Embassy, Mrs. Dunning, March 2, 1953, NARA, RG220, Box 1.

45. Memorandum, Department of State, "Governments Entitled to Participate Under Article 11 of the Peace Treaty in Decision with Respect to War Criminals Sentenced by the IMTFE," April 29, 1952, in NARA, RG84, Japanese War Criminals, Box 1.
46. Summary of Meeting, February 19, 1953, of Representatives of interested governments on procedure to deal with Class A war criminals, NARA, RG220, Box 1.
47. Memo for Ambassador, "Class A War Criminals Conference," Jules Bassin, March 3, 1953, in NARA, RG84, War Criminals – General, Box 28.
48. General Working Files, copy of report from Mr. Dunning, "Loose Ends with respect to Class A War Criminals," April 10, 1953, NARA, RG220, Box 5.
49. General Papers Re A, B, + C War Criminals, From Kenneth Young, Direction of Northeast Asian Affairs to Arthur R. Ringwalt, American Embassy to London, June 3, 1953 in NARA, RG220, Box 1.
50. Ibid.
51. Telegram from Dulles to American Embassy Tokyo, March 25, 1953, NARA, RG220, Box 5.
52. Telegram, Murphy, American Embassy, Tokyo to Secretary of State, March 26, 1953 in NARA, RG84, War Criminals – General, Box 28.
53. Ibid.
54. Ibid.
55. Foreign Service Dispatch, John M. Steeves, US Embassy Tokyo to the Department of State, October 2, 1952, NARA, RG220, Box 5.
56. Ibid.
57. Wilson et al., *The Japanese War Criminals: The Politics of Justice After the Second World War*, 189.
58. Utsumi Aiko, *Sugamo purizun*: senpantachi no heiwa undō (Tōkyō: Yoshikawa Kōbunkan, 2004), 147–48 cited in Ibid., 195.
59. Foreign Service Dispatch, John M. Steeves, US Embassy Tokyo to the Department of State, October 2, 1952, NARA, RG220, Box 5.
60. Wilson et al., *Japanese War Criminals: The Politics of Justice After the Second World War*, 191.
61. Dai-016 Kai Kokkai Honkaigi Dai 29, July 30, 1953.
62. Higurashi, *Tōkyō saiban*, 360.
63. Wilson et al., *Japanese War Criminals: The Politics of Justice After the Second World War*, 193–194.
64. Ibid., 194.
65. Nakajima Takeshi, "The Tokyo Tribunal, Justice Pal and the Revisionist Distortion of History," *The Asia-Pacific Journal*, Vol 9, Issue 44 No 3, October 31, 2011. http://apjjf.org/2011/9/44/Nakajima-Takeshi/3627/article.html (accessed June 13, 2016).

66. Ibid.
67. Ibid.
68. Wilson et al., *Japanese War Criminals The Politics of Justice After the Second World War*, 196.
69. Ibid.
70. Dispatch from the American Embassy in Tokyo, Purpose of the People's Convention on Immediate Release of War Criminals (Translation), January 13, 1953, NARA, RG220, Box 5.
71. Ibid.
72. Ibid.
73. Working Papers Re A, B, +C War Criminals, Folder 1, Dispatch from William Leonheart, American Embassy Tokyo to State Department, Legal Advisor, July 6, 1953, in NARA, RG220, Box 5.
74. Ibid.
75. Letter E. Stanley Jones to Edward Snow, April 24, 1953, NARA, RG220, Box 5.
76. General Files 1952–1958, Walter Simon, "Fear Escape of War Criminals in Jap Prison, "September 19, 1953, in NARA, RG220, Box 5.
77. General Files, 1952–1958, "Gist of the Enforcement of the Last Release Movement Policy, Sugamo Management Committee," September 1, 1953, in NARA, RG220, Box 5.

CHAPTER 10

From Criminals to Spirits: Class A War Criminals

HIDING BEHIND THE CURTAIN OF "LEGALISM"

The classification of war criminals into Classes A and BC created a confusion during the post-institutional phase of the Trial as its main stakeholders created different expectations for each group. As noted in Chap. 9, Class A war criminals were stigmatized as "the worst ones" by Japanese public opinion and by the Japanese government. They were seen as a benchmark against which the success of the release process could be assessed. Once Class A war criminals were released, the release of BC war criminals would be quasi automatic. Nevertheless, the classification only indicated the type of crime and the rank of its perpetrator, not the seriousness of the crime. In addition, terms such as "major" interchangeably used for Class A war criminals and "minor" for Class BC war criminals fostered this logical but erroneous perception not only for the Japanese government and people but the Allies themselves.

In 1945, it was of utmost importance for the Allied powers to mete out stern justice to individuals whose names were publicly sound—Hideki Tōjō, besides Emperor Shōwa, was leading as the Japanese equivalent of German Kaiser Wilhelm II. Among the BC war criminals facing justice for conventional war crimes and crimes against humanity, however, were those guilty of crimes such as vivisections and bacteriological testing which were considered to be some of the most heinous crimes. The classification of war against peace as "the supreme crime" at the IMT at Nuremberg was a consequence

A. Babovic, *The Tokyo Trial, Justice, and the Postwar International Order*, New Directions in East Asian History,
https://doi.org/10.1007/978-981-13-3477-1_10

of the desire to justify its centrality to the Tribunal's prosecutorial effort. In this regard, for the majority of the Allied powers' governments, Class A war criminals were not necessarily the most problematic or worst criminals to deal with. In other words, the release of Class A war criminals was not a sine qua non of the release process for Class BC criminals. These misunderstandings were a source of frustration and confusion that stressed the unfolding of the clemency and parole program on both sides.

In 1953, the Clemency and Parole Board (CPB) received the first recommendations for the release of Class A war criminals from the Japanese Ministry of Foreign Affairs—notably for Jirō Minami, Shunroku Hata, and Takazumi Oka. In March 1953, the former IMTFE Chief Prosecutor Joseph Keenan was on a private visit to Tokyo where he met with Prime Minister Yoshida and other officials and received an audience with the Emperor.[1] The encounter naturally led to a discussion on the war criminals, albeit not officially. The Japanese press reported that the US government requested the ex-Prosecutor's views on the war criminals' parole which were to be decisive on the matter. In his grandiloquent-like manner, Keenan said that quasi almost all of the 12 Class A war criminals "[could] be released without danger to world peace."[2] Ironically, Keenan was still framing the narrative around golden age Class A war criminals in terms of world peace, whereas the peace promised to be maintained and war crimes deterred, by the UN Charter and war criminal tribunals in 1945, respectively, had been usurped in not so faraway battlefields of the Korean Peninsula. Few months later, Keenan visited the CPB where he voiced his opinions on Class A war criminals with respect to their rank and the potential threat they posed to postwar Japan. Although the IMTFE obviously failed at educating the Japanese, General Snow's notes[3] of the meeting captured Keenan's candid view of what goals the Trial was meant to fulfill. It was not so much about the deterring effect, but rather it was used to "inform Japanese people of how they got into war," and "to reduce effect of exulted function of defendants on the people."[4] These words explained the challenges of the prosecution to convict the representatives of each phase of the war faced with meager evidence. In that context, the multiple criteria that were used relied on their rank, reputation, and visibility during the war in order to assure their conviction. In Keenan's evaluation Minami and Araki were described as not "rabble-rousing" which recommended them for clemency, while he held some reservations for Hata due to the high rank he held in the Army. As the only field marshall, Hata was one of the key figures in the China phase of the Trial—convicted of negative criminal responsibility and war crimes committed on a large scale and over a long period of time by his troops in China—although his conviction was made upon prima facie evidence.[5] Kenryō Satō, lieutenant general, who had never held the highest-level cabinet or army posts, and Okinori Kaya, minister of finance, both Tōjō's protégés were recommended for clemency as they were not "fanatic and war promoters." Having in mind that these individuals were charged with aggressive war charge, these labels came as a posteriori confession on the arbitrary choice of defendants. Among those pre-approved for clemency by Keenan was Naoki Hoshino, one of the prominent entrepreneurs and political figures in Manchukuo, and later chief of cabinet in the Tōjō Cabinet. Keenan considered that he would be "of more use outside prison," probably referring to his entrepreneurial skills that were needed in the process of Japan's economic revival. Interestingly, Keenan suggested a careful reexamination of one of the most important defendants at the Trial, the Lord Keeper of the Privy Seal and Advisor to Emperor Kōichi Kido as he thought that "he might have been wrongfully prosecuted." In 1947, Keenan cross-examined Kido in order to elicit from him any information about the Emperor's role in the decision-making process preceding the Pearl Harbor Attack which he thought would support the larger occupation policy of exonerating the Emperor from criminal responsibility. Initially, his cross-examination was supposed to be conducted by Comyns-Carr, the British prosecutor at the IPS, who was in charge of studying Kido's dossier, but at the last moment Keenan bluntly took over without any prior preparation or consultation with other members of the IPS, thus ruining the opportunity for getting important information from "this intelligent and formidable witness."[6] The rest of Class A "villains," according to Keenan, were all listed as more or less dangerous. For instance, Kingorō Hashimoto was branded as an unrepentant "fanatic war monger"; Takazumi Oka, navy vice-admiral, was depicted as a bitter fanatic; and Hiroshi Ōshima, the former Japanese ambassador to Germany; was described as "the most dangerous man in confinement." The list also included Shigetarō Shimada, navy minister during the Pearl Harbor Attack, and Teiichi Suzuki, army general.

In 1953, as the anti-US climate was reaching higher peaks, rumors that Communist China and the Soviet Union were willing to repatriate the Japanese war criminals in their possession further frustrated the Allied powers' "legalistic plan" for the release of war criminals. To be more precise, Japanese POWs were prosecuted in the Communist China Trials in the 1950s where their main purpose was to reeducate the Japanese, contrary to the Allied powers' criminal courts that dwelled on retribution. The Chinese accorded a lot of importance to the trials as a tool for "shifting the imperial mindset" and for making the Japanese express themselves, face their misdeeds, and repent whereas the Chinese appeared as benevolent—the approach was legal, psychological, and political. The Communist Party calculations went beyond benevolence. The Communists Chinese wanted to affirm themselves as capable and legitimate rulers of China and establish relations with Japan,[7] as well as secure its legal presence on the international scene as they lost their opportunity at the Tokyo Tribunal.[8] In the Soviet Union, they were held in concentration camps, while few of them were adjudicated in the Khabarovsk trial. As neither Communist China nor the USSR signed the Peace Treaty with Japan, they had the liberty to organize their own trials. All the Japanese captured by both countries were referred to as "war criminals," not prisoners of war. This strategic move potentially had serious ramifications at various levels. On the one hand, it would add more fuel to the already enflamed Japanese public opinion against the US, their ally, which was slacking its pace of releasing the war criminals behind its legalistic policies, while the Communist countries showed benevolence in dealing with the Japanese. This situation contrary to common sense and logic gave a powerful political tool to the leftist and neutralist elements in Japan to gain more sympathies among the population.[9] The refusal to grant clemency to Class A war criminals Araki and Minami could be evaluated against Communist magnanimity.[10] Neither China nor the USSR was included within the release process by the Allied powers, but they found an effective way to exert influence upon and manipulate emotions of the Japanese population towards the US.

The members of the Japanese House of Representatives met with Walter Robertson and Robert J. G. McClurkin in September 1953 to communicate their fears and urge the US to further speed up the release since the Communist threat loomed large.[11] On October 12, 1953, the Japanese Red Cross helped repatriate 1274 Japanese "war criminals" from Moscow, among which were military and civilians.[12] According to the data held by the Ministry of Foreign Affairs of Japan, there were 68,000 Japanese prisoners of war and civilians in the hands of the Soviets and Chinese who were serving their sentences as war criminals. The situation became more precarious with both the Philippines and China pardoning and releasing war criminals[13] which created the impressions that the Asians did their part, but not the Americans. Furthermore, the release of North Korean and Chinese Communists who had been captured by the Allies in the Korean War and their non-prosecution for atrocities committed against the Americans and United Nations' POWs was one of the first failed tests of postwar international criminal law principles adopted in 1945. What's more, the illegality of waging war, its criminality, along with war crimes and crimes against humanity were disregarded in favor of more pressing matters, and no country wanted to get embroiled in another round of fastidious criminal proceedings. The UN General Assembly Resolution condemning, in vague and unspecified terms, the atrocities against Americans and the UN POWs was released only to appease the Congress and public opinion at home.[14]

The recommendations for clemency of Minami, Araki, and Hata were discussed between the Allied governments' representatives in November 1953. The US supported clemency on the grounds of old age and health for Minami and Araki, who were to be supervised by the attorney general of Japan, but postponement of Hata's case for a later date as he was convicted on counts of war crimes (BC Class) to which the Netherlands, Pakistan, and France all concurred.[15] The Commonwealth countries formed a conservative block that opposed any form of clemency suggesting they would agree to a temporary release for a hospital treatment, upon which they should return back to prison.[16] The UK and Australia were opposed to clemency, even on the grounds of old age which they considered to be insufficient according to their domestic law—the most they could offer was to eventually agree to release the three on parole in 1959. The Australian position was particularly conservative not only because of the suspicions harbored towards Japan and their popular opinion being hostile to the Japanese but also because their criminal system only recognized medical parole and reduction of sentence; hence they were careful about establishing precedents. Australians did not heed much about the fear the US felt as a response to the peaceful offensive by the USSR and "opposed what seemed like US effort to force the issue."[17] In January 1954, a special medical parole was approved by the majority governments only for Minami, 78 years old, who left Sugamo Prison, while Araki, 75, was left for later consideration.

Months prior to Prime Minister Yoshida's official visit to the US scheduled for November 10, 1954, the Japanese Embassy in Washington was laboring hard to persuade the US government to prepare some tangible policies that would speed up the release of war criminals. Embassy officer

Takeuchi pointed at the speedy clearing of German prisons which was frustrating to the Japanese government, as well as the unrest among the war criminals confined in Sugamo that could potentially escalate in the absence of some ameliorations.[18] At this point, war criminals were becoming assertive in demanding a political solution to the issue as they had a clear awareness "that public opinion was an important force behind them, not Yoshida or the US."[19] Ambassador Allison urged Secretary of State Dulles to seize the opportunity and find a solution to the problem, before it was too late. In Allison's words, "failure to attack this problem effectively is bound to cause our broader interest here to suffer increasingly."[20] He rightly observed that "the Japanese attitude was hardening on number of fronts"[21] in light of utmost irritation around the static issue of war criminals and the Bikini Atoll incident. Finally, he warned that this might be the last opportunity to take the maximum benefit of the present situation by offering something of value for Yoshida, still, without jeopardizing US interests.[22] The US could objectively promise to speed up the release of a considerable number of war criminals, while the remaining ones, those who committed egregious crimes, could never be paroled or at least not in the near future.

In 1954, an important change brought about the solution that would speed up the release process while preserving the veil of legality that was of the utmost importance to the US and some of its allies. The expedite judicial review solution was a victory for the legalists in the US government against the repeated calls for granting amnesty or pardon from the Embassy and various State Department officers that was rejected on the grounds that it would nullify the legality of the war crimes program. It was a step forward towards resolving the anti-US "psychological climate not conducive to Japanese cooperation."[23] The US reviewed the CPB parole procedure in responding to the pressures and repeated warnings coming from the Political Division of the US Embassy in Tokyo. It was suggested that "the US government should elaborate a policy or concept as to the time limit in which the war criminal problem can be liquidated."[24] On July 12, 1954, the President approved the CPB proposal for a change in the basic rules governing parole mechanism—one-third of the sentence for those with sentences of 30 years or over and 15-year rule for lifers—which resulted in an all-encompassing 10-year rule which allowed all prisoners to become eligible for parole after having served 10 years of their sentence.[25] In addition, upon the recommendation of the State Department, the CPB agreed to review all the cases and recommend them to the President,[26] with the exception of the Class BC hard-core cases, by the end of 1955 which meant that the war crimes program would be almost liquidated.[27] If the old rules were to remain, the lifers, all of the Class A war criminals, would only become eligible for parole in 1959.

Simultaneously, during 1954, all of the ten remaining Class A war criminals were recommended for clemency by the NOPAR, four of them based on old age, as they were over 70 years old, while the remaining seven were the ones most involved in the aggressive war policy line according to the Board. The Board recommended that in the absence of credible medical records justifying earlier release on medical parole, all the cases would become pending.[28] Recommendations for special medical parole for Hata, whose medical situation was worsening, and Oka, who was not seriously ill, were a thorn in the eye to the CPB as they were also convicted of two other categories of crimes, which could have repercussions for BC war criminals and for those involved in the Pearl Harbor Attack, respectively.[29] For these cases, the CPB required the veracity of Japanese medical reports to be confirmed by an American doctor. Ambassador Allison strongly discouraged this course as it could be interpreted by the Japanese government as questioning of their good faith in applying Article 11 of the Peace Treaty and would create a situation reminiscent of the occupation days.[30] Especially so in the light of the death of Bikini Atoll victim Aikichi Kuboyama and the fact that other governments did not ask for a double confirmation which would additionally enrage the Japanese. In the end, the chairman of the board acquiesced, but still on his own initiative forwarded the Japanese medical report to an army doctor through the US Army Judge Advocate General (JAG) for a comment.[31] The US did not reach a decision on the two, "but not to make impression of dragging their feet," before the other Allies, they attributed the non-decision to the resignation of their Department of Justice Board member.[32] Contrary to Japanese expectations, the US was not always setting an example for other countries by simply approving the recommendations, quite the opposite. The US Embassy in Tokyo feared that if such information leaked to the Japanese, it would come at a high cost for the US. Both Hata and Oka were granted special medical parole by the majority vote from which the US eventually decided to abstain.[33]

In November 1954, the Allied governments were slowly starting to act in concert regarding the Class A war criminals—the ten-year rule was proposed by the New Zealand delegate and the US as a legal basis for their parole, thus making them eligible in 1955 or the beginning of 1956 the latest.[34] The most conservative governments, Australia and Britain, were opposed to this proposition, while France, Pakistan, and the Dutch which supported early clemency and release agreed to these more liberal policies regarding Class A war criminals. Australia was willing to follow the US lead as long as it did not have to be the initiator, due to its domestic concerns.[35] For the Dutch, Class A war criminals could be processed quicker as the justification for its Parliament, and public opinion could be provided "under considerations of international nature."[36] The remaining task was for the Allied powers' respective governments to formulate their positions with respect to individual cases keeping in mind the ultimate goal that was "to dispose of this problem as rapidly as possible."[37]

In the words of J. Graham Parsons, Officer of the US Embassy in Tokyo, during his visit to Washington in November 1954, Yoshida missed his chance to achieve more tangible results regarding the war criminals issue which was not of primary importance for him. Instead, he considered this topic should be left for discussion to lower-level officers who accorded much more attention to it.[38] Although Yoshida's modest efforts regarding war criminals' release did not score high among his diplomatic achievements, things were taking their natural course. Japanese public opinion became intransigent and Yoshida's political base was crumbling, whereas an overall anti-US climate took root. The internal conflict between "political" and "judicial" approaches was slowly converging towards an urgent political solution. It became clear that the war crimes program would have to get the tint of political and finally take more seriously into consideration the diplomatic and geopolitical aspect of its relation with Japan, instead of clinging onto keeping the war criminal program judicial enough. The war criminals question and the insistence on its judicial character were taking toll on the implementation of other important policies, especially related to defense.[39] The Assistant Secretary for East Asia and Pacific Affairs Robertson acknowledged that together with the State Department Legal Advisor, Phleger, who previously vigorously protested a political solution, the issue will be brought to the attention of the Secretary of State.[40]

Difficult Road Towards the Release

The medical parole was the only way in which the Allied powers could effectively justify the release of Class A war criminals on humanitarian grounds but also show themselves as compassionate and merciful towards aged and sick men they did not want to see dying in prison.

In its recommendations for clemency of Class A cases who were over 70, the Japanese government advanced a clause from its Code of Criminal Procedure of 1948 according to which the execution of sentence for prisoners who are at least 70 years old could be stayed on moral grounds. However, not all the Allies were willing to accept the Japanese Criminal Code clauses, but advanced their own as an impediment for casting their favorable vote. The US position was quite prudent when it came to medical parole; the Board was favorable to casting a vote for reasonable requests, but it deplored that the Japanese government in many cases failed to demonstrate the detailed medical condition or ailment of Class A war criminals as they were not all old and sick. The Board concluded that granting them all medical parole would be a farce.

Sadao Araki is a case in point. His application dragged on for two years due to the stark opposition from Commonwealth governments. As the initial application for Araki did not comprise a medical report or any information indicating ailment, his dossier was placed together with other Class A war criminals who were considered for clemency or regular parole. The French government was the most flexible as it was prepared to grant special treatment to Class A war criminals over 70—Minami, Araki, Hata, Shimada, and Kido.[41] The US was concerned that the group releases would jeopardize the proper procedure of reviewing each case on its merits. It was forgotten that these men got into the dock as being part of the group, tacitly or deliberately, which conspired to plan and wage aggressive war. They were only then considered on an individual basis but for their official position within the cabinet. In November 1953, during governmental consultations, the Commonwealth nations were all opposed to any form of clemency based on old age and proposed 1959 as the year to consider parole for Class A war criminals who were not applying for medical parole. According to the Australian penal system, life sentences were considered as 21 years' sentence with remission of one-third for good behavior which would reduce the sentence to 14 years; hence the prisoner would become eligible in 1959.[42] In October 1954, the Canadian government proposed that as Araki was not involved in aggressive policies after 1939, whereas others were, he could be distinguished from other Class A war criminals.[43]

At that time, the US representative proposed that the system of parole, the ten-year rule approved by the president, could also be extended to Class A war criminals who were all serving life sentences.[44] In February 1955, Secretary of State Dulles complained to Jules Bassin, legal attaché in Tokyo Embassy, that the NOPAR medical reports were out of date which posed difficulties in deciding the cases and fed the idea that an American doctor should examine the prisoners directly.[45] The State Department entered into all sorts of legal technicalities to support these requests. In case of medical examination of applicants by an American doctor, the State Department explained that Japanese Law No. 103 contained a provision under which the Japanese government should allow the interested government to send an official to inspect the conditions of the execution of sentence and interview the prisoner.[46] In March 1955, the NOPAR provided a medical report for Araki, 78, that diagnosed him with kidney atrophy due to arteriosclerosis and prognosis was not bright—"recovery is slow and the prospect of recovery extremely poor" concluded the report.[47] On June 14, 1955, the Allies' representatives agreed to grant a special medical parole to Araki.[48] Furthermore, in Hata's application the NOPAR deliberately understated the offenses committed, at his request, in order to make a strong case for clemency and parole.[49] The US was calculating its position in anticipation of other Allies' votes; concretely the CPB agreed that in case of the casting vote, the chairman should oppose clemency, while in case the majority was pro-clemency, he should align.[50] In that sense, the US was not necessarily setting an example for others but was using the positions of other governments to secretly preserve its time-consuming legalistic policies, a time credit that the US had already started to lose.

The medical parole requested for Shigetarō Shimada was pending as the defense member of the Board considered that it would be difficult to release him on a medical parole given the serious offenses he was involved with as navy minister.[51] The member referred to Shimada's support for policies of killing survivors of sunken ships. This offense did not gain prominence at the IMTFE, but his subordinates pleaded guilty in *United States of America v. Hisashi Ichioka, et. al* case in the Yokohama Trials.[52] Together with Kingorō Hashimoto, he was described as "bad eggs," and as they did not suffer from any serious illness, the prospects they would be released were slim in 1954. In his letter to the Embassy in Tokyo, Director of Northeast Asian Affairs from State Department Noel Hemmendinger deplored the almost set in stone rigidity of the US war crimes program: "it was extremely unfortunate that our position is so inflexible [w]hile the other Governments are developing more liberal attitudes as a result of our pressures, our position is remaining static."[53]

This rigidity was reflected when in March 1955 Shimada was granted a medical parole by the majority vote of the interested governments, on the occasion of which the US did not vote and stayed aside as it could not reach position on the case.[54] Hashimoto, although recommended for medical parole by the NOPAR and despite the fact that he had already been hospitalized in 1952, diagnosed with gastric ulcer which might have later developed into cancer, was not granted medical parole. Released on parole in September 1955, he died soon after on June 29, 1957, of lung cancer.[55] It is possible that in case of Shimada, his military record—the top-ranking military officer responsible for his troops' war crimes in USS Panay Incident and portrayed as a staunch promoter of a military control over government, and aggressive war policies through his membership in the Imperial Rule Assistance Association—weighted against the unclear or suspicious diagnosis on his medical record in the deliberations of the CPB. It appears that the US was publicly pretending to be liberalizing its position, while the minutes of the CPB and voting history show that there was a difficulty of loosening the grip of the CPB trio that promoted strict judicial procedures. On numerous occasions the US abstained from voting, shielded by Allied deliberations that were secret in nature. For many of the defendants who were released, the US, contrary to Japanese expectations, did not play an instrumental role. As time passed by, Commonwealth countries started liberalizing their policies which became more receptive of the idea that parole could be granted to Class A war criminals.

The Hatoyama Cabinet and the Shifting Policies: *Jyūnen Hito Mukashi*

A major shift took place with the Hatoyama Cabinet that finally dealt with the war criminals issue at the top governmental level contrary to the previous years where it had been almost exclusively relegated to the lower level where the respective embassies and the CPB were in charge with slight interventions of the State Department and President Eisenhower. In 1955, Allison warned against the pressure placed upon Japan to increase its defense spending which would backfire on the US and introduce considerable resistance to the establishment of the solid foundations for long-term cooperation.[56] Japan was deeply frustrated for not being an equal that could "influence US policy to same degree as major NATO powers"[57] and pursue policies that are in line with its national interest rather than "result of external pressures."[58] This bred a feeling among the Japanese of their country being treated "as second-class nation."[59] The shift in the US policies was to primarily focus on building a solid political and economic basis in Japan which would bring improved confidence and a sense of responsibility and hence become its bouncing-off place for a more robust military buildup.[60]

On December 10, 1954, Ichirō Hatoyama was elected the Prime Minister who ousted Yoshida from power. This change in power would have major repercussions not only for Japanese foreign policy but also for Japanese war criminals, including Class A. In his address before the Diet on January 21, 1955, he talked at the very beginning about his intention to finally resolve the deploring issues of repatriation of the Japanese detainees from abroad and war criminals still detained in Sugamo by appealing to the countries concerned.[61] Prime Minister Hatoyama was determined to urge the US government to speed up the release of war criminals meant to be eligible for parole only in 1959 by considering a reduction of sentence. He argued that US public opinion, often advanced as an excuse by America to justify the reluctance in the release process, should understand that ten years after the war, the Japanese were eager to liberate themselves from the remnants of war and ensure the general release of prisoners and their full freedom which proved to be impossible under the present parole system. During the same month, Foreign Minister Shigemitsu voiced his stance on foreign policy priorities which were the return of Okinawa and resolution of war criminals issue. Shigetmitsu did not hide his deep frustration with the inequality reigning the US-Japan relation—"it is truly distressing to see the scars of the war before our eyes at a time when cooperation with the democratic, free nations is being stressed."[62]

The general elections planned for February 27, 1955, brought before the US, specifically the Secretary of State Dulles, the question of the timing when the decision regarding the release of Japanese war criminals could be announced to provide maximum benefits to the US. Ambassador Allison suggested that as it was expected that the conservatives would win two-thirds of the seats, the announcement before the elections would not contribute to a strengthening of the conservative position and might also be plagued with accusations of American ulterior motives. This option lost appeal to the fact that all the parties across the political spectrum were also eager to see war criminals released as they considered it "as politically motivated and unwarranted influence in Japan's internal affairs."[63] Allison favored the announcement to be given after the elections as a strategic move that would set the US off to a good start in its interaction with the new government and clear the current anti-US environment of tensions so that the negotiations on more important matters could finally take place.[64] Anxiousness over the possibility that the Soviets could offset the US in releasing the Japanese "war criminals" before elections prompted Allison to ask the government to make a final decision as soon as possible.[65] To the disappointment of the State Department officers in charge of the Far East, Dulles refused the recommendation to announce the release of all Class BC war criminals as he thought it would provoke negative reactions on the German side, considerations of which still actively managed to "prejudice" more resolute steps on the Japanese side.[66] The solution that was contemplated was to place the definite authority of granting parole and clemency upon the CPB which would remove the President from the decision-making chain and speed up the process. However, McClurkin was rather pessimistic that all war criminals could be released by the end of 1955 having in mind "the legal approach that dominated the thinking of the Board,"[67] but decided to stay engaged in pressing further for the resolution of Japanese war criminal questions when such opportunity arose.[68]

The amendment to the executive order which would delegate the presidential prerogative to make the final decision regarding the grant of clemency and parole to the CPB stopped the stream of paroles for a few months which further frustrated the Japanese.[69] This decision was deemed necessary in light of relieving the President of such burdensome procedure and in view of other considerations in two countries' relations[70]—one of them being that the clock was ticking for the Americans to show some tangible results on the war criminals' agenda. Although the CPB acquired the authority to act independently, there was no major evidence that the release process was moving forward which seriously started to press and worry the increasingly frustrated officials from the US Embassy in Tokyo and the State Department, who represented the first line of defense against the Japanese pressures, and prompted them to urge for some concrete rules or measures to be adopted that would result in improved relations with Japan.[71] In May, the CPB set the target date, the end of 1956, by which the decisions regarding the BC Class war criminals should be made, except for the hard-core category.[72] For its part, the CPB almost commended itself for the principled and legalistic approach the American war crimes trial program in the Far East had taken.[73] Regarding Class A, the CPB announced that only one Class A war criminal, Kenryō Satō, would be eventually paroled in 1956, thus implying that the remaining ones would be paroled throughout 1955.

In February of the same year, the officer from the Japanese Ministry of Justice Yokomizo traveled to the US to discuss the issue of war criminals with William Sebald and Richard Finn, the State Department officers in charge of Far Eastern Affairs. At this point, the Japanese started expressing frustration over the pace of US release of German war criminals, while the Soviets were ready to release all of the war criminals in their custody. Given the lack of any better answer, Sebald framed his argument legalistically that the Soviet prosecutions of the Japanese for war crimes were not undertaken on any valid international basis.[74] Complaints were coming from the Foreign Ministry Office regarding the discrepancies between Japan and Germany. Throughout 1954 two-thirds of German war criminals were released against only one-fifth of the Japanese.[75]

Under Shigemitsu, the efforts of the Ministry of Foreign Affairs took the shape of a diplomatic offensive. On August 15, 1955, on the occasion of the tenth anniversary of the end of war, the Foreign Ministry sent a verbal note to the US requesting the release of war criminals from Sugamo.[76] The recommendation for the release was prepared by the NOPAR which expected the postwar decade to bring a halt to and remove all vestiges of the war era and principally release the war criminals from confinement. This would be a stepping stone to the deeper and more mature relations between the two countries. Symbolically, this initiative was in line with the Japanese saying *jyūnen hito mukashi* or "ten years make an epoch" which implied that at this turning point the past should be released so that a new basis could be laid for an improved future.[77] On June 3, Shigemitsu expressed what he saw as a major impediment to improved US-Japan relations by saying that "Japan wants to cooperate with the US, but with war criminals still kept in Sugamo, their families and relatives are hardly likely to feel cooperative,"[78] as reported by *Yomiuri*. Eikichi Araki, Governor of the Bank of Japan and the first postwar Japanese Ambassador to the US, also believed that bilateral relations could not be "cemented" without clearing the war criminals' problem which would in return have dramatic impact upon the Japanese attitude towards the US.[79] On July 19, 1955, the House of Representatives passed a resolution urging for the release of all "war prisoners" or *senso jukeisha*[80] referring to those detained in the Soviet Union and war criminals' problem in reference to the Allied powers which should be finally concluded a decade after the end of the war. Tadanori Nagayama, in his speech before the Diet, made a reference to inmates who were 70 or over 70 whose detention was being inobservant to humanitarian considerations. He used the opportunity to refute the Tokyo Tribunal that he called "an arbitrary court" and "revengeful measure" which was contrary to international law and human rights, thus an offense to legalism cherished by civilized nations.[81]

At the end of August 1955, Shigemitsu's week-long visit to the US where he met with Secretary Dulles and other officials was instrumental for discussing key matters burdening bilateral relation. During these talks, in an informal manner, Kishi expressed his view on what he considered the main impediments to the healthy US-Japan relations—that is, military bases in Japan, lack of independence in making its own defense budget and the issue of contributions to the US forces, and finally the detention of war criminals.[82] Unashamedly, Kishi made a remark to US officials that "he and the Foreign Minister had spent some time in Sugamo Prison and could not but be emotionally concerned in obtaining the release of those still in prison as soon as possible,"[83] and expressed his hope that "the United States would take a 'bold stand' and settle this problem once and for all."[84]

On the last day of Shigemitsu's visit to the US, *Asahi* and *Sangyo Keizai* reported, in reference to Reuters dispatch, that Australian Foreign Minister Richard G. Casey revealed that the US and other countries agreed to adopt a more "lenient"[85] attitude towards war criminals and gave the US "a considerable free hand"[86] in resolving the issue during the ongoing negotiations with the Japanese. On September 8, 1955, the representatives of the Allied powers' governments once again discussed the adoption of the ten-year rule for Class A war criminals that had been previously proposed by New Zealand and the US. France and Pakistan, in view of their interest for a prompt liquidation of the war criminals issue, offered their support for the proposal. The Dutch representative expressed his disapproval of adopting any rules or "automatic system of parole" which would prejudice the judicial review of each parole application on an individual basis, and said his government would agree to consider Class A war criminals eligible for parole after they have served ten years of their sentence. The Dutch were the last line of resistance among the eight Allies. They feared that the automatic release on parole for the major Japanese war criminals would make them adopt the same decision regarding the still confined Japanese minor war criminals and German war criminals they held. In the words of the officer from the US Embassy in Hague, the Dutch held "bitter personal memories" and it was politically difficult for them to justify any such lenient position before its Parliament and public opinion.[87] The New Zealand representative considered that the Dutch were just acting for the record and as the decision would be adopted by the majority governments, it would not be as harmful for them.[88] In the end, the governments agreed that the rules by which the majority decision was achieved and the vote cast should remain secret when the decisions for Class A war criminals' parole were notified to the Japanese government,[89] among others not to hurt the results of the negotiations related to the Dutch civilian internees compensation.[90] On September 17, 1955, the representatives unanimously granted parole to Kaya, Hashimoto, and Suzuki after having completed ten years in confinement.[91] *Asahi Evening News* dedicated its front page to the release of the three Class A war criminals, reporting that despite "Shigemitsu's personal pleas,"[92] the Allies refused the wholesale release pointing fingers at the Dutch due to "bitterness at war crimes and inadequate reparations."[93] Hoshino was paroled on December 13, 1955, while Kido and Ōshima were released three days later, after being granted parole by the Allies, while the Netherlands abstained from taking vote.[94]

The governments agreed that no special restrictions, other than those already existing under the Japanese law, would be imposed upon the parolees.[95] The Japanese Embassy tried to press for Satō's earlier release by manipulating the dates of his arrest, but to no avail, and as had been previously mentioned, he was paroled only on March 31, 1956, which meant that Sugamo was finally cleared of Class A war criminals. However, Sugamo was still inhabited by "hard-core" BC war criminals who had committed such heinous crimes that the CPB could no longer find the appropriate basis for their parole.

The Secretary of State recommended that the CPB be abolished which the Board observed as an end to the judicial procedures regarding the Japanese war criminals: "if there exist political or diplomatic problems that render desirable a termination of the present judicial solution of the war criminal program and the substitution of a political solution, the Board has no objection."[96] Harumi Takeuchi, section chief of the American Bureau of the Japanese Foreign Ministry, worried that the release of Class A war criminals, considered to bear greater responsibility for war than those at the "working level," without the simultaneous release of the Class BC war criminals "hue and cry," was to take place in Japan.[97]

Criminals to Men: The Diplomatic Success of the Kishi Cabinet

Kishi's election in February 1957 came as a gift to the American elite and diplomats for his proactive stance towards Japanese rearmament. In the words of Ambassador MacArthur II, he was the man "he could 'do business' with,"[98] and hence urged Washington that it had to seize the opportunity to respond to the Japanese demands for change resulting from a deep sense of frustration and subordination emanating from the unequal security treaty, the Okinawan issue, and trade restrictions with China. Already in 1954, he was "an American favorite"[99] for the position of the prime minister, but conservatives chose Hatoyama instead. Ironically, Kishi was the middleman in connecting the military with the zaibatsu in order to secure investments for the industrial development of Manchuria, Tōjō's Minister of Commerce and Industry at the time of the Pearl Harbor Attack who signed the declaration of war against the US, and a golfing partner of Joseph Grew.[100]

On March 31, 1956, almost all of the Allies' countries, even the most conservative ones, expedited the release process. The Netherlands and Australia both cleared Sugamo from the war criminals they had prosecuted while Communist China had repatriated a large number of Japanese war criminals. Only the US, technically Japan's closest ally, was unable to release the 133 remaining criminals, 50 of whom were under consideration for parole. Under the ten-year rule, many of them were eligible for parole, but the CPB refused to consider their cases or to reduce their sentences to make them eligible still on the grounds of the gravity of crimes committed.[101] In the eyes of the Japanese, the US was gaining the reputation of being "warden of Sugamo."[102] In the light of the Okinawan land issue and discrimination of Japanese textiles, the prospects for amelioration of their bilateral relation only looked bleak.[103]

Given that fact that the German Mixed Parole Board had German members, Shigemitsu urged the US to consider transferring the right to grant clemency and parole for the still imprisoned war criminals in Sugamo to the Japanese government.[104] This was refused on the grounds that such action would have consequences for German war criminals who would likewise have to be released. It would further complicate the matter from the point of view of the need to revise the provisions of the Bonn-Paris conventions and thus place the revision before the Congress that had already been unsupportive of paroles for Dietrich and Peiper,[105] and in relations to Germany which placed the utmost importance to the resolution of the criminals issue.[106] The Germans and Japanese kept an eye on the pace and method of release of war criminals by the US in both nations and constantly drew comparisons in order to get concessions. For instance, in Japan, out of 800 war criminals sentenced by the US, 133 remained in prison as of March 1956, while in Germany out of 665, only 31 remained.[107] The CPB kept refusing Allison's urges to release all of the Class BC criminals to whom it retorted that the Board "can't just be moved about like a chess in handing of the cases," and that if a political solution was to be implemented it should be done under someone else's guise.[108]

The public activity of released Class A war criminals was attracting attention. The *Yomiuri Shimbun* editorial reported about radio lectures given by Araki, Hashimoto, Suzuki, and Kaya which were "reminiscent of wartime atmosphere." Hashimoto was planning to come back to political life, while Araki stated that "Japan was not defeated in a sense" thus appearing as if they left their responsibility for war the day they left Sugamo.[109] The editorial took a rather critical approach in stating that they should exercise prudence in what they do and say as "their patriotism in the newly created postwar political circumstances were unnecessary"[110] and that now when the Japanese people left most of their war memories behind "the words of Class A war criminals may serve them like narcotics."[111] In November 1955, Araki's article "Recollections of my life in Sugamo prison" appeared in the monthly magazine *Bungeishunjū* that exposed the lax treatment of prisoners in Sugamo which alarmed the representatives of the Allies and once again cast doubt upon the good faith of the Japanese government in carrying out Article 11 of the Peace Treaty. Prison life in Sugamo somewhat emulated life in Japanese society as the prisoners were entertained by kabuki plays, concerts, and baseball games aimed to distract them from daily misery and resentment according to his account. Inmates were offered vocational guidance and allowed leave of absence for 30 days which many of them used to get employment. In the words of the article, Class A war criminals were given a better treatment than others, and Araki hoped than the remaining prisoners would be released soon. Representatives of the Allies, especially Britain and Australia, were irritated by these stories as that meant that the monthly reports they received from Sugamo were deceitful and that the attitude of the Japanese government now threatened "to harm the parole program."[112] While Araki was himself defensive in that his account was distorted, the Ministry of Justice and the Prison Officers all refuted the veracity of the stories as "exaggerated," while the Foreign Ministry's War Criminals Office was worried about repercussions this might have for the remaining Class BC war criminals detained in Sugamo. The US Embassy in Tokyo advised other representatives to take no action as the Japanese government was expected to put an end to this kind of statements which were bad for its reputation. Araki was also reported to have bitterly criticized his trial and blamed "the late President Roosevelt for 'inveigling' Japan into war."[113]

Roy L. Morgan, the former IPS American chief interrogator, in 1955–1956 occupying the position of the advisor to the Japanese Prime Minister, was informed that Hayato Ikeda, Takeo Miki, Nobusuke Kishi, and Ichirō Kōnō were determined in helping Hatoyama remain in power after April 1956. One of the prewar senior politicians the group was promoting for Diet membership and potentially as Hatoyama's successor was the paroled Okinori Kaya, finance minister in Tōjō Cabinet and member of technical committees at both the London Naval Conference in 1930 and the Geneva Disarmament Conference.[114] In an interview for *Mainichi* in 1957, Morgan who worked on Kaya's dossier admitted that his choice was solely guided by his cabinet position at the time of the Pearl Harbor Attack and that there were other candidates who could have been added instead.[115] He went on further to say that in later stages of the trial the evidence was adduced about his opposition to war, up until the receipt of the Hull Note which was read by the Japanese as an ultimatum. Morgan's account as a former IMTFE American associate prosecutor eased the war responsibility stigma that had been placed upon Kaya who was at that time active as a consultant in industrial circles, government, and planned on engaging into politics again by running in the electoral campaign for the Diet.

In 1956, Japanese frustration over non-repatriation from Communist China and the USSR, along with the US dragging its feet over the remaining war criminals, peaked—it meant "Japan's inferior international standing,"[116] a feeling of being treated as a "second-class" power, a feeling that Japan had suffered from at the end of World War I. The Japanese government's progress on rearmament and defense issues and its anti-Communist cause were directly impeded by the war criminals issue that in the eyes of the Japanese mind "symbolize[d] national sacrifices for guilt incurred by the entire Japanese nation."[117] The release of Class A war criminals provoked criticism of lesser war criminals still being imprisoned testifying to the persistence of the aforementioned confusion between the two classes. In Japan's understanding the Japanese military and civilian leaders who plunged Japan into a war they lost and the atrocities their troops committed were considered to be "forgiven" and "cleared" the day the US and Japan signed the treaty of reconciliation which over the course of time, due to their protracted detention, made them appear as national martyrs and not war criminals. Subsequently, for Japanese elites this issue represented an essential irritant and "psychological impediment"[118] to military buildup that would allow Japan to contribute to the free world and cherish its commitments. Even the Japanese who supported the rearmament could no longer understand the US foreign policy incoherence in demanding Japan to rearm, but at the same time keeping the Japanese as war criminals in Japanese prisons.

The Japan-Soviet negotiations scheduled in the end of 1956 further added drama among Washington's officers; Robertson was particularly worried that the normalization of Japan-Soviet relations would lead to unconditional amnesty for Japanese "war criminals" which would have a detrimental impact upon the US diplomatic stance towards Japan.[119] Despite their territorial issues, the USSR and Japan resumed their diplomatic and trade relations in December 1956. During the same month, the Soviets returned 1025 former prisoners to Japan after commuting their sentences and claimed that all prisoners were released to which Japan did not agree. Allegedly, there were additional 10,000 Japanese prisoners somewhere in the USSR.[120] Other than Stalin's thirst for revenge towards Japan, the Soviet attitude towards the issue of Japanese war prisoners can be placed within the broader context of decline of the Japanese Communist Party since 1949, the need for labor to carry out Stalin's modernization programs, and overall dissatisfaction with the US occupation of Japan.[121] Nevertheless, by this time, as expected, the US looked bad in the eyes of its ally.

The newly elected Prime Minister Kishi required the US to grant pardon for all Class A war criminals as he had plans for some of them, principally for Kaya to engage politically as noted above. The pardon was ruled out as a solution as it would jeopardize the war criminal problem and cause public indignation. The options under consideration for the US were termination of their parole supervision or reduction of sentences to time served. This request did not come out of concern that as parolees they would be constrained to assume public office, which was the case under the Japanese Criminal Code, but having in mind that the Japanese considered the IMTFE judgements to be "foreign judgements," these usual restrictions would not be applicable as they were not considered as war criminals under Japanese domestic law. Eisaku Satō, the Diet member and Kishi's younger brother, in his meeting with Ambassador MacArthur II, emphasized the importance of clearing the paroled war criminals of "criminal stigma," and wiping out their guilt so that the source of anti-American feeling can be removed.[122] Satō was primarily pleading for civilians, singling out Kaya as a close friend and advisor to Kishi, while he was ready for a sellout of the Class A military so that civilians could reclaim their honor and banish their war guilt.[123] Kaya made a successful comeback to public life in both political and financial circles as a "senior" colleague who was entitled to support from his subordinates to "regain his 'rightful place,'"[124] the same way Kishi did when he was released from prison; this revealed a deep-rooted "pattern of thought" and political culture of loyalties among the Japanese elite.[125] He was expected to run for a seat in the Lower House with Liberal Democratic Party (LDP) support and, in the future, to replace Ikeda in the position of Minister of Finance.[126]

Until the CPB was abolished, on December 3, 1957, it held the position that a distinction could be made between the civilians and the military among Class A war criminals from which it would be possible to reduce sentences to time served for the former, and terminate parole supervision for the latter, having in mind the serious nature of the crimes they had perpetrated. This would mean that Kaya, Kido, and Hoshino would have their sentences reduced, while the remaining eight would have their parole supervision terminated only.[127] The State Department particularly worried about the interpretation of the term "termination of parole supervision," as they wanted to avoid the possibility of the Japanese interpreting it as if the parolees were discharged of their sentence.[128] The US again took special care at this stage not to jeopardize in any way the judgement and sentences imposed by the IMTFE—it was ready to go with the alternative option, as the other governments were likely to go further.[129] However, in that case the Japanese government would be placed in an unfavorable political position as it would have to amend Law No. 103 that allowed for parole supervision only for the duration of the sentence, which meant that their sentences would have to be reduced. Another facet of the problem was that suspending parole supervision for Class A war criminals but continuing it for Class BC would be troublesome.[130]

As the general elections in Japan scheduled for May 1958 approached, the US was hurrying to liquidate the war criminals problem "in time to give Kishi record of final accomplishment on at least this one troublesome problem,"[131] while the Japanese Embassy was under pressure to rebrand the Prime Minister's friend Kaya for the upcoming elections.[132] When the

CPB was abolished, the Japanese government formed a new board, independent from NOPAR, that assumed the CPB role of recommendation for clemency and parole for the remaining 45 Class BC war criminals to the Secretary of State.[133] The Board wanted to settle the war criminals issue as soon as possible to which the US did not oppose, as, after all, Japan was supposed to rehabilitate these criminals into their society.[134] Graham Parsons, from the US Embassy in Tokyo, made a remark that this persistent matter "created disproportionate political problems that we [the US] did not want to have."[135] Although not directly related, this rather favorable move by the US government in respect to the Japanese war criminals coincided with the lenient sentence pronounced by the Japanese court in the Girard case which was also adding strain to US-Japan relations throughout 1957.

The Japanese government made a request to other interested governments for the reduction of sentences to time served for all Class A war criminals. The Canadian representative questioned the reasons for such demand in view of lax restrictions that had been placed upon parolees and the French government was concerned about the repercussions that treating the major Japanese war criminals as a group, and not on an individual basis, would have for IMT major convicts in Spandau.[136] On April 7, 1958, the Allied powers agreed to comply with all Japanese requests, thus putting an end to the IMTFE saga. In his reply note, Japanese Foreign Minister Aiichirō Fujiyama related to Class A war criminals as *A kyū kankeisha* or Class A-related persons instead of *A kyū senpan* Class A war criminals.[137] This is how the Japanese Class A war criminals ceased being stigmatized as "lawless international wrongdoers"[138] which allowed them to leave their wartime criminal record behind and subsequently the severe social stigma they were exposed to.

Men to Spirits: Class A War Criminals Were Forgiven

The fast transition from the Pacific War strategy to the Cold War strategy created confusion within the US administration which was also reflected in the dilemma surrounding the release process of war criminals.[139] Class A war criminals were all released on parole and then had their sentences reduced; there was no pardon involved; thus their sentences were not invalidated from the point of view of the Allies. However, the fact that they were released and thus cleared from war stigma does imply that domestically they were no longer responsible, they were forgiven. The IMTFE judgement had been observed as a foreign judgement, imposed as a part of the occupation, which, for the Japanese, lost meaning after the occupation ended. In Japan, war responsibility is marked by dichotomy between its domestic and international perceptions of it. Domestically, although Japan accepted the IMTFE judgement by the Peace Treaty, the war guilt is perceived as being cleared in both domestic and international contexts with the end of occupation and through the release of the war criminals. However, at the international level its war responsibility is still valid but also problematic due to Japan's ambivalent stance towards it, especially in its relation to South Korea and China. In addition, parole and reduced sentence for the IMTFE defendants also signified that Japan was institutionally forgiven by the Allies which signed the Peace Treaty with Japan. For Japanese, this pertained to an old era that Japan was slowly surpassing as it regained its place in international relations as a Western ally. Especially so, in the 1960s which was the era of economic prosperity for Japan in which the concepts of "prewar," "militarist Japan," no longer resonated with the society, and consequently, war criminals who were an inseparable part of that era no longer had any meaning in the newly created circumstances.[140]

During the same period, debates about the nature of the Pacific War were animating the press which was divided between aggressive and self-defensive natures of the war.[141] The prevalent view was still that of aggressive war which called for the avoidance of war and a pacifist stance to infuse the dominant historical narrative, thus extending the rationale of the Tokyo Tribunal's judgement.[142] In 1970, Zhou Enlai and Kim Il-sung fiercely accused Japan of its militaristic revival and for becoming "a dangerous force of aggression in Asia."[143] They went further on to accuse Prime Minister Satō of serving US imperialistic ambitions in the Vietnam War, conspiring new war against North Korea and having pretentions to seize Taiwan.[144] In the same year, Richard Minear's *Victors' Justice* publication refuting the legal, historical, and procedural validity of the IMTFE further reinvigorated views of the far right that Japan fought a self-defensive war and should no longer subscribe "to the Tokyo trial view of its history" which was met with strong criticism from the leftist who at that time still considered that the Tribunal is a symbol of peace and that war responsibility should not be negated. On October 17, 1978, the seven Class A war criminals were secretly consecrated to Yasukuni Shrine. Yasukuni Shrine commemorates the spirits of the IMTFE defendants, and it is "ideologically loaded"[145] as it revers the war dead as Shinto gods, thus glorifying the Japanese imperial past.[146] In the domestic arena, it constantly gives rise to debates about the meaning of war crimes trials, and in the international realm, it provokes suspicion about Japan's stance towards its war responsibility and the Tribunal's verdict it had accepted by the virtue of the Peace Treaty.

Notes

1. From American Embassy Tokyo to the Department of State, April 9, 1953, NARA, RG220, Box 28.
2. Ibid.
3. General Snow's notes regarding Appearance of Chief Prosecutor Keenan on June 8, 1953, General Files, NARA, RG220, Box 5.
4. Ibid.
5. Yuma Totani, *The Tokyo War Crimes Trial: The Pursuit of Justice in the Wake of World War II* (Cambridge (Massachusetts): Harvard University Press), 2008, 187–89.
6. Yuma Totani, *The Tokyo War Crimes Trial*, 36–38.
7. Barak Kushner, Men to Devils, Devils to Men: Japanese War Crimes and Chinese Justice (Cambridge: Harvard University Press, 2015), 269–282.
8. Ibid.
9. General Files, 1952–1958, Memorandum of Conversation, Department of State, September 25, 1953, in NARA, RG220, Box 5.
10. Weekly notes, November 7, 1953, in NARA, RG 84, Japanese War Criminals, Box 1.
11. General Files, 1952–1958, Memorandum of Conversation, Department of State, September 25, 1953, in NARA, RG220, Box 5.
12. The Weekly Notes for Tokyo, Department of State, November 21, 1953, in NARA, RG 84, Japanese War Criminals, Box 1.
13. *Mainichi*, Editorial, "War Criminal Issue," January 11, 1954, in NARA, RG84, War Criminals—General Files, Box 28.
14. Telegram, Dulles to American Embassy, Tokyo, October 30, 1953, in NARA, RG84, War Criminals—General, Box 28.
15. Weekly notes, November 7, 1953, in NARA, RG 84, Japanese War Criminals, Box 1.
16. Ibid.
17. General Working Files, Dispatch from Ottawa, December 1, 1953, Dispatches regarding Class A war criminals, November 25, 1954, NARA, RG220, Box 5.
18. Working Papers Re A, B, + C War Criminals, Folder 2, Telegram from Allison to Secretary of State, May 21, 1954, in NARA, RG220, Box 9.

19. Ibid.
20. Ibid.
21. Ibid.
22. Ibid.
23. Working Papers Re A, B, + C War Criminals, Folder 2, From Mr. McClurkin to General Snow, June 13, 1954, in NARA, RG220, Box 9.
24. Memorandum from Kenneth T. Young, Department of State to General Snow, March 24, 1953, NARA, RG220, Box 5.
25. Working Papers Re A, B, + C War Criminals, Folder 2, Draft Yoshida Paper, Japanese War Criminals, October 19, 1954 in NARA, RG220, Box 9.
26. Working Papers Re A, B, + C War Criminals, Folder 2, From Mr. McClurkin to General Snow, June 13, 1954, in NARA, RG220, Box 9.
27. Ibid.
28. Memo, "Clemency of Seven Class A War Criminals," P. Brumby to Mr. Parsons and Mr. Bassin, May 28, 1954, in NARA, RG84, War Criminals—General, Box 28.
29. General Working Files, October 6, 1954, NARA, RG220, Box 4.
30. Telegram, from Allison to Secretary of State, September 25, 1954, in NARA, RG 84, Japanese War Criminals, Box 1.
31. Weekly Notes to Tokyo, October 2, 1954, Jules Bassin in NARA, RG 84, Japanese War Criminals, Box 1.
32. Ibid.
33. Minutes, October 25, 1954, NARA, RG 220, Box 1, folder: Minutes CPB, M-64.
34. Working Papers Re A, B, + C War Criminals, Folder 2, Summary of Meeting of Representatives of Interested Governments on Class A War Criminals, November 22, 1954, in NARA, RG220, Box 9.
35. Working Papers Re A, B, + C War Criminals, Folder 2, From Peaslee to Secretary of State, July 9, in 1954 in NARA, RG220, Box 9.
36. Working Papers Re A, B, + C War Criminals, Folder 2, Summary of Meeting of Representatives of Interested Governments on Class A War Criminals, November 22, 1954, in NARA, RG220, Box 9.
37. Ibid.
38. Letter, Informal, J. Graham Parsons, US Embassy Tokyo to Mr. Noel Hemmendinger, Office of Northeast Asian Affairs, December 21, 1954, in NARA, RG 84, Japanese War Criminals, Box 1.
39. Memorandum for the Files, American Embassy, Tokyo, December 20, 1954, in NARA, RG84, War Criminals—General Files, Box 28.
40. Memorandum for the Files, American Embassy, Tokyo, December 20, 1954, in NARA, RG84, War Criminals—General Files, Box 28.
41. Memorandum for the Record, Mr. Pelletier, French Embassy, Mrs. Dunning, March 2, 1953, NARA, RG220, Box 28.

42. Summary of Meeting, November 5, 1953, of Representatives of IMTFE Governments with Respect to Class A War Criminals in NARA, RG84, War Criminals—General, Box 28.
43. Summary of Meeting, October 5, 1954, of Representatives of Interested Governments on Class A War Criminals in NARA, RG 84, Japanese War Criminals, Box 1.
44. Ibid.
45. Dulles, Department of State to Bassin, American Embassy, Tokyo, February 14, 1955, in NARA, RG 84, Japanese War Criminals, Box 1.
46. State Department to American Embassy, Tokyo, September 10, 1954, in NARA, RG 84, Japanese War Criminals, Box 1.
47. Records of CPB, Class A War Criminal, Araki Sadao, March 4, 1955, in NARA, RG220, Box 1.
48. CPB, Minutes, June 20, 1955, Minutes, NARA, RG 220, Box 1, folder: Minutes CPB, M-78.
49. CPB, November 2, 1953, NARA, RG 220, Box 1, folder: Minutes CPB, M-41.
50. Ibid.
51. Minutes, November 29, 1954, NARA, RG 220, Box 1, folder: Minutes CPB, M-66.
52. General Working Files, November 17, 1954, NARA, RG220, Box 5.
53. Letter, Mr. Noel Hemmendinger, Office of Northeast Asian Affairs to J. Graham Parsons, American Embassy, Tokyo, December 3, 1954, in NARA, RG 84, Japanese War Criminals, Box 1.
54. Minutes, April 4, 1955, NARA, RG 220, Box 1, folder: Minutes CPB, M-73.
55. Records of CPB, Class A War Criminal, Hashimoto Kingoro, Telegram from MacArthur, American Embassy Tokyo to Secretary of State, July 18, 1957, in NARA, RG220, Box 9.
56. Telegram From the Embassy in Japan to the Department of State by Allison, Tokyo, January 10, 1955, FRUS 1955–1957, *Japan,* Volume XXIII, Part 1 (Washington: United States Government Printing Office: 1991).
57. Ibid.
58. Ibid.
59. Ibid.
60. Ibid.
61. Dai 021 Kaikokkai Honkaigi Dai 5-gō, January 21, 1955. http://kokkai.ndl.go.jp/SENTAKU/sangiin/021/0512/02101220512005a.html (accessed August 3, 2017)
62. CPB, Clemency Efforts in 1955, "Shigemitsu to talk about Foreign Policy," *Kyodo,* January 21, 1955, in NARA, RG220, Box 9.

63. Working Papers Re A, B, + C War Criminals, Folder 2, Telegram from Allison to Secretary of State, February 1, 1955, in NARA, RG220, Box 9.
64. Ibid.
65. Ibid.
66. Letter, Robert J.G. McClurkin to Allison, February 4, 1955, in NARA, RG84, War Criminals—General Files, Box 28.
67. Ibid.
68. Ibid.
69. General Working Files, Memorandum, From Mr. Hagen, CPB, to Mr. Snow, FE, May 12, 1955, NARA, RG220, Box 5.
70. Working Papers Re A, B, + C War Criminals, Folder 2, Letter from Herbert Brownell, Jr., Attorney General to the Secretary of State, February 21, 1955, in NARA, RG220, Box 9.
71. Letter, J. Graham Parsons, American Embassy, Tokyo to Mr. Noel Hemmendinger, Office of Northeast Asian Affairs, March 14, 1956, in NARA, RG84, War Criminals—General Files, Box 28.
72. General Working Files, Memorandum, From Mr. Hagen, CPB, to Mr. Snow, FE, May 12, 1955, NARA, RG220, Box 5.
73. Ibid.
74. Working Files Re A, B, + C War Criminals, Folder 2, Memorandum, Japanese War Criminals, February 16, 1955 in NARA, RG220, Box 9.
75. Letter, Ryuiji Takeuchi, Minster in charge of European and American Affairs Bureau to Graham Parsons, American Embassy, Tokyo, February 3, 1955, in NARA, RG84, War Criminals—General Files, Box 28.
76. Working Papers Re A, B, + C War Criminals, Clemency Efforts in 1955, Dispatch from Embassy in Tokyo to Board of Clemency and Parole, August 15, 1955 in NARA, RG220, Box 9.
77. Working Papers Re A, B, + C War Criminals, Folder 3, "Decision on a recommendation for general release of war criminals," (Translation), Matsusuke Shirane, NOPAR, July 25, 1955, in NARA, RG220, Box 9.
78. Working papers Re A, B, + C War Criminals, Folder 3, Dispatch form Windsor G. Hackler, American Embassy to Tokyo to State Department, July 1, 1955, in NARA, RG220, Box 9.
79. Ibid.
80. Kokkai kaigiroku, Shūgiin, Honkaigi, dai-43-gō, July 19, 1955. http://kokkai.ndl.go.jp/SENTAKU/syugiin/022/0512/02207190512043a.html (accessed September 23, 2017).
81. Ibid.
82. Memorandum of a Conversation, Department of State, August 31, 1955, FRUS 1955–1957, *Japan,* Volume XXIII, Part 1, Washington: US Government Printing Office, 1991, 107.
83. Ibid.

84. Ibid.
85. Working Papers Re A, B, + C War Criminals, Folder 3, Telegram from Parsons, American Embassy to Tokyo to Secretary of State, August 29, 1955, in NARA, RG220, Box 9.
86. Ibid.
87. Telegram, Mr. Ronhovde, US Embassy, Hague to American Embassy, Tokyo, August 30, 1955, in NARA, RG84, War Criminals—General Files, Box 28.
88. Telegram, Department of State to American Embassy, Hague, August 25, 1955, in NARA, RG84, War Criminals—General Files, Box 28.
89. Summary of Meeting of Representatives of Interested Governments on Class A War Criminals, September 8, 1955, in NARA, RG84, War Criminals—General Files, Box 28.
90. Telegram, Mr. Ronhovde, US Embassy, Hague to American Embassy, Tokyo, August 30, 1955, in NARA, RG84, War Criminals—General Files, Box 28.
91. CPB, Minutes, September 26, 1955, NARA, RG 220, Box 1, folder: Minutes CPB, M-84.
92. Working Papers Re A, B, + C War Criminals, Folder 3, Telegram from Allison to Secretary of State, September 13, 1955 in NARA, RG220, Box 9.
93. Ibid.
94. CPB, Minutes, December 19, 1955, NARA, RG 220, Box 1, folder: Minutes CPB, M-89.
95. Working Papers Re A, B, + C War Criminals, Folder 3, Summary of meeting of representatives of interested governments on Japanese Class A war criminals, December 6, 1955, in NARA, RG220, Box 28.
96. December 27, 1955, Report of Clemency and Parole Board for War Criminals, NARA, RG 220, Box 1, folder: Minutes CPB.
97. Letter, J. Grapham Parsons to Robert J.G. McClurkin, September 10, 1955, in NARA, RG 84, War Criminals—General Files, Box 28.
98. Schaller, *Altered States: The United States and Japan Since the Occupation* (New York: Oxford University Press, 1997), 130.
99. Schaller, *Altered States: The United States and Japan Since the Occupation,* 76.
100. Schaller, *Altered States: The United States and Japan Since the Occupation,* 124.
101. Records of CPB, General Files, 1952–1958, Conrad E. Snow to Robert Upton, March 16, 1956, in NARA, RG220, Box 6.
102. Telegram, Allison to Secretary of State, June 30, 1956, in NARA, RG84, War Criminals—General Files, Box 28.
103. Ibid.

104. Records of CPB, General Files, 1952–1958, Memorandum Shigemitsu to Allison, Tokyo, March 18, 1956, in NARA, RG220, Box 6.
105. Joachim Peiper was sentenced to death in the Dachau trials in Germany for his involvement in the Malmedy Massacre in 1944; however his sentence was commuted to life imprisonment.
106. Records of CPB, General Files, 1952–1958, Richard D. Kearney, Assistant Legal Adviser for Far Eastern Affairs to Mr. Noel Hemmendinger, Disposition of Japanese War Criminals, June 12, 1956, in NARA, RG220, Box 6.
107. Records of CPB, General Files, 1952–1958, Memorandum Shigemitsu to Allison, Tokyo, March 18, 1956, in NARA, RG220, Box 6.
108. Records of CPB, General Files, 1952–1958, Memorandum, July 3, 1956, in NARA, RG220, Box 6.
109. "Released War Prisoners Held Talkative," *Yomiuri Shimbun*, Editor's Note, April 16, 1956.
110. Ibid.
111. Ibid.
112. "Felon story repudiated by Gaimusho," *Nippon Times,* October 16, 1955, in NARA, RG 84, Japanese War Criminals, Box 1.
113. "Calls Trial Disgrace," *Washington Post*, May 2, 1956, NARA, RG220, Box 6.
114. Letter, "Political Situation—Japan," Legal Attache, US Department of Justice to the Ambassador, January 3, 1956, in NARA, RG 84, Japanese War Criminals, Box 1.
115. Ernest Hobrecht, "Prosecutor Admits Kaya Was Found to Have Opposed War—Postnote To Tokyo War Crimes Trial," *Mainichi*, May 7, 1957, in Records of CPB, Class A War Criminal in NARA, RG220, Box 5.
116. Intelligence Report, "Japanese sentiment for release of war criminals," Department of State, Office of Intelligence Research, June 14, 1956, NARA, RG220, Box 6.
117. Ibid.
118. Ibid.
119. Records of CPB, General Files, 1952–1958, Memorandum, Department of State, Japanese War Criminals, October 3, 1956, in NARA, RG220, Box 6.
120. William F. Nimmo, *Behind a Curtain of Silence: Japanese in Soviet Custody, 1945–1956,* 83–97.
121. Ibid.
122. Records of CPB, General Files, 1952–1958, Memorandum by R.H. Lamb, War Criminals, From American Embassy Tokyo, May 13, 1957, in NARA, RG220, Box 6.
123. Ibid.

124. The Rehabilitation of Okinori Kaya, Class A War Criminal, US Embassy Tokyo, William B. Coolidge, June 19, 1957 in NARA, RG 84, Japanese War Criminals, Box 1.
125. Ibid.
126. Ibid.
127. CPB, Minutes, October 21, 1957, NARA, RG 220, Box 1, folder: Minutes CPB, M-111.
128. Records of CPB, General Files, 1952–1958, Telegram, American Embassy Tokyo to Department of State, July 9, 1957, in NARA, RG220, Box 6.
129. Records of CPB, General Files, 1952–1958, Telegram, MacArthur, American Embassy to Tokyo to Secretary of State, July 12, 1957, in NARA, RG220, Box 6.
130. Records of CPB, General Files, 1952–1958, Telegram, MacArthur, American Embassy to Tokyo to Secretary of State, July 30, 1957, in NARA, RG220, Box 6.
131. Records of CPB, General Files, 1952–1958, Memorandum, Thomas S. Estes, Office of Professional Responsibility to Mr. Hagen, CPB, January 21, 1958, in NARA, RG220, Box 6.
132. Ibid.
133. Records of CPB, General Files, 1952–1958, Telegram, Dulles to American Embassy Tokyo, December 19, 1957, in NARA, RG220, Box 6.
134. Memorandum, "Japanese War Criminals," November 27, 1957, in NARA, RG84, War Criminals—General (1957), Box 28.
135. Ibid.
136. Memorandum, "Class A War Criminals," November 5, 1957, in NARA, RG84, War Criminals—General (1957), Box 28.
137. Yuki Takatori, "'Equal Punishment for All'—Japan's View of the Tokyo Tribunal," *Virginia Review of Asian Studies* 17 (2015): 12.
138. Ibid.
139. Yoshinobu Higurashi, *Tōkyō saiban* (Kodansha: Tokyo, 2008), 388.
140. Higurashi, *Tōkyō saiban*, 386–387.
141. Ibid.
142. Ibid., 388.
143. Schaller, *Altered States: The United States and Japan Since the Occupation*, 229.
144. Ibid. 229.
145. Barack Kushner, *Men to Devils, Devils to Men: Japanese War Crimes and Chinese Justice* (Cambridge: Harvard University Press, 2015), 313.
146. Ibid.

CHAPTER 11

International Criminal Tribunals: *Cui Bono?*

The Tokyo Tribunal benefited the Allied powers in providing for them the venue to assert the principles upon which they based the immediate postwar international order—illegality of aggressive war, and, implicitly, its criminality. The focus on Japan's misdeeds shifted from the Allied powers which used law to consolidate their World War II gains by prohibiting alterations of the status quo. This law and criminal tribunals were strategic in nature in a sense that they served as a vehicle for furthering the Allies' larger diplomatic and security goals. In the larger context of the Cold War, however, these policies proved to be shortsighted and rigid to adapt to the newly created geopolitical dynamics in which Japan was becoming an ally. The criminality of war and individual criminal responsibility for it had not been applied since. The passions of the Pacific War had barely settled; the Cold War triggered other wars in Asia which demonstrated that even in the presence of law peace was precarious. The IMTFE project, understood as extending well into 1956, as an example of retribution for waging aggressive war, or at least, challenging the status quo, stood against the background of great powers' colonialism, engagement in proxy wars, and interventions which deeply eroded the Tribunal's legality and legitimacy. Already in November 1954, the United Nations General Assembly, where the project of codification of international criminal code based on Nuremberg principles was discussed, the US delegate Charles H. Mahoney explained that "the project for a code of crimes under international law in

A. Babovic, *The Tokyo Trial, Justice, and the Postwar International Order*, New Directions in East Asian History,
https://doi.org/10.1007/978-981-13-3477-1_11

today's world is impractical and inappropriate,"[1] while it refused the possibility that its citizens could be subjected to an international agency which would apply the said code.[2] International law did not outlaw war; on the contrary, it prohibited one specific form of war which is unilateral use of force for changing the status quo or regulating international disputes. All other forms of war or use of force short of war were permitted.

When it comes to state responsibility for war, states have been playing around legal exceptions of the collective security actions, in the form of military humanitarian interventions, or extensive interpretations of self-defense that often take guise of an aggression. For instance, in the current East Asian regional order led by the US, a status quo power, whose hegemony has been challenged by China, a revisionist power, there is a potential for military conflict on the basis of the explicitely prohibited unilateral changes to status quo. Where does the aggressive war start, and under which conditions? China is changing the status quo by building artificial islands, as it claims, for self-defense purposes. Law, when accompanied with power, is an evolving, powerful thing. When it comes to criminal responsibility for crime of aggression, it can be said that it is still there where the Allies left it in the 1940s. It has not been defined more closely, and the ICC, which has material jurisdiction for this crime, has never had a case of crime of aggression before it.

The legislating role performed by the Tribunals has also its positive aspects, especially when it addresses victims' needs, at least in the form of recognizing or further refining the rule. For instance, in case of the Tokyo Trial, although an imperfect example, rape was recognized as a part of crimes against humanity although it was used for evidencing crime of aggression.

The role of the Tribunals is to apply law but also to make law through their decisions and determination and interpretation of what law is. This aspect demonstrates selectivity of the law, and more so, in the arena of international relations. International criminal law is not consistently applied; it needs to weigh pros and cons in each case. In short, the practical aspects of the Tribunal, strategic value of particular situation, its cost, both material and political are taken into consideration. It is not a universal and consistent instrument. It is an instrument of hegemony, not in all its spheres, but in the international criminal sphere, it is usually imposed. International criminal justice is not perfect and that should be the departure point of any critical analysis addressed on their behalf.

Furthermore, the Tribunal provided a highly linear historical narrative on Japan's conspired and aggressive Fifteen Years War. The important parts of the narrative were enshrined in the Tokyo Judgement that had gained a certain degree of authority when it comes to a hegemonic view of history that fits into legal narrative that is by its nature fragmented. On the other hand, silence in the judgement on other events that could be equally qualified as criminal was intentional. Tribunals also tend to forget events that are out of sync with the history of the victor. These events lose relevance in the efforts of postwar reconstruction.[3] The question is whether the Tokyo Trial had historical consequences or did it close the dark chapter of Japan's history? It can be argued that historical consequences of the Trial have been palpable, especially when it comes to its relations with neighbors. As the book has shown, forgiveness was institutional, but did not come from victims, the Chinese and Koreans. These nations were completely left out from the indictment, tribunal, and judgement—at that time the Tokyo Tribunal had a laser-sharp goal—it was not supposed to relieve victims, but victors. As they did not get their share of judicial relief, they are seeking it themselves or through their governments. The case of comfort women is an illustration of this seeking. In that sense, the Tokyo judgement keeps the dark chapters of Japanese colonialism alive and is susceptible to cause disputes. Historical issues are always prone to states' strategies of linkage. Economic or security issues can sometimes entail "historical retaliation."

Furthermore, the most notorious Japanese leaders were stigmatized for crime of aggression that was not established as a part of positive law at that time. For them, waging war went from being a political mistake to ultimately becoming a crime. In that sense, the Tokyo Trial was educational only in the sense of demonstrating what could possible happen to those who wage aggressive war unilaterally, as instrument of national policy. It did not truly educate them in the sense of providing a venue from them to reflect deeper on one's guilt and role in the conflict and repent. It was pedagogical in the sense that it attracted a wide attention and publicity for its moral and political narrative. The atomic bombings and the Soviet entry into the war had been perceived as immense injustice which, in turn, influenced not only the Japanese leaders' but also the Japanese people's capacity to reflect upon their own guilt. The ultimate release of the war criminals, based on institutional forgiveness, protracted periods of their incarceration, and perceived sense of injustice resulted in societal perception and portrayal of war criminals as being victims and martyrs. In the practice of modern international tribunals, the release after the defendant has served two-thirds of its sentence is automatic. Law forgives, but this does not mean that victims' grievances are being addressed. That is why these post-institutional or post-trial phases are equally important and can be transformative of the overall Tribunal's legacy and its intended "pedagogical" role. This phase also reveals that justice is not a static phenomenon, immune from circumstances in which it is taking place; it is always in motion.

Individualization of war crimes guilt, especially for high-leadership positions, is certainly beneficial as it prevents the whole nation from being stigmatized for the political decisions of a few. It carries, however, a lot of risks, one of them being forgoing a larger debate within all levels of one society about war, the role of citizens, intellectuals, and business in the war machine. The Tokyo Trial is, in that sense, a gross simplification of war responsibility that always transverses deeper into social strata. The Tribunal produced "highly schematic and simplified histories"[4] in which the antecedents of conflict [...] are elided.[5] Laws are unable to write history, yet the records of the Tokyo Tribunal are full of poorly patched historical narratives construed around weak and indirect evidence which was interpreted in the light of a colossal amount of studies, documents, and treaties used by the prosecution.[6] Illustratively, "great men" theory purported by the Tribunal eliminates all other individuals or circumstances that led to the atrocity. In 1919, the Versailles Commission refused prosecution on the basis of authorship pointing out at complex, multifaceted circumstances leading to war. In Japan, that larger picture of war history and war experience of the Empire was not digested and processed. It had created a historical vacuum and ignorance towards more diversified historical narratives. In the case of Japan, the experience of the occupation, war crimes trials, extreme devastation, and poverty together with rapid changes in Japan's status helped speed up the process of forgetting and amnesia. The Allied powers, especially the US, played an important role in that aspect. They fulfilled their mission of getting relief or satisfaction in terms of majority judgement that confirmed that Japan's war was unique and aggressive, relieving the Allied powers from bearing the burden of their wartime misdeeds. The Japanese could also admit that they got their judicial relief in the form of Pal's dissenting opinion that was, extensively, extrapolated to fit the narrative of complete absence of guilt. Indeed, it vindicated the absence of criminal, but not political or moral responsibility. In Japan, to the present day, these topics are conflated. Crudely put, the fact that the Japanese reject the legality of the actions qualified as crimes by the Tribunal does not mean that they did not happen or that their political character should not be discussed.

The first international criminal tribunals established on an ad hoc basis by the UN Security Council after the IMT and IMTFE precedents were the International Criminal Tribunal for ex-Yugoslavia (ICTY) and International Military Tribunal for Rwanda (ICTR). The tribunals established in the 1990s, and even the International Criminal Court that is permanent in nature, completely misunderstood the role that IMTs played in the immediate postwar period and thus overestimated what international tribunals can and cannot do.[7] No matter how sophisticated international criminal law and its case law has become, rules of procedure and evidence in these modern embodiments of transitional justice, their institutional design and quality of justice remain plagued by a similar criticism that had been addressed to their historical counterparts. Therefore, it is crucial to understand what are international tribunals capable of delivering which is the point that concludes this book. It is important to take these conclusions as lessons from a detailed single case study of the Tokyo Tribunal which could be further tested through a study of modern international criminal tribunals.

International criminal tribunals are not exclusively victim oriented, they do not aspire to address the totality of the atrocity committed in a given conflict setting. They are not benevolent institutions, they are infused with larger policies and serve to advance national or strategic interests of sponsoring states or state they choose to patron. They are not universal and consistent in their application, there needs to be a strategic value and political will for them to come to life and address particular war or injustice. International criminal tribunals are not interested in emotional, complex, irregular historical narratives. International criminal tribunals cannot provide for reconciliation as they produce linear, over-deterministic narratives. They cannot be free from political and ideological influences. They cannot have independent prosecutors. They cannot reeducate politicians or military they prosecute. They are elitist in nature. On the other hand, international criminal tribunals can produce and advance international criminal law and its case law. They can produce a hegemonic version of history. They can attract wide publicity and attention. They can stigmatize the elites, but their narratives can also stigmatize entire nations. They can address instances of atrocity. They can hinder peace process. They can render collective war responsibility redundant. They can forgive and rehabilitate. In essence, they are institutions in the making, susceptible of improvement, but in case they are chosen as an instrument in post-conflict societies, there should be a clear awareness of what the sponsoring states want to achieve and how these can meet those needs. In the end, *cui bono*?

International criminal tribunals are of greater benefit to states that are sponsoring them but that does not mean they cannot be of benefit to states whose leaders are prosecuted, or victims, although to a lesser degree.

Notes

1. General Working Files, "Are We Men or Murderers?," *The Saturday Review*, February 19, 1955, NARA, RG220, Box 5.
2. Ibid.
3. Holger Afflerbach and Hew Strachan, *How Fighting Ends: A History of Surrender* (Oxford University Press, 2012).
4. Gerry Simpson, "International Criminal Justice and the Past," in Gideon Boas, William A. Schabas, and Michael P. Scharf, eds., *International Criminal Justice: Legitimacy and Coherence* (Cheltenham: Edward Elgar Publishing, 2012), 134–35.
5. Ibid.
6. Richard Ashby Wilson, *Writing History in International Criminal Trials* (New York: Cambridge University Press, 2011), 1.
7. Peter Maguire, *Law and War: An American Story* (New York: Columbia University Press, 2001), 212.

The manufacturer's authorised representative in the EU is Springer Nature Customer Service Centre GmbH, Europaplatz 3, 69115 Heidelberg, Germany. If you have any concerns regarding our products, please contact ProductSafety@springernature.com

Printed and bound by CPI Group (UK) Ltd, Croydon, CR0 4YY
25/09/2026
02222897-0019